Kate Remembered

At the age of seventy-five, Katharine Hepburn, four-time Academy Award winner, opened her door to biographer A. Scott Berg – then thirty-three – and so began a special friendship. Over the next twenty years and to the end of her illustrious life, Kate used their many hours together to reveal all that came to mind, often reflecting on the people and episodes of her past and occasionally on the meaning of life.

   Recording heretofore untold biographical details of her entire phenomenal career and her famous relationships with such men as Spencer Tracy and Howard Hughes, *Kate Remembered* is a book about love and friendship, family and career, Hollywood and Broadway – all punctuated by unforgettable lessons from an extraordinary life.

American River College Library
4700 College Oak Drive
Sacramento, CA 95841

Further Praise for *Kate Remembered*

'Rather wonderful . . . One of the best books of 2003'
Sunday Herald

'Scott Berg is a terrific writer'   *Glasgow Evening Times*

'A tender and wholehearted tribute to one of acting's great personalities'   *Edinburgh Evening News*

'Berg's account . . . charms and encourages the reader to feel as warmly towards [Hepburn] as he does'   *Irish News*

'An excellent read is this lovingly written memoir of a very special lady'   *Irish Independent*

'Compelling . . . Berg allows Hepburn to come alive like a character in a story'   *Sunday Tribune*

'Berg finds joy in [Hepburn's] longevity, and admires her humility, humour, charm and candour. His memoir is an extended love-letter'
Catholic Herald

'*Kate Remembered* is for fans of Hepburn and old Hollywood who want to spend a little more time in the presence of a real star'
South Wales Argus

Kate
Remembered

KATHARINE HEPBURN
A Personal Biography

A. Scott Berg

POCKET
BOOKS

LONDON • SYDNEY • NEW YORK • TORONTO

First published in Great Britain and Ireland by Simon & Schuster, 2003
This edition first published by Pocket, 2004
An imprint of Simon & Schuster UK Ltd

Simon & Schuster UK is a Viacom company

Copyright © A. Scott Berg, 2003

This book is copyright under the Berne Convention.
No reproduction without permission.
All rights reserved.

The right of A. Scott Berg to be identified as author of this work
has been asserted in accordance with sections 77 and 78 of the
Copyright, Designs and Patents Act, 1988.

3 5 7 9 10 8 6 4 2

Simon & Schuster UK Ltd
Africa House
64–78 Kingsway
London WC2B 6AH

www.simonsays.co.uk

Simon & Schuster Australia
Sydney

A CIP catalogue record for this book
is available from the British Library

ISBN 0-7434-1563-9

The ten-line excerpt of Phelps Putman's 'The Daughters of the Sun' (as published in
The Collected Poems of H. Phelps Putman, edited by Charles R. Walker, 1971)
is reprinted with the kind permission of Farrar, Straus and Giroux.
The following photographs are used with the kind permission of the following
owners: Archive Photos: frontispiece and pages 136 and 168; the Academy of
Motion Picture Arts and Sciences: pages 8, 216, and 312; Corbis/Bettmann-UPI:
pages 26, 68, and 274; Getty Images: page 108; G. P. Putnam's Sons: page 362;
Nick Vaccaro: page xiv.

Printed and bound in Great Britain by
Bookmarque Ltd, Croydon, Surrey

to

KEVIN MCCORMICK

Contents

	Author's Note	*xi*
I.	A Private Function	*1*
II.	Making a Difference	*9*
III.	Curtain Up	*25*
IV.	Morning Glory	*60*
V.	Katharine of Arrogance	*97*
VI.	In Bloom Again	*121*
VII.	Yare	*149*
VIII.	Guess Who Came to Dinner	*191*
IX.	Always Mademoiselle	*241*
X.	Travels with "My Aunt"	*273*
XI.	Queen Anne's Lace	*317*

Author's Note

Over the past thirty years, I have written three biographies. Each of these books is part of a larger plan I have long been devising, a collection of objectively told life stories of great American cultural figures of the twentieth century, each representing a different wedge of the Apple Pie. (Thus far, I have written about a book editor from New England, a motion-picture mogul from Poland, and an aviator from the Midwest.) This book falls outside that plan.

The subject at hand has certainly led a fascinating life and impacted the times in which she lived. She more than merits a full-scale biography. Alas, I am not the one to write such a book because I am, quite frankly, incapable of writing about her objectively. For one thing, I believe—unabashedly and without qualification—that Katharine Hepburn established the greatest acting career of the twentieth century, perhaps ever. And for another, Katharine Hepburn was a close friend of mine for two decades. Quite frankly, I walked into her life adoring her; and over the next twenty years, my admiration for her only swelled.

This book is, thus, not a critical study of either Katharine Hepburn's life or her career. It is, rather, as true an account of her life as I can present, based on countless hours of private conversations during which she reminisced. Even more than recalling events, Miss Hepburn often used our time together to reflect, an exercise in which I don't think she indulged with anybody else. And so, more than *my* remembrances, this book intends to convey hers.

As our conversations would invariably turn to her past, I soon felt that she was using me less as a sounding board than as an anvil against which she could hammer some of her emotions and beliefs. Consequently, this book reveals an unusual relationship in a unique life, one lived large—and largely according to her own rules. More important, it sets down many of the stories of that life as she saw them, full of sentiments she felt should not be made public until her death. Ultimately, then, it is not just a story of the poignant final years in which I knew her; it is a tale of a great theatrical personality and the better part of the century that was the stage for her distinguished life.

I

A Private Function

I've never felt so intimidated ringing a doorbell.

Even though she and I had become friendly in the past few months over the telephone and I was standing at her front door in New York City at her invitation, I was genuinely nervous about our first meeting. And I've never been especially starstruck.

But this was different. Katharine Hepburn was the first movie star I had ever noticed, and she had been my favorite ever since—the only actor whose plays and movies I attended just because she was in them.

On that Tuesday—April 5, 1983—I arrived at Third Avenue and Forty-ninth Street with fifteen minutes to spare. So I walked around a few neighboring blocks until 5:55 p.m. Then I slowly walked east on Forty-ninth Street until I was a few doors from Second Avenue— number 244. I stood on the sidewalk for another minute and a half, until the second hand on my watch ticked toward twelve. I opened the little black iron gate, stepped down into the well at the curtained front door, and pressed the button. The bell let out a ring so shrill, I could practically feel all four floors of the brownstone shake.

Nobody answered. After a long pause, a short woman with black hair poked her cherubic face out of an adjacent door, the service entrance, and said, "Yes?"

I said I had a six o'clock appointment with Miss Hepburn. Was I at the wrong door? "No, no," she said. "I'll let you in." She came to the front door, and I heard two heavy locks tumble. This was

Norah Considine, who cooked and cleaned. She said Miss Hepburn was expecting me.

I entered the vestibule and left my raincoat on a bench at the foot of the steep, narrow staircase, with its metal pole for a handrail. Another woman appeared from the kitchen—gray-haired, bony, with a neckbrace; and we introduced ourselves. She was, as I presumed, Phyllis Wilbourn, Hepburn's companion and majordomo. "Oh, yes. Go right up," she said in a sandy-throated English accent. "Miss Hepburn's expecting you." At the top of the landing, I could look into the rear living room, where the last of that day's light was coming in from the garden.

Before I had even entered the room, I heard the unmistakable voice from inside. "Did you use the bathroom?"

"I'm sorry?" I said, now standing in the doorway and seeing Katharine Hepburn for the first time.

She sat to the right in a comfortable-looking chair, her feet in white athletic shoes propped up on a footrest. She appeared to be amazingly fit for a seventy-five-year-old then recovering from a serious car accident. She looked restored and relaxed, her skin tight against the legendary cheekbones, her eyes clear, a soothing pale blue, her hair a ruddy gray, all pulled off her face and pinned up into her trademark knot. She wore no makeup and flashed a big movie-star grin, exuding charm and energy. She was wearing khaki pants, a white turtleneck under a blue chambray shirt, and she had a red sweater tied loosely around her neck. As I approached her, I tried to take in as much of the room as I could—the high ceiling, pictures on the walls, a fire blazing in the fireplace, nothing ostentatious except for huge bouquets of flowers everywhere.

"Did you use the bathroom?" she asked again, before I had reached her.

"No."

"Well, don't you think you should?"

3

"No, thank you. I don't think that's necessary."

"Well, I think you should probably go back downstairs and use the bathroom first." I repeated that I didn't think it was necessary but that I would do my best.

Two minutes later I returned; and as I reached the top of the stairs, she asked, "Did you use the bathroom?"

"Well, actually," I said, "I did, thank you."

"Good. You know my father was a urologist, and he said you should always go to the bathroom whenever you have to . . . and you see, you had to. So how do you do? I'm Katharine Hepburn."

"Yes, I know you are." We shook hands, and from her chair she looked me up and down and smiled. "You're tall." A little over six feet, I told her. "Tennis?" No, I said, but I swim regularly and work out with weights at a gym. "Boah." A little boring, I concurred, adding that it was the most time-efficient form of exercise for me.

"Do you smoke?" she asked.

I started to laugh—feeling as though I had walked into a production of *The Importance of Being Earnest*—and said, "No, Lady Bracknell, I don't." She laughed and said, "I used to. Gave it up. Disgusting habit. Well, I hope you drink."

"Fortunately," I said, "I do." With that, she sent me to the table behind her, on which sat a wooden African mask of a woman with unusually large, wild eyes and prominent cheekbones. "Somebody sent me that," she said. "It looks just like me, don't you think?" Except for the tribal paint, it did. Next to it sat a large wooden tray with several bottles of liquor and three thick glass goblets. "Do you see anything there you like?" I did—a bottle of King William IV Scotch. She asked me to make two of them, according to her specifications—which meant filling the glass beyond the brim with ice, pouring a shot of the whiskey slowly over the cubes, then topping it with soda. She directed me to sit on the couch to her right, white canvas covered with a red knit throw. She took a sip, then a gulp of her drink and said, "Too weak." I doctored it. "Yours looks too weak," she said. Fearing a replay of the bathroom episode, I stood my ground, saying, "I feel the need to stay one ounce more sober than you."

While we discussed the interview I had come to conduct with her, Phyllis Wilbourn climbed the stairs. I started to get up, as the neck-braced septugenarian appeared a little wobbly; but my hostess assured me she was just fine. "You've met Phyllis Wilbourn?" Miss Hepburn inquired, as the older woman passed a tray of hot cheese puffs. "My Alice B. Toklas."

"I wish you wouldn't say that," Phyllis insisted. "It makes me sound like an old lesbian, and I'm not."

"You're not what, dearie, old or a lesbian?" she said, laughing.

"Neither." With that, Phyllis fixed her own drink, a ginger ale, and sat in a chair opposite us; and I continued to soak up the room. Hepburn watched me as I gazed at a carved wooden goose hanging on a chain from the ceiling. "Spencer's," she said. Then I noticed a painting of two seagulls on some rocks.

"Do you think that's an exceptional picture or not?" she asked.

"It's amusing," I said. "Fun."

"Me," she said, referring to the artist.

The fire was dying, and Hepburn asked if I knew anything about fireplaces. I told her I was no Boy Scout but that I could probably kick a little life into it. "Let's see," she said, preparing to grade me in what was clearly an important test. I used the pair of wrought-iron tongs to turn a few logs over, and they went up in a blaze. She was visibly pleased. "How about those on the mantel?" she asked, referring me to a pair of small figurines, nude studies of a young woman. "Me," she said.

"You sculpted these?" I asked.

"No, I posed for them." Upon closer scrutiny, I could see that was the case and that she was pleased again.

5

Over the next few minutes, we made small talk—about my hometown, Los Angeles, our mutual friend director George Cukor, who had died there just a few months prior, and our impending interview. She asked how much time I thought I would need, and I asked, "How much have you got?"

"Oh, I'm endlessly fascinating," she said, smiling again. "I'd say you'll need at least two full days with me."

As my fire-tending had made the room warmer, I stood and removed my blue blazer, which I set on the couch. "I don't think so," said Hepburn gently but firmly. "Now look, I want you to be as comfortable as you like. But look where you've put that jacket. It's right in my sight line, and it's, well, somewhat offensive."

"Yes," I said, "I can see that." As I started to put it back on, she said that wasn't necessary, that there was a chair on the landing and I should just "throw it there"—which I did. Upon re-entering the room, I instinctively adjusted a picture on the wall, a floral painting which was slightly askew.

"Oh, I *see*," said Miss Hepburn with great emphasis; "you're one of *those*." She smiled approvingly and added, "Me too. But nobody was as bad as Cole Porter. He used to come to this house, and he'd straighten pictures for five minutes before he'd even sit down. Listen, while you're still up, I'm ready for another drink. How about you?"

Again I made mine the weaker. It was not that I was afraid of falling on my face. It was more that I felt as though I were now walking through an RKO movie starring Katharine Hepburn, and I didn't want to miss a single frame of it.

As the clock on the mantelpiece bonged seven, Miss Hepburn said, "Look, I only invited you for drinks tonight because I wasn't sure how we'd get on, but you're more than welcome to stay for dinner; there's plenty of food. But I can tell by the way you're dressed, and I must say I like that tie, you've got another date. It's probably better if you go anyway because we're starting to talk too much already, and then we won't be fresh for the performance tomorrow. Shall we say eleven?" I explained that I did, in fact, have a dinner date; but for her I would happily break it. "No," she said, "we don't want to run out of things to say to each other." We shook hands goodbye, and I exited the room, grabbing my jacket from the chair.

When I was halfway down the stairs, I heard her shout, "Use the bathroom before you leave!"

II

Making a Difference

T he first time I didn't meet Katharine Hepburn was in April 1972.

I had graduated from Princeton University the preceding year, having written my senior thesis on Maxwell Perkins, the legendary editor at Charles Scribner's Sons who had "discovered" and developed F. Scott Fitzgerald, Ernest Hemingway, Thomas Wolfe, and at least another score of the most significant writers in the United States between the World Wars. Even after submitting the thesis, I considered it a work in progress, a first draft of a full-scale biography of the man I considered the most important but least-known figure in American literature—a Harvard man whose ancestors went back to seventeenth-century New England, and a New York book editor whose vision ushered American literature farther into the future than any of his contemporaries. He was a Manhattan Yankee. While he chose to live most of his adult life as a Connecticut commuter, in the mid-1930s his highly theatrical wife, Louise, insisted they and their five daughters move to the city, into the house she had inherited from her father, a brownstone in the area called Turtle Bay, at 246 East Forty-ninth Street—next door to Katharine Hepburn.

For several years the Perkinses called New York their home. Except for its allowing him to work extra hours with his most challenging author, Thomas Wolfe—who was then constructing *Of Time and the River* according to Perkins's blueprint—Max Perkins dreaded urban dwelling. Louise, on the other hand, thrived. A talented actress and writer who lacked the drive and discipline to pursue an artistic career, she happily filled her days with city life. She found excitement in just living next door to her favorite star of the stage and screen. She was so stimulated, she even wrote a play about Napoleon's sister Pauline as a vehicle for Miss Hepburn—a work she did not hesitate to bring to her neighbor's attention. The two women became good acquaintances, though it privately ate at Louise being so close to the very model of everything to which she aspired and yet was so far from attaining.

Katharine Hepburn and Max Perkins never met. Never comfortable in any kind of theater, he had no interest whatsoever in show people. Perkins's stars performed on paper. But he enjoyed having a figure so glamorous living so close and privately delighted in the constant bustle at 244. His wife's excitement over their famous neighbor amused him; and stories of the fabled actress brought out a touch of the voyeur in him. While he occasionally strained to get a peek at her, the closest he ever got to laying eyes on Katharine Hepburn was in espying a bust of her that sat by one of her drawing room windows.

So in the spring of 1972, when I was diligently approaching everyone I could find who ever knew Max Perkins, I decided I had to interview Katharine Hepburn. To be honest, whatever testimony she might offer would be far from crucial. The fact is, I simply wanted to meet Katharine Hepburn, and I felt I had a good excuse.

Growing up, I was always crazy about television and the movies, but I never had any great interest in meeting movie stars. Disappointment seemed inevitable. But as has long been the case with many—from truck drivers to presidents—Katharine Hepburn was always the exception. From the first time I had watched her old movies on television and in revival houses and her new ones as they appeared in theaters, I wanted to meet her. By the time I had graduated from college, I had seen all of her signature films—not such an easy task in those pre-video days.

Most fans suffer the problem of visiting their own best hopes upon their idols; but to her legions of fans around the world and across the century, Katharine Hepburn somehow seemed different from other movie stars, one whose natural beauty was probably just as striking even without Hollywood lights and makeup, one whose dialogue probably crackled with humor and intelligence even without others writing for her, one whose presence doubtless outshone any postures and gestures a director might have taught her. The greatest movie stars, the few genuine icons of the cinema, become so because we believe they are sharing actual pieces of themselves on the screen, a delusion fans nurse to heighten the fantasy. With Hepburn, however, such qualities were always assumed more than imagined.

Working on my Perkins book at home in Los Angeles, I had heard that Katharine Hepburn lived perpetually in transit but that the best way to reach her was through her California address, where her life was at its most calm. I presumed Katharine Hepburn still received hundreds of letters a week with dozens of requests for interviews; but somehow I figured mine would appeal to her because the subject would be so unexpected. My father, a television and motion-picture writer and producer, obtained the Los Angeles address for me, and I sent a brief but earnest typed letter to 9191 St. Ives Drive, on the Beverly Hills border, just a few blocks above the Sunset Strip. Months passed, during which time I interviewed dozens of witnesses far more appropriate to my work—such writers as James Jones, Alan Paton, Taylor Caldwell, Marcia Davenport, Erskine Caldwell, and Martha Gellhorn. I mentally wrote off the letter I had written Hepburn.

Then one day an envelope arrived, addressed in strong, jagged handwriting. Inside I found my letter to Katharine Hepburn, now filled on both sides of the page with the flamboyant script that had adorned the envelope. This handwritten response apologized for taking so long to get back to me but explained that her mail was in a constant state of flux; furthermore, she added, she really did not see any reason for us to meet as she had never met Max Perkins. She went on to write that she used to look out her windows and see the beautiful Perkins daughters, and that Louise Perkins was "a lovely-looking creature—reaching for something on her own which she never could attain, I felt—living in the shadow of a remarkable man." As for Perkins himself, she added, she used to spy on him walking "up and down Forty-ninth Street either conversing or in happy silence with my driver . . . who was known as the 'Mayor of Forty-ninth Street.' I always hoped that someday he would speak to me," she noted, in conclusion. But he never did. The letter ended abruptly with neither complimentary close nor signature—merely "K.H."

I wrote back to thank her and to suggest that just those few outpourings indicated that a good interview might unlock more memories. She never responded. Frankly, she had already delivered more than I expected; and so I felt I had no business imposing any further. I finished my biography six years later and mailed a copy to her, again hearing nothing in reply.

The next year, in the spring of 1979, I embarked on my second book, a biography of Samuel Goldwyn. He was the "Great Independent" of the Hollywood producers, a man who helped establish four motion-picture companies that had withstood fifty years of economic earthquakes—Paramount, MGM, United Artists, and the Samuel Goldwyn Company. His second wife, a former starlet named Frances Howard, had broken into show business in summer stock in Rochester, New York. There she fell in with (and in love with) a pudgy up-and-coming director of enormous talent, George Cukor. Strangely, his homosexuality only intensified their friendship, allowing them to become intimate in all ways but one. When the divorced Sam Goldwyn—with his fabled temper, twenty-one years her senior, and no matinee idol—proposed marriage, Frances ran straight to George, who quickly assessed her career opportunities. "Marry him, Frances," he said. "You'll never get a better part!"

George Cukor and Frances Goldwyn remained close all their lives—and beyond, as you will see; and the Goldwyns' son—Sam, Jr. ("Sammy" to those who knew him as a boy)—immediately arranged for me to meet with this crucial primary source. Beyond his remarkable career, Cukor was also famous for having one other "best friend"—Katharine Hepburn, whom he had directed ten times, including several pictures that were among the very best work either of them ever did. The talents and temperaments of actors and directors—be it D. W. Griffith with Lillian Gish, John Ford with John Wayne, William Wyler with Bette Davis—often click that way, providing outstanding results. For my money, no actor-director team in motion-picture history ever topped Hepburn and Cukor—especially when it came to romantic comedy. In fact, Hepburn's small house on St. Ives was actually the guest cottage on the Cukor estate that Spencer Tracy had rented as the home away from his legal residence with his wife, the home Hepburn had shared with Tracy.

I went to 9166 Cordell Drive (around the corner from St. Ives) for the first time at eleven in the morning on September 11, 1979, a blazingly hot day, into the 100s. The Cukor house was walled off from the road. At a door in the middle of the wall was a small wooden box, containing a telephone. I picked up the receiver, announced myself, and was admitted into the yard. A lawn swept down to the right toward a Romanesque pool area, where Cukor was standing with what appeared to be a team of houseboys, gardeners, and pool attendants. He suggested that one of the downstairs guestrooms in his big white house would be the coolest place for us to sit and talk. En route we toured much of the house, passing portrait-filled walls, with Hepburn represented everywhere—in paintings, photographs, even a pair of puppets of her and Spencer Tracy.

Cukor was a most animated talker—at a fast clip, with a lot of hand gestures; and we talked for several hours. I scribbled notes in a pad as "television tables" were set before us with large chef's salads and tall glasses of iced tea. A little before three, a handsome young assistant checked in on Cukor, whose energy was flagging, and I stood to introduce myself. "Oh, I know who you are," he said. "Miss Hepburn talks about nothing but your book whenever she's here."

Suddenly reminded, Cukor said that Kate was eager to meet me, that he would arrange it when she was next in California. Before I left, Cukor insisted on showing me the rest of his house—a beautiful living room with a large-paned picture window and Chippendale and Regency furniture that was fancy without being fussy; an oval room with a copper fireplace and a parquet floor and Georges Braque and Juan Gris represented on the walls; and, finally, his secretary's office, every square inch of which seemed to be covered with signed photographs of the greatest actors of the century. "Funny how they always call me a 'woman's director,'" he said with some irritation, pointing out pictures of many of his leading men—John Barrymore, W. C. Fields, Leslie Howard, Jack Lemmon in his first film, Ronald Colman in his Oscar-winning performance in *A Double Life*, and Rex Harrison in his, *My Fair Lady*. We met many more times over the next few years and became friends.

The second time I didn't meet Katharine Hepburn was in 1981, when she came to Los Angeles while appearing in Ernest Thompson's *The West Side Waltz*. I saw the play, and Cukor arranged for us to meet at dinner after the run; but the invitation arrived at a time when I had to be in New York. So there I was getting to know many of Hepburn's coevals—most of the remaining stars from the "golden age of Hollywood"—actresses whose careers had wound down while hers was humming. And I was still missing the one I was longing to meet.

At the end of 1982 I received a telephone call from Rust Hills, the fiction editor of *Esquire*. He explained that the magazine wanted to mark its impending fiftieth anniversary by producing its "greatest issue ever." Toward that end, *Esquire* was asking fifty authors to write about one of the fifty people in the last half-century who had "made a difference" in the way we had lived. Knowing I was deep into my Goldwyn research, Hills figured that I would think of motion pictures as the most popular art form of the 1900s and that I might select a mogul—probably Goldwyn—whose career might illustrate the "difference" he had made. I hesitated, largely because I was still in the midst of my research and was not ready to write up my findings, not even in a magazine piece. "But this would be a great opportunity for you," Rust Hills kept insisting, reminding me that I would be in the company of Mailer and Cheever and Updike.

"I definitely want to contribute a piece," I assured him, "but I'm not prepared to write about one of the moguls." After a moment's thought, I said I had a better idea. "What about Katharine Hepburn?"

"Oh no," he said. "We've already decided that we don't want any movie stars. And we only want to write about men."

"Now look," I said, "I'd like to give this some serious thought . . . but I could make a very good argument right now that Katharine Hepburn is a lot more than a movie star. And one other thing . . ." (I was suddenly recalling Cary Grant's response to Jack Warner's offer to play Henry Higgins in *My Fair Lady*—that not only did he not want the part but that if Rex Harrison didn't play it, he didn't even want to see the movie.) "If there are not going to be any women represented in the issue," I said, "not only do I not want to write for it, I don't even want to read it. I think you guys are going to be in big trouble if Eleanor Roosevelt isn't one of the fifty people who have 'made a difference.'" I suggested we both think about it.

By the time Rust Hills called back a week later, I was perfectly clear about my choice of subject and why. I explained the singularity of Katharine Hepburn's career, the "greatest in Hollywood history," I said. I dramatized my point with the fact that she won her first Academy Award for Best Performance by an Actress in a Leading Role the very year *Esquire* was founded and her unprecedented fourth Best Actress Oscar just that March. Thus, I explained, her career spanned *Esquire*'s years precisely. She was the only leading lady in the history of the medium to sustain a major career over five decades, I said, and she was still in demand. As if that was not enough, I added, she was one of the few movie stars who had performed regularly on the stage. Even more important, I argued, was the role Hepburn had played off the screen, as a model, even a hero, for at least three generations of women.

Hills reiterated that his editor in chief, Lee Eisenberg, simply did not want to include any women in the issue, and certainly not an actress. "Then how about this," I argued, "—why not do forty-nine men and one woman, Hepburn, as the person who made the biggest difference in the way men have changed their act over the last fifty years, that Hepburn best illustrates how the role of women had metamorphosed since the 1930s and how men had been forced to play at the top of their games just to keep up? The modern woman that Hepburn symbolizes," I said, "has kept men on their toes for years."

Thinking of a handful of actors I thought the men at *Esquire* would consider their gods, I built my case: I suggested that Cary Grant was never so jaunty and appealing as when he was playing off Katharine Hepburn in *Holiday, Bringing Up Baby,* and *The Philadelphia Story*; Spencer Tracy, I said, was never so spunky and attractive as he was when keeping up with Hepburn in *Woman of the Year* and *Adam's Rib* and *Pat and Mike*; Jimmy Stewart was never so lusty and swaggering as he was in *The Philadelphia Story*, the only role for which he won an Oscar; Henry Fonda was never so prickly as he was on Golden Pond, in the role for which he won his only Oscar. And Humphrey Bogart never proved himself so doughty as when his Charlie Allnut shaped up for Hepburn's Rosie Sayer in the role for which he won his only Oscar.

To make the Hepburn piece even more special, I suggested that instead of writing about her, I would interview her, allowing her to talk about the preceding five decades and *Esquire* to publish the most piquant bits of the transcript. After making my hard sell, I backpedaled, explaining that I felt funny making so strong an argument when I did not know Miss Hepburn and had no idea whether she would be remotely interested in cooperating. "But," I said, "I think I can at least arrange a meeting." Early that spring, Rust Hills asked if I would come to New York and present my case to Lee Eisenberg.

I did. During the meeting, he said they were already making room for a few women on their list . . . but that he was adamant about not including any other Hollywood personalities. I said that was important to me as well, because that would be part of my pitch to Hepburn, that she would be the sole representative of motion pictures in this gala issue.

I wrote to Hepburn, addressing my letter this time to her New York address, though I believed she was somewhere in Connecticut, where she had made headlines after becoming involved in a potentially fatal car crash near her weekend house in Old Saybrook the preceding December.

Less than a week later my phone rang, and the unmistakable voice said, "Mr. Scott Berg, this is Katharine Hepburn. Is this really a good idea?"

I was completely taken aback, not only to have Katharine Hepburn on my phone but to be plunging right into the discussion without any preamble. "Miss Hepburn, you're great to—"

"I mean, all these magazines are so slick," she said, "and *Esquire* is the slickest of the slick. Is this really a good idea?"

I explained that I thought it was, that I shared many of her reservations, but this promised to be something out of the ordinary. I underscored the seriousness of *Esquire*'s intentions by pointing out that she would be one of very few women presented at all, that ours would be the only piece in a question-and-answer format, and—my ultimate selling point—that she would be the only representative of Hollywood. That appealed to her the most. But she said she could not set a date right away, as she was still recuperating from her car accident and staying with her sister Marion and brother-in-law in Hartford. I asked what had happened—"Was it a snowy day? Were the streets icy?"—and inquired about her medical status, asking, "Are you on any dope?"

"Dope?" she asked. "I'm the dope. It was the most beautiful day I had ever seen, and I was driving my friend Phyllis from Fenwick back into the city; and there was a magnificent blue sky and I was so busy going on and on about how beautiful it was that I just drove right off the road and into a telegraph pole! No, it was the middle of the morning and no, I was cold sober, thank you very much."

Both women, then in their seventies, got banged up badly. Phyllis Wilbourn, who had by then been in Hepburn's employ for more than twenty years, suffered a fractured wrist and elbow, two broken ribs, and neck injuries; Hepburn's right ankle fractured in so many places, she said, it had been "hanging on by a thread." The ambulance driver was prepared to take her to the hospital in New Haven, the nearest major medical center; and there was already talk of amputating her foot. But Hepburn insisted on going to Hartford Hospital, where her father had been a surgeon and where her brother

Bob practiced. "A brilliant orthopod," she said, "glued my foot back on." For the next few weeks, she said, she would be stuck where she was—playing a lot of Parcheesi with her family. "Look," she said, "take this number down, and we'll talk again."

"With pleasure," I said.

"Call me tomorrow. Same time." I looked at the clock and realized we had been on the phone for more than an hour.

Over the next few weeks we chatted almost every day—discovering we shared mutual friends, political persuasions, and a passion for chocolate. I sent her boxes of dark chocolate turtles and almond bark from Edelweiss, her favorite confectionary in Beverly Hills, and a copy of *The Man Who Came to Dinner,* the Kaufman and Hart classic about a curmudgeon who breaks his leg and moves into an unsuspecting household, wreaking havoc on everybody's lives.

By March 1983, Hepburn was ambulatory again—still in a cast and on sticks—charging back into her former routine. We arranged our interview session for the first Wednesday and Thursday in April, and she suggested I stop by for an introductory drink the preceding Tuesday at six sharp. "But only," she said, "if you think this is really a good idea." And so, there I was on Wednesday, April sixth—my second time at at 244 East Forty-ninth Street—on what many consider one of the most desirable blocks in Manhattan.

Once an actual bay, roughly shaped like a turtle, the area had been filled in after the area's settlement in the seventeenth century; and except for a few stray businesses that use the name in this midtown East Side neighborhood, Turtle Bay has come to refer to the block of houses on Forty-eighth and Forty-ninth streets between Second and Third avenues, which back onto a private communal garden. These narrow four- and five-story houses have long been magnets for artists, home to a lot of literary and theatrical greats—including E. B. White and Robert Gottlieb (my editor at Alfred A. Knopf, the publishing company he headed), Harold Prince, Ruth Gordon and Garson Kanin at 242 East Forty-ninth, and, of course, Max Perkins at 246, a house then owned by Stephen Sondheim. Hepburn's house at 244 distinguished itself from the rest of the row with its decorative wrought-iron balustrade on the second floor, outside the three front windows, the center of which was crowned with a triangular arch.

I rang the terrifying bell for the second time in my life that morning at eleven on the dot. On this occasion, however, Hepburn herself opened the door. "Scott Berg," she said, "you're late."

"I'm not," I protested. "I'm right on time, to the second."

"You're ten years late."

As if I hadn't been hers before I ever arrived, I was now utterly captivated, all but having become a Shaw character, the romantic poet hopelessly in love with the older Candida. "I feel like Marchbanks," I said to her as I followed her up the stairs. After a few steps, however, I stopped. "If you will excuse me," I said, "I would like to use the bathroom first."

Upon joining my hostess in the living room, I placed a small tape recorder on the table between us and made a few sound checks. I explained that I had never taped an interview before but that it was necessary in this instance because of the question-and-answer format. Then I removed my jacket and left the room to set it on the chair. "You're learning," she said, as I returned to the couch and pulled out my pages of questions.

In the second before I pushed the "record" button, she anxiously blurted, "What's the first question?"

"Don't worry," I assured her. "You know all the answers."

"No," she insisted, "I have to know the first question."

"You want the first question?" I asked. "Okay. What's the capital of Kansas?"

"Wichita!" she said. "No, no. Topeka!"

"Right. Let's go. . . ."

For the next two days, from eleven until five, we sat in the living room discussing not only Katharine Hepburn's career but also the development of Hollywood as seen through her eyes—those of an insider who chose never to own a house there, so that she might always remain an outsider. I kept my questions on a fairly professional path, seldom trespassing into the personal. Her memories were vivid, and she was charming and funny; but I was constantly struck by how little thought she had given to her own actions and to those of people around her. Hepburn, I learned, always lived in the moment; and once an event had been completed, she was on to the next. There was no looking back.

Lunches quietly appeared and disappeared during our taping sessions; and my subject asked each afternoon if I wanted to stay for dinner. I suggested that it might be best if I did not, to keep us fresh. "We don't want to run out of things to say to each other," I reminded her. After a day of calling her "Miss Hepburn," she said, "Look, I think you should call me Kate."

"Okay, Kate," I said. "And I think you should call me . . . Mr. Berg."

By the end of the second day we had covered her entire career, from the movies she saw as a child (with her father every Saturday night, at the Empire, Strand, or Majestic theater in Hartford, where she became infatuated with William S. Hart, the great stone-faced cowboy) to the script she was then trying to get produced, the story of an old woman who hires a hit man to put old people out of their misery. We had talked about fifty feature films in which she had starred, a dozen television movies, and twice as many stage productions. She answered everything with candor, I felt, trying to bring originality even to the basic questions she had heard hundreds of times. The only question she refused to answer concerned the years between 1962 and 1967, the one hiatus in her career, during which time I knew she had cared for the ailing Spencer Tracy. "I never talk about that," she said when I reached that period. We quickly proceeded to discuss *Guess Who's Coming to Dinner,* their last picture together.

Once we finished, Kate asked if I would like her to show me the rest of her house. For the first time, I entered the front living room, larger than where we had been sitting, and full of interesting artifacts and mementos, including the white bust of her that Maxwell Perkins used to see. There was also a television set, situated in such a way as to suggest nobody ever watched it. In fact, I noticed, it was not even plugged in.

One flight up was Hepburn's bedroom, a big bright room with a high ceiling and fireplace, overlooking the garden. The bed had a dozen pillows on it, of all shapes and sizes. A small painting of a man reading a newspaper, his back to the artist, sat on the nightstand; the close-cropped white hair was enough to reveal that this was Spencer Tracy. "I never could get his face just right," she explained, ". . . except when I sculpted him." She produced a small, accurate bust she had made.

She led me into the bathroom, one unimaginably crude for a movie star. An old freestanding sink with two taps; a small tub with a big, plain showerhead hanging directly overhead, not protruding on an angle from the wall; some drawers and shelves with pictures of family and Spencer Tracy; threadbare towels; Colgate Tooth Powder; Albolene face cream. A second bedroom, at the front of the house, had become an extension of her closets, with athletic shoes, shirts, and a lot of red sweaters everywhere. She said there was a comfortable guest room upstairs.

As we headed down, Kate asked if I had plans for the weekend. She was going "up country," she said, to Fenwick, her country house in Connecticut; and she felt our interview was just getting started. "Look," I said, "we've got much more material than *Esquire* could ever possibly use. But I would love to see Fenwick." She suggested

I appear at Forty-ninth Street the next day at noon, at which time her driver planned to collect her and Phyllis. In fact, I had an appointment the next day—an interview for my Goldwyn book, which I could not break; and so I suggested that I would get up there on my own steam, by dinnertime. She said the trains to Old Saybrook were few and asked if I really wanted to bother renting a car.

We went down to the kitchen together, where we found Phyllis lying on a small daybed in the corner, reminding me that she had been the more seriously injured in the December car accident. "Do you have a good sense of direction?" Hepburn asked me, in the same tone that she had used two days earlier when asking about fireplaces. I told her I did, and she began to reel off the route to Fenwick, a sock-shaped peninsula off the Connecticut coast at Old Saybrook, where the Connecticut River empties into the Long Island Sound. She ran through the directions again, making them more complicated the second time. I assured her I could find the way. Not convinced, she threw a pop quiz at me. "Okay," she said, while we stood in the kitchen, "which way is south?" As I looked around to get my bearings, she muttered to Phyllis, "It's hopeless. We'll never see him again."

"I'll be there, Kate," I said, as I leaned down to kiss her on the cheek. She gave me a hug and a big pat on the back and said, "I used to be taller. I've already shrunk an inch or two." With that, she slammed the heavy door behind me, sending me out onto Forty-ninth Street, yelling, "Don't be late."

III

Curtain Up

I saw a play that night called *K2*. On a spectacular set that recreated the second-highest peak in the world, an interesting drama unraveled: In quest of the summit, one of a pair of climbers becomes injured, forcing the other to choose between returning to base camp or remaining with his teammate; this incited a dialogue about survival. In the end, he chooses to remain with his climbing partner, leaving the two to perish together.

At least, I think that's what the drama was about, for my mind wandered throughout the performance. I kept reliving the comedy I had stepped into during the preceding three days, one that volleyed between "drawing-room" and absurdist. I kept wondering why this virtual stranger, whose reclusiveness among movie stars was second only to Garbo's, had made herself so available to me. Katharine Hepburn and I had certainly gotten along and shared a few laughs, but that did not explain why somebody almost as famous for shutting people out as she was for her acting was suddenly opening her doors to me.

The next morning I interviewed Blanche Sweet, one of the earliest stars of the silent screen (her career began in 1909) in her small apartment downtown. Just shy of eighty-eight, she was still a beauty with sharp insights and a sharp tongue. She was full of happy recollections of her days as one of Samuel Goldwyn's leading ladies. But she was equally saddened by the way in which her career plummeted when pictures began to talk. Upon further reflection, she proudly asserted that her run of nearly twenty years was, in fact, as long as any actress could ask for in the medium, no matter what the era. "Even the great ones," she said, "can't stay a star longer than that. Some of the men get to go longer; but for women, it's always about youth. Pickford and Garbo knew when to quit. Gish became a character actress; Crawford became a cartoon, playing axe-murderers. And Bette Davis was doing orange juice commercials. Orange juice for God's sake!" she shrieked. "Bette Davis!"

"Only one that I can think of," said Miss Sweet, "got through the minefield, and that was—"

"I know who you mean," I said, not revealing my recent connection, "and she's still going strong."

It was early afternoon when I left Blanche Sweet, picked up my rental car, and crossed the Triboro Bridge. One hundred miles out of the city, I exited the Connecticut Turnpike and drove through Old Saybrook—a charming small town, with one shop-lined main street. As instructed, I carried on until the road ended. ("Be sure to stop there, or you'll end up in the Connecticut River," Hepburn had warned.) I took a right onto a narrow causeway, over an inlet dotted with swans, and made the first left on the other side. "First right, past the flagpole, left at the tennis courts—just keep heading south and east; you can find east, can't you? It'll be afternoon, so the sun will be setting in the west, so you go where the sun isn't setting. You can do that, can't you? And it's the house farthest south and east."

It was, in fact, hard to miss—a long, white brick house, three stories in the middle dropping to high-gabled two-story wings, rising from a long spit of land. A rush-filled pond ran the length of one side of the house, the Long Island Sound the other, so that it practically sat as an island on an island. At the approach of a dirt driveway was a hand-painted sign: PLEASE GO AWAY. As I drove under some trees, game birds flew out, into a cold, gray sky. It was a little after four when I rounded a bend and pulled into a large parking area.

The front door was ajar, so I rapped on it as I entered a big foyer. Phyllis came to greet me and announced that Miss Hepburn was swimming. She directed me outside, where, between some stone jetties, I saw Katharine Hepburn's head bobbing in the Sound. I walked across a patch of lawn, then a strip of sandy beach, buttoning my coat. "Now listen," she shouted, "you are absolutely crazy if you don't come in for a swim." I put my hand in the water, which seemed to be in the fifties. "I'd be crazy if I did," I said. "It's a little cold, isn't it?"

"Only for the first few seconds," she explained. "And then you're numb."

She breaststroked in and grabbed her towel from the rocks. "And it feels so good when you get out." She was wearing a one-piece black bathing suit, which she still filled nicely. Despite her lagging injured foot, she exuded enormous power—strong shoulders and arms and legs. "South," I said, pointing across the water to Long Island. "East," I said, pointing to one of two lighthouses along the river. "Good boy," she said with a smile. "Ask Phyllis to show you to Mother's room, and I'll meet you in the living room in a few minutes."

While I re-entered the house through its center porch, Hepburn went up some stairs at its west end, where there was an outdoor shower, which she used. By the time Phyllis and I had climbed the wide wooden stairs to the second floor, Kate had come down the long corridor of the bedroom floor and poked her head into the choicest guest suite—"Mother's Room"—an ample sitting room (with windows on two sides) and bedroom, overlooking the water, with its own bath. There was nothing fancy anywhere, unfinished wood paneling, comfortable furniture, books on the desk and the nightstand, a fresh bar of Ivory soap on the sink. "Is this okay?" she asked.

Smelling a fire burning downstairs in the living room, I was suddenly seized by the notion that if a seventy-five-year-old woman with a bad foot could find it within her to hobble out to the water and swim, surely an able-bodied thirty-three-year-old should be able to do the same. I quickly changed into a bathing suit and went down the corridor, which was lined with several other similar bedroom suites, though none seemed as large or well-situated as mine. I ran down the stairs toward the beach, and just kept running, headfirst into the water. Having got that far, I figured I owed it to myself to stay in as long as I could. After no more than forty-five seconds, I retreated, my body having turned blue. I took a hot shower outside on the upstairs deck, steam billowing into the cold air, before dressing. Then I meditated for twenty minutes, as I had for close to ten years, and joined my hostess in the living room.

She was already seated on the couch at the end closest to the large fireplace, her foot up on a stool, in the big, wonderful room. Windows on the south looked onto the water, as did the bay window to the east, before which sat a wide bench filled with pots of plants and flowers. Big vases of cut flowers bloomed everywhere, amid several odd objects Hepburn had collected over the years—a small antique sled, two massive slabs of wood chained to the ceiling, and on the mantelpiece, spools of yarn in different colors, a cut-out wooden marksman taking aim, and two odd-shaped hunks of what looked like white stone, which—after making me guess—she revealed were elephant teeth. Decoys, stuffed birds, and other replicas of waterfowl were tucked here and there. "Now don't you feel better?" she asked, referring to my swim.

"I felt better the second I got out."

"Well, that's really the point, isn't it? And now you've earned your drink." On a table at the entrance to the room sat a big tray with all the fixings for cocktails. Kate was already drinking what I learned was her usual starter, a goblet full of grapefruit juice on the rocks, which she had just finished. Then she liked that same glass refilled with ice, her shot of Scotch, topped with soda. I made the same for myself in a clean goblet and sat in one of the white wicker chairs opposite her on the other side of the fireplace. Several small, dim lamps were lighted all around the room. She clutched a pillow, on which was needlepointed a motto that had been carved into the fireplace of her first childhood home, the words of Charles Dudley Warner, a former editor of *The Hartford Courant*: LISTEN TO THE SONG OF LIFE.

She asked what had taken me so long after my swim, and I said that I had been "listening to the song of life"—that I had been meditating. "Is that like contemplating your navel?" she asked. No, I said, it was more like settling down, and getting my mind and body, maybe even a little of my spirit, in tune. "Oh, I *see*," she said in a tone she would later use whenever she heard anything that sounded a little otherworldly. "But don't you find it a bothersome waste of time?" she inquired. That was my fear at first, I told her; but I quickly learned that meditating twice a day actually bought me more time, energizing me. She wasn't buying much of what I was saying, certainly none of the metaphysical aspects. But when I described the physical effects, the nuts-and-bolts effects of meditation, she pressed for details. For the rest of her life, I discovered, she was insatiably curious, always fascinated by things she did not know about or understand. After hearing all the information she could absorb, she would assert her own position. "You're not going to start meditating on me in the middle of dinner, are you?" she asked.

The evening drill at Fenwick was similar to that in New York: Phyllis appeared with a few plates of hors d'oeuvres—usually small shrimp with a Louis sauce on one and small hot dogs with honey mustard on another. I offered to get her a drink, which she always considered, then requested a ginger ale. Because Norah did not make the weekly journey to Old Saybrook—having a family of her own in New Jersey—dinner was prepared by Phyllis or any number of people helping in the kitchen, including the driver and sometimes Kate herself. The meals would appear on trays—always served first, Kate placed hers on a plump pillow on her lap; mine and then Phyllis's were set on television tables.

There was always variety to the huge meals, but the tray at every dinner was essentially the same. We started with a large cup of soup—either beet with dill or zucchini with shallots, served hot or cold, depending on the weather—with thin Portuguese bread, which had been buttered then toasted. The main dish was either steak, curried lamb, or fish, sometimes a roast chicken, occasionally roast beef, for which Phyllis would prepare her specialty, Yorkshire pudding. The plate always contained some potato, usually au gratin or baked, and a vegetable alongside a few spoonfuls of boiled carrots and celery. By the time the third tray had been set down, Kate was usually halfway through her plate. Wine was always offered, but nobody ever accepted, as she and I happily sipped our Scotch-and-sodas. By the time the trays were cleared, we had usually moved on to a second Scotch. Dessert was always ice cream; and at my first dinner at Fenwick, Kate told me that her brother Dick had just cooked up an extraordinary batch of hot fudge, which we must have. Phyllis brought in the big scoops of coffee ice cream drowned in thick, bittersweet sauce, accompanied by a plate of Norah's lace cookies with walnuts, practically paper thin. Kate always asked if I wanted "any coffee or tea or funny tea" (which meant something herbal), which neither of us ever had.

By seven-thirty, dishes, trays, and tables had been cleared, and Phyllis had retired to the kitchen. I boldly approached the large country fireplace and placed a few more logs on, under the chatelaine's watchful eye—"Not too close to each other," she insisted. "Make them fight for the flame." She asked me to throw a piece of driftwood on top, because it crackled and emitted colorful sparks. She asked about our interview in New York, if it had been satisfactory; and I said she had gone well beyond the call of duty. "Good, good," she said, "because I didn't want you to feel shortchanged in the Spencer department."

"I think we covered those films more than adequately," I said.

"Mmmmm," she said in a way that would become familiar to me over the years, dropping several tones, suggesting that she could easily agree but that the issue at hand could be improved upon. I looked into the flames and, while jabbing the logs with a heavy wrought-iron poker, asked, "Was there something more you wanted to say?"

In fact, there was. Raising her glass for me to refill, she began to walk me through her twenty-six-year relationship with Spencer Tracy, starting with their meeting on the MGM lot in 1941 and going up to his death in 1967. We had covered some of the same ground in New York. But this time she didn't talk about the making of their movies, only about the nature of their relationship, what began as mutual admiration and quickly ripened into the most important experience in her life—"because for the first time," she said, "I truly learned that it was more important to love than to be loved."

The fire died; and it was close to midnight. "Oh," she said, looking at the clock, "I never stay up this late." Kate directed me in the placing of the heavy screens in front of the fireplace and in locating the switches for each of the lamps in the living room.

"Now, what do you like for breakfast?" she asked. I explained that I was very easy, a few pieces of fruit and some water. "No eggs, no cereal, no coffee?" No, honestly, just a few pieces of fruit and some water. "Fine," she said, "you'll find it all in the kitchen there, and whenever you're ready, bring your tray into my room." We walked up to my room, where she and I turned down the bed—which involved her folding and placing the comforter at the foot of the bed in such a way that one pull (should it become necessary in the middle of the night) would cover the entire bed. She plumped the pillows, checked on the towels, came over to peck me on the cheek, and said, "Nightie-night." She closed the door and was gone.

I was just unbuttoning my shirt when she walked right back in to drop a curious remark before leaving for the night. "You have a good memory," she asked, "don't you?"

I always thought it was pretty good. But I stayed up until two scribbling page after page.

Sleeping at Fenwick feels like drifting on a boat at sea. The wood of the house creaks gently, in harmony with the lapping tide and the distant foghorn. I awakened to the sound of gulls. After meditating in my sitting room (yes, twice a day), I padded down to the large kitchen—which held enough appliances for two households, as I would soon discover was the case. I found a tray waiting on the counter—with a grapefruit already sliced and separated, glasses and plates, and a fruitbowl—and a note saying, "See me. K." I poured some juice from the nearest of the two refrigerators and selected some fruit and carried my tray upstairs, knocking on Hepburn's open bedroom door.

The master apartment was actually two rooms, with a picture-lined little hallway leading past a small bedroom suite into Kate's huge room, practically as large as the living room directly beneath. The south- and east-facing windows allowed morning light to pour in. A fire crackled in the small fireplace. Unlike the other rooms I had seen, this one had red brick walls and was only trimmed in wood. It was a scene of orderly clutter, slithering books and scripts here, smooth stones and marble objects there. A rack held a dozen (mostly straw) hats; and cut flowers and her own paintings (by then, her representational though slightly fanciful style had become recognizable to me) were everywhere. Propped high in her bed on a mound of pillows, Kate—in white pajamas and a thin and faded red

33

robe—sat reading the newspaper. Her hair was combed up and she was glowing; she wore spectacles low on her nose. A rattan chair and ottoman sat by the fire, which she instructed me to push closer to her bed, so that I could use the footrest as a table and face her while I ate. "Did you sleep all right and did you find everything you need?" she asked. I assured her I did and asked how late she had slept. "I'm usually up with the sun," she said, "or just before." At that hour, she explained, when the world was hers alone, she went down to the water—summer or winter, snow or shine—and swam.

She looked at my tray and said, "That looks pretty meager. Don't you even take coffee?" No, I said, just water and juice, which I mix with psyllium husk.

"Psyllium husk?" she asked, in a shocked tone. "You take psyllium husk?" As I prepared to discuss this fiber's gastric benefits, she added, "I thought I was the only one who knew about that. You know, Howard turned me on to psyllium husk forty-five years ago. I've taken it every day since." I was surprised—not that she too was a regular user but that she had dropped so casually the name of Howard Hughes, her most reclusive alleged paramour.

She had worked through her own breakfast of grapefruit and toast and dry cereal—having recently given up shredded wheat, which she would crumble, she told me, for granola with dried fruit—and was pouring the last cup of what had been an entire pot of coffee. "Are you sure you don't drink coffee in the morning? What do you use to turn on the motor?" Actually, I explained, I meditate each morning as well as at the end of each day, and that charged me up. "Christ," she said, rolling her eyes, "how much is there to think about?!!"

Over the next half hour we discussed the news—she kept current in all sections of the paper, except the business pages—and talked about our options for spending the day. The agenda was so full, I kept forgetting that she was still recovering from a car accident.

I removed the breakfast trays to the kitchen, showered, and we met in the foyer, where Kate was suiting up for a chilly morning. She was wearing some old khaki pants, a black turtleneck, and an overshirt, and was putting on a ratty, torn jacket. "What is that made of?" I asked. "Dog hair?"

She was only partially amused. "You don't approve of my jacket?" she asked. I said it was not a question of approving; I just wondered what it was. It turned out to be a removable lining from an old coat, one that had not belonged to her in the first place, which she somehow had walked off with twenty-five years earlier. From a barrel in the front hall, which was filled with old golf clubs and walking sticks, she grabbed a proper cane and handed me a long, narrow piece of driftwood which she thought became me.

We went out the front drive and headed over the lawn toward the beach to the east of the house. Once we hit this rocky part of the shore, I suggested that perhaps this was not the best place to walk on an ankle that had recently been shattered. But she insisted this was the best way to strengthen it. I asked if that was a medical opinion, and she said no, "a sensible one." We walked at a good clip, toward a far jetty of huge granite blocks which, she said, had once served as ballast on America-bound ships. We climbed atop this rugged walkway of unevenly cut boulders and began to walk out to the far lighthouse in the Sound—one built in the 1860s, she said, as a companion to the lighthouse of one century earlier several hundred yards up the river. We were about a quarter of the way out when we reached a point that was going to require a good leap from one boulder to the next. Noticing her sizing up the challenge, I said, "Why don't we head back?" No, she insisted. She could not press on, but it was important that I get all the way out to the lighthouse, that I must go to the far side of the tower so that I could get the view looking out to the sea and then looking back to the house. She waited for me, sitting on one of the rocks, while I ran all the way out and took in the spectacular view, a strong wind slapping my face on the run back.

Returning to the house, Kate gave me some of the history of Fenwick. It had once been a great farm but, by the early 1900s, had been subdivided, becoming a private summer enclave principally for Hartford insurance executives. Kate's father, Dr. Thomas Norval Hepburn, who practiced in Hartford, bought a big, Victorian-style house at the end of a cluster of summer homes, and sent his family down there for the season, joining them as often as possible. The houses surrounded what was then a private golf course and tennis courts. Everybody there knew everybody there. It was an ideal place for boating and fishing and swimming and diving, all of which Kate mastered early on. "Paradise!" Kate said, whenever she talked about Fenwick. She told me then how, as a child, she developed not only into a superb all-around athlete but also a tomboy—calling herself "Jimmy." She pointed out the pier from which she learned to dive— swandives, backflips, halfgainers, you name it.

"I was fearless," she said, ". . . and lawless." Time and again, Kate told me over the next twenty years that she and her siblings were raised with "no rules—except the golden one." The Hepburns lived largely by their own code, which often meant pushing limits and beyond, forcing them to develop their own moral compasses. She told me how she and a friend also used to break into houses, for example, just to create mischief. When damage had been done, her father would generally take care of it, letting Kate's own shame stand as her punishment. Her conscience was enough to inform her that she would have to make any necessary financial adjustments. For major infractions, he believed in spankings. In fact, Kate often spoke of how most "modern parents" had become afraid of their children. "Children need boundaries," she said, in one of her few psychological observations, "so they can know how far they have to go to get beyond them."

Freedom fostered creativity. When the Bishop of New Mexico preached in Connecticut one Sunday about the plight of the Navajos and their need for a new victrola, young Kate and some friends produced a stage version of *Beauty and the Beast*. Kate grabbed the choicest role for herself—the Beast; and the children raised seventy-five dollars for the Native Americans.

Kate wanted to show me the rest of Fenwick on that cool but clear day. Normally, she explained, we would go on bicycle; but her foot was clearly hurting. In the large garage sat a golf cart, which I backed out and which she "backseat drove" as I tooled along some curvy roads through some high grass to the northeast corner of Fenwick, right along the river. We passed a few old houses, which she adored, and a number of large "monstrosities" that were being built in what was fast becoming an all-too-fashionable locale. Kate was not averse to the newcomers—for people pretty much stuck to themselves there, treating her like any other neighbor—nor even the building of new houses. It was the lack of good taste and common sense, building houses beyond the proportions their land dictated. She introduced me to an elderly man coming out to his mailbox, one Charlie Brainard, whom Kate had known from Hartford and Fenwick for close to seventy years. "Charlie and I remember when all this was our playground," Kate said affectionately.

"We're still pretty lucky to be living here," he said. "It's still fun."

"Charlie," she said with a toss of the head, "we're pretty lucky to be living anywhere." Knowing a good exit line when she heard one, she rapped her cane on the steering wheel of the golf cart, and we were off again, to see the inner lighthouse—which required our walking across other people's property. Whether the owners were home or not did not matter. Fenwick was still her playground, and she always seemed to draw strength just watching the flow of the Connecticut River. She told me that her family's original house in

Fenwick was completely destroyed by the hurricane of 1938, and that she had built the present house—larger and stronger.

Heading back toward the Hepburn house, and then beyond, she reminded me that the river connected Fenwick to Hartford in the north. (I told her I was no stranger to the Connecticut River, as I had spent a great deal of time along its banks even farther north, in Windsor, Vermont, which had been Max Perkins's summer and ancestral home. She seemed a little surprised—not that I knew *her* river, but that it extended beyond her territory.) "Republican," she said as we drove around, "all very Republican." She was speaking of the Hartford insurance families, her neighbors and summer friends.

"We were always left of center," Kate said of her family, thinking how the Hepburn brood must have appeared to the rest of the upper–middle class in Hartford. "I'm sure they considered us extremely eccentric, a tribe of wild Indians." And with good reason:

Dr. Thomas Norval Hepburn and his wife, Katharine Houghton Hepburn, were unlike any of their peers, and they prided themselves on the differences. While both were active members of their community, they—and their six children—had always stood slightly apart.

Tom Hepburn came from two Virginia families—the Hepburns and the Powells—both of which had suffered economically during the Civil War. His father was a poor Episcopalian minister, his mother a proper lady who believed women did not get a fair deal in life and that they should obtain proper educations. "He was very good-looking," Kate said of her father, "and he adored women." He had been a great athlete at Randolph-Macon College and studied medicine at Johns Hopkins.

Katharine "Kit" Hepburn was almost two years his senior, the daughter of Caroline Garlinghouse and Alfred Augustus Houghton (pronounced HO-ten, not HOW-ten). She was, in many ways, the woman Tom's mother might have become, had she been born a generation later. Alfred Houghton grew up in the shadow of his dynamic brother Amory (prounounced AM-ree, with a short "a"), who built the Corning Glass Company. Alfred suffered from depression; and one day, after visiting his brother, without explanation, he put a bullet through his brain—leaving a young wife and three daughters.

Not long after that, Caroline Houghton, Kit's mother, learned that she had stomach cancer and that her days were numbered. She knew her wealthy in-laws would see that her girls would never starve, but she did not want them to be subjected to their very reactionary ways. ("*Very* Republican," said Kate.) Their only life-insurance policy, Caroline Houghton hammered into her children's heads, would be a college education.

She moved her family to Bryn Mawr, Pennsylvania, where there was a new college, with a wonderful reputation, for Kit and a prepatory school next door for the younger girls. When Caroline Garlinghouse Houghton died at thirty-four, her three children were farmed out to one relative, then another. Although rich Uncle Amory oversaw their finances, Kit stood up to his conservatism and insisted on his paying for her college education—something he considered a worthless enterprise for women. Katharine Houghton graduated from Bryn Mawr College, and her two sisters followed.

One of the sisters, Edith, went on to Johns Hopkins to study medicine, where she met Tom Hepburn. They became friends and fencing partners. Then he met her older sister, who quickly fell for him and found a teaching job in Baltimore, just to be near him. Without much money between them, they soon married, confident of opportunities for a bright young doctor and his college-educated wife. Over several offers from hospitals in New York, they chose the small, prosperous city of Hartford and moved into a house across the street from the Hartford Hospital. They promptly had two children, a boy named for him and a girl—born May 12, 1907—named for her. Kate.

"Venereal disease was being discussed by my parents as long as I can remember," Kate told me that day. In fact, I later learned, it had been a topic of conversation among Houghtons and Hepburns before that. Edith Houghton never became a doctor (ultimately marrying a classmate, Donald Hooker, instead); but she did travel to Germany to study the hottest medical topic of the day. And she came home sufficiently informed and inflamed to incite several around her. Venereal disease was, of course, directly related to prostitution, which had all sorts of sociopolitical ramifications, including the white-slave trade and teenage pregnancy. Thus, venereal disease was directly linked to issues relating to the oppression of women, a connection that was not lost on either Dr. or Mrs. Hepburn.

Kate would never forget the regard her mother held for *her* mother, how the young Caroline Garlinghouse Houghton had died so young, full of expectations for her girls—envisioning something more than traditional homemaking, pleasing a husband, and raising children. "And there was Mother," Kate said of those early years of marriage, "thrilled to be Mrs. Hepburn. But she was also a woman with a really good mind and an advanced degree. She was a wonderful speaker and an attractive woman. And she felt she should do more with her life. She became restless—a real rebel without a cause."

One day Dr. Hepburn noticed in the newspaper that Mrs. Emmeline Pankhurst, the English suffragist leader, was speaking in town that very night. He insisted they attend, and an activist was born. Mrs. Hepburn became the head of the Connecticut Woman Suffrage Association and later a friend and colleague of birth control advocate Margaret Sanger. She worked at the grassroots level—trotting young Kate out in parades and having her pass out pamphlets—and took on all opponents up to and including local newspaper editors and the mayor. "But Mother's secret," Kate would tell me repeatedly—and this was true of the most effective early feminists—"was in remaining extremely feminine. She dressed beautifully, she tended to her husband, she showed off her well-groomed children. And then, while she was pouring the mayor a second cup of tea, she would discuss with great intelligence some great injustice being heaped upon his female constituents. And then she'd smile and say, 'More sugar?'" Dr. Hepburn supported his wife in all her campaigns.

As regularly as possible, he came home from work at teatime, so that he could spend time with his children—discussing adult matters with them, playing with them, challenging them to support unpopular causes. More than once, the Hepburns had rocks thrown through their windows.

Four and then six years after Kate was born, the Hepburns had two more children, both boys, named Richard and Robert. Five and seven years after that came two girls, Marion and Margaret (known as Peg). Each pair was born in a different house in Hartford, each house a little bigger than the last. There "Jimmy"—pairing off with her older brother, Tom—used to race the trolley cars down Farmington Avenue on her bicycle. She said there was not a single tree in town she could not climb, not even an especially dangerous one on Hawthorn Street. She delighted in telling of the neighbor who called Kate's mother and said, "Mrs. Hepburn, Kathy is on the top of the hemlock tree . . ." and how Mrs. Hepburn replied, "I know, Mrs. Porritt, please don't frighten her or she might fall out."

Kate and I rode in the golf cart to the western side of Fenwick, beyond the tennis courts, to a few gridded streets with pleasant-looking houses. "You must meet Marion," she said. "Hey," Kate yelled, as we walked unannounced into a handsome place, then undergoing renovation. Marion appeared, obviously a Hepburn. While very pretty, she was less glamorous than Kate, her face rounder and her features less pronounced. Then came her handsome, white-haired husband, Ellsworth Grant, whom Kate had warned me was very rich. They were the parents of the actress Katharine Houghton, who had played Kate's daughter in *Guess Who's Coming to Dinner*. Kate introduced me, saying, "This is Scott Berg, my biographer."

"Whoa," I said, shaking hands with our hosts, who were somewhat taken aback themselves, knowing there had been a lifelong interdiction against giving writers personal access to the family. "Let's not get ahead of ourselves."

"Well," said Kate, "I mean he's learning everything there is to learn about me . . . because now he's writing a piece about me for a magazine. Think of him as 'the man from *Spy*,'" a reference to the magazine for which the Jimmy Stewart character worked in *The Philadelphia Story*. "Now this is Marion and Ellsworth Grant," she said. "They've been married forever, they've been in love with each other forever, and they've been sleeping with each other since they were fifteen."

"Katty!" said Marion. "Kate!" said I. And Ellsworth stood silent, grinning.

"Well, it's true," said Kate, "and you should be proud of it, because you're still a damn good-looking couple. Now what are you doing to this place?" We trooped through the house, upstairs to the master bedroom, where Kate decided the bed was terribly positioned. "Now look," she said, "you've absolutely got to move this bed. I mean, it's crazy. You've got one of the most beautiful views in the world, and you're not even waking up to it. Move it over here and you'll wake up to glorious sunrises, looking out onto the water. It's insane otherwise."

"Well," said Ellsworth, "we like it here."

"But what's the point?" said Kate, now exasperated. "I mean what's the point of living in one of the most beautiful spots in the world, with one of the most beautiful views right out your window, and you're refusing to look at it? You're hopeless. The both of you,

I mean, just hopeless. It's a waste, this whole house is utterly wasted on the likes of you two. . . ." And we were off.

Back at Kate's house we went into the kitchen to scare up lunch. Phyllis was already at work, preparing chicken salad. "Don't forget to slice the grapes," Kate told her, obviously for the thousandth time. "Vertically, not horizontally," she added, turning to me to explain that they tasted different if they were cut across their equators. At the far end of the kitchen, between the second refrigerator, the cabinets, and a stove filled with boiling and steaming pots of all sizes, their lids clacking, hurtled a big man—tall and stocky—in a red sweatsuit and wearing a rooster cap, complete with cockscomb. Kate introduced me to her brother Dick. He offered a huge, hamlike hand.

"Welcome," he said, holding a big spoon to my mouth. "Now taste this." It was turkey soup, very hot, filled with vegetables. "Now, what would be good in that?" he asked, as he made his way to the cabinet in search of spices. He returned to the stove with cayenne pepper, then he removed a macaroni-and-cheese casserole from the oven and stirred a saucepan full of candied grapefruit rinds. "Now try one of these," he said, handing me one of the cooled candies.

Kate was hungry, so we retreated to her side of the kitchen, where Phyllis was finishing the trays of chicken salad and green salad and toast and milk and zucchini soup. Each of us picked up a tray, though Kate paused at the counter to grab a dark chocolate turtle out of a two-pound box before entering the dining room. After cleaning our plates, Kate asked Phyllis to see if any of the pots on Dick's stove contained hot fudge. One did; and we made huge sundaes.

"Now we can rest," Kate said. "Just read the papers or take a nap, or, no, better that you see the town, and then we can come back and swim before dinner." Although her young driver from New York was there at the house, she suggested that we let him rest. So I took the two of us across the causeway in the white town car she leased from Hertz—"That's the telegraph pole I drove into, nearly killed Phyllis, nearly killed me too"—then turned left into the village of Old Saybrook.

We stopped first at Walt's, a small grocery which Kate claimed had the best meat anywhere. She picked up steaks for dinner and a slab of unsliced bacon; and she grabbed a bag of bagel chips, which she proceeded to consume as we walked through the market. By the time we reached the checkout stand, she had to tell the checker who weighed what remained in her bag of chips to double it. She signed for the groceries. Then she took me through Patrick's Country Store, a charming shop with a lot of plaid, woolen goods. She couldn't find anything she wanted, but she insisted I meet the proprietor. We made a final stop at James Gallery and Soda Fountain, to pick up a few items, some newspapers and—so long as we were there—didn't I want an ice-cream cone? I felt I had already eaten enough for two days, but she insisted that James had the best ice-cream cones anywhere. So she ordered maple walnut in a honey cone, and I went with chocolate in a plain cone. "You can't order a plain cone," she said. "They're so boring. It's like eating cardboard. They always taste stale."

"Well, this one is rather good," I insisted, "crisp, crunchy, and it doesn't fight the flavor of the ice cream the way your honey cone does." She simply shook her head as though she could not comprehend anything so outrageous. "Get me out of here," she said, muttering, "I never heard of anyone eating a plain cone."

We returned to the house; and though it was getting cloudy and cold, Kate was ready for a swim. I joined her and found my tolerance for the cold water had increased in just one day. Or maybe it was being in the water together and not being willing to get out until she had. After a few minutes, we both headed for the outdoor shower. By the time we met downstairs again, it was starting to rain. Kate suggested I start a fire while she rustled up a game of Parcheesi. "You do know how to play Parcheesi, don't you?" she said.

"Oh sure," I said, remembering Parcheesi from my childhood—you throw some dice and you move some green plastic pieces toward home. "Well, you couldn't be worse than Phyllis," said Kate with a competitive edge in her voice that I had not heard before, "so she'll play with Dick, and you'll be my teammate." Dick—without his rooster hat, revealing a completely shaved head—entered the living room with a tray of mocha-flavored candy he had just cooked up. (Overcooked, actually, so these thin squares that were meant to be chewed had become hard candies of sugar, chocolate, and very strong coffee.) Everybody grabbed one while we set up the gameboard and chose our colors. "I have to be blue," insisted Kate.

It became apparent after my first couple of throws of the dice that the game was not exactly the one I remembered and that I had stepped onto a no-nonsense playing field. Kate looked at me with utter disgust, now stuck with me as her partner. Then I made the mistake of saying, "How hard can it be to pick up? I mean, it's sort of like Chutes and Ladders. Seven-year-olds play this."

"Well, clearly you don't have the brains of a seven-year-old!" she asserted, suggesting that I was missing all the subtleties of this ancient Hindu game. As she took to moving my green men strategically around the board, Dick leaned over and slapped her hand. "You can't do that," Dick shrieked. "He has to move his own men. It's simply not fair otherwise."

"But my partner is a complete idiot," she countered. "He doesn't have a clue what he's doing, and it's simply not fair for me to be penalized like this."

Dick held his ground. "You chose him," he insisted. "You could have chosen Phyllis. But you took a chance on somebody new."

"But I didn't know he was a complete idiot."

We were all on our second or third candies by now, and the caffeine was kicking in. The tempo of the game had discernibly picked up, as had our tempers. I was truly getting the hang of the

45

game's subtleties—such as they were—but after one unfortunate roll of the dice on my part, Kate stood up and said, "I give up. This is hopeless. I mean he's positively hopeless." Dick insisted she sit down, that she had to play this game to the bitter end, which I kept praying would come soon. I like to think the slight tremble in my hands was the result of the candy. But now the tables began to turn, and after one of Kate's moves, Dick offered, "That was a great mistake on your part." For the next several minutes they argued how Kate should have made her move. On Phyllis's next turn, Kate criticized her. On mine, my opponent Dick took to offering me advice, with which Kate disagreed. "Now look," I said, "you've all put me in a terrible spot. On one hand I feel I should listen to my partner, but on the other, Dick appears to be the best player and is on the verge of winning the game."

"Dick is not the best player," said Kate. "I've been beating him at Parcheesi all his life." I followed my partner's strategy.

"Well, you're not going to beat him today," he said, making what everybody had to concede was a brilliant throw of the dice (and let's remember, we're throwing dice here!), which took advantage of my vulnerable position. On Kate's next roll, Dick started in again, pointing out the errors of his older sister's plays. Meantime, Phyllis slowly and silently kept rolling dice and moving her little red markers, until at last she threw her hands in the air and shouted, "I won! I won!" And sure enough, she and Dick had.

"I protest this game," Kate said with great authority, "on account of my having to play with a complete idiot."

"I resent being called an idiot," I said, "just because I didn't win this idiotic game. It's mostly luck anyway." At this, Dick took umbrage, claiming that it's actually a game requiring great intelligence and a sense of strategy . . . which he suggested Kate was too impulsive ever to master. "Oh, you're all a bunch of idiots, real idiots," Kate said, putting the game away.

"But I won! I won!" said little old Phyllis with great glee.

"Yes, dear, you won," said Kate. "Now why don't you do something important, like get our dinner going."

I announced that I was going upstairs for a little peace and quiet.

"Yes," Kate suggested, "you *meditate* on how you lost us that game."

During dinner—warm beet soup and plates heaped high with vegetables, baked potatoes, steaks, and broiled tomatoes ("You must always have the wet of the tomato," Kate explained, "with the dry of the beef")—we talked about my current work, how I was attempting to paint a giant mural of Hollywood from its beginnings, through the life of Samuel Goldwyn. Kate loved the idea, insisting that he was the most colorful and compelling of all the movie moguls. "Of all those pirates, and they were all pirates," Kate asserted, "I think he was the only one with a sense of humor."

I told her about the play I had recently seen, *K2,* and its conclusion of the two mountain-climbers being left to die. Kate insisted the playwright had made a terrible mistake, dramatically and morally. The injured man, who could not go on and who was only jeopardizing the life of the second man, she said matter-of-factly, should have thrown himself off the edge of the mountain. "In offering his life, he would have saved a life. As it is," she said, "he is responsible for two deaths. That would have made for a much better play. Really satisfying."

While Phyllis was off doing the dishes, Kate got to reminiscing about her family. That, she said, was the great advantage she had had in her life and her career, what gave her "a leg up." Life is "tough," she said, but one could have no greater support system than a family, people who knew all your weaknesses and loved you anyway. Her parents were obviously great examples of courage, common sense, and nonconformity. Also, I realized, narcissism.

I never heard Kate speak a single word that did not honor her mother or father. Often she would say how "lucky" she was to grow up in so vital and stimulating an environment. And yet, in that conversation and many thereafter, I often detected annoyance in her voice and traces of ill will between the lines. There was a discernible resentment toward her father's bluster, a trait that bordered on bullying. All Hepburns were encouraged to exercise their rights of free will; but there never seemed to be a way to win his approval. Simply following meant you were weak; defiance meant disrespect—both of which were frowned upon.

Kate's love and respect for her mother was frayed with frustration as well. While Kit Houghton Hepburn was a genuine feminist pioneer, largely at her husband's instigation, Kate came to develop a filial impatience that her mother didn't blaze trails farther into the frontier. She appreciated the strides Kit had made for herself and other women; but she suggested to me more than once that had her mother stood up to her husband, she might have become a national figure, like Margaret Sanger. But Dr. Hepburn was not about to let her abandon him and their children.

So there was a Catch-22. Kate always felt she benefited enormously from the strong family structure provided by the presence of two parents. And yet she always harbored some resentment toward her father for imposing his will, for standing in his wife's way. At an early age, she became determined not to let men tell her what she could or could not do.

Kate's siblings were as important to her as her parents, providing compassion and companionship in the world she had created for herself, one from which most people would be shut out. While her brothers and sisters obviously delighted in her extraordinary success and her exciting presence, she knew they all had paid a certain price.

Each of the Hepburn siblings developed large personalities as well, in reaction to their dynamic parents as much as to Kate. She had become an international celebrity by the time they were teenagers; and so, her two sisters sometimes seemed more like her own children. Marion, she felt, was the most intellectual of the lot, passionate about history, and active in local historical societies; but Kate often remarked that she tended to be "very social"—perhaps in reaction to being ostracized because of her parents' extreme views—a tendency she didn't really understand. Marion, she said, "always wanted to belong." Peg, who had graduated from Bennington College, proved to be the most opinionated of the clan, strong and articulate. She lived a hard physical life, independent, a divorcée running a cow farm upstate.

The Hepburn boys were equally disparate from one another. Bob, the most passive of the children, found happiness in order. He became a Harvard-educated doctor, and was mild, thoughtful, and highly congenial. Dick, on the other hand, next in line after Kate, was voluble and theatrical, with a booming voice. Kate believed he suffered most from her success. For Dick was highly intelligent and artistic, a Harvard graduate himself, who long yearned for a life in the theater. A fine musician, an amusing raconteur, and a skillful playwright with wicked powers of observation, he could never escape being identified as Katharine Hepburn's brother. He wore his resentment like a badge. Without his ever quite making a name for himself in the world, Kate made him her responsibility, allowing him to become a kind of ward of the castle.

By the time I had played my first game of Parcheesi at Fenwick, Dick's first marriage had dissolved and his four children had grown, leaving him to move into the west wing of Kate's house. In some ways, he was a case of arrested development, a big kid. But he was extremely knowledgeable, well-read, and wise about people. So much so, Kate said, that he ultimately opted not to compete. Kate took full responsibility for his predicament and became his sole support. In the past he had sometimes provoked her to rage; but by the time of my first visit, I realized that he could only irritate her. "What can I do?" Kate would say about him over the years. "He's my brother."

And so, they forged their own version of domestic tranquillity, sharing the house in Fenwick though sometimes going entire weekends without seeing each other as they maintained separate sides of the same kitchen.

All of Kate's siblings had children, and she spoke lovingly of her nieces and nephews. She was always happy to see them, and just as happy, she said, to see them go. Her closest and most complicated relationship was with the actress Katharine Houghton, who called her "Aunt [ont] Kat" and who, between career moves, often lived upstairs on the fourth floor in Turtle Bay.

That night, as rain pelted against the windows at Fenwick, I asked Miss Hepburn if she regretted not having children of her own. "I would have been a terrible mother," she said point-blank, "because I'm basically a very selfish human being. Not that that has stopped most people from going off and having children."

She proceeded to illustrate her main point. "Let's say I have a little child," she explained, "and it's seven o'clock at night and Baby Johnny or Baby Janey suddenly comes down with a one-hundred-and-three-degree fever. And I've got twelve hundred people waiting to see me that night at the St. James Theatre. Now some of those people, I'm thinking, have waited months for their tickets, and some of them have scraped together money they can't really afford and arranged baby-sitters so that they can have their special night that year. And now little Johnny or little Janey is in pain and screaming and yelling. And there's no question what I have to do. I would walk into that baby's room, and take a pillow, and smother that adorable child!"

"I'm terrifying," Kate said, after a dramatic pause. "But I'm smart enough to know I'm terrifying. And that's why I didn't have children."

Without provocation, Kate went on to talk about the defining moment of her own childhood, a story that all but determined a life of coolness and compassion. In 1920, at Eastertime, Mrs. Hepburn sent Kate, almost fourteen, and the older brother she adored, Tom, to New York City, for a holiday. They stayed in a charming brick house in Greenwich Village with one of Kit's friends from Bryn Mawr, an attorney named Mary Towle. For several days, they went sight-seeing with "Auntie," taking in a stage production of *A Connecticut Yankee in King Arthur's Court,* based, of course, on the work by Hartford's foremost citizen, Mark Twain. The selection of that play resonated especially for Tom, then fifteen and a half, who attended the Kingswood School in West Hartford, the campus of which had been one of Twain's former homes.

Tom was growing up to be tall and handsome, but he had been a diffident boy—in many ways not his father's son. He lacked the swagger. As a young boy he developed facial tics and later suffered from St. Vitus's dance, an ailment then attributed to stress. Dr. Hepburn expressed no great concern, noting simply that his father had walked through life with a shaking head. Mrs. Hepburn came to believe that perhaps the pressures of so dominant a father, one who seldom parceled out praise, might have been difficult for Tom. In time, however, Tom outgrew the condition, becoming confident at school—popular, athletic, and a very good student. As many of the neighborhood kids still considered the Hepburns outsiders, a colony unto themselves, Kate felt unusually close to her older brother. "Jimmy" even wore his clothes.

On the Saturday of their spring break in New York, the children went to bed around ten, after Tom had entertained Kate and his godmother, playing banjo for them. The next morning he did not come down from his attic bedroom for breakfast. At nine, Kate went to inquire. When he did not answer her calls, she went into the unfinished studio—only to find him, next to the bed, hanging from some torn sheeting that had been tied to a rafter. Kate ripped down the sheet and felt her brother's skin. It was cold.

The thirteen-year-old was in too much shock to remember precisely what happened next. In her memory, she ran to a doctor across the street, shouting that her brother was dead. A woman at the doctor's house said that if he was dead, he didn't really need a doctor. In time, adults wandered onto the scene; Kate's parents came down to New York. She sailed with them on a ferry to New Jersey, where they had her brother's body cremated. During the crossing she saw, for the first time, her mother cry. She never saw as much from her father.

For days, people grasped at explanations. Kate recalled that there had been a hanging incident in *A Connecticut Yankee* that had intrigued Tom; and Dr. Hepburn recalled that Tom had been fascinated with a story the doctor had told of being able to fake a hanging, by tightening up one's neck. But the more she thought about the theories, the less likely they seemed. The truth was this family had already been plagued with three suicides. And even considering Tom's eventual success at school, Kate suggested, "He was never really charged up quite like the rest of us. I had heard that maybe a girl had rejected him—who knows, maybe a boy. Whatever it was, he simply could not cope."

Whatever it was, nobody in the family talked about the incident for years. Whether it was accidental or intentional, over lost love or newfound feelings, young Tom Hepburn was dead and not all the deliberating in the world could bring him back. Nor, I was to see, would he ever be completely laid to rest. His ashes were buried in the Cedar Hill Cemetery in Hartford, but there were no family visits. Tom would haunt Kate for the rest of her life, and she argued one scenario then another in search of an explanation. While she simply could not understand why he would take his own life, she was willing to accept that he had. "There's just so much about people," she concluded, "that we can ever really know."

Dr. and Mrs. Hepburn refused to allow gloom to permeate their lives. Previous generations on both sides of the family had treated disappointments and depression, indeed, mental illness, simply by forcing themselves above it or swiftly succumbing. Moaning and complaining had never played in their house; and now it was simply not tolerated. All the Hepburns were encouraged to move on with their lives with even greater intensity. Over and over, I would see that this incident affected Kate more than she realized—keeping her from ever delving into the past or even dwelling in the present. Like the rest of her family, she listened to the Song of Life—the refrain of which was always, "Get on with it."

The tragedy hit Kate hard. (She would be loath to say it hit her the hardest, because that would suggest complaining.) A sensitive teenager going through her awkward years—a strong freckle-faced tomboy becoming an unusual-looking young woman—she entered her own private crucible. In a town where the Hepburns had been considered odd, the suicide, veiled in mystery, stigmatized them even further. Kate dealt with her renewed feelings of isolation by role-playing—becoming stronger, prouder, even haughtier. She learned to mask her feelings, to create one persona that would greet the world while she hid another that she would fight to keep private. She would cloak her loneliness and insecurities with a personality that could entrance. She was becoming an actress.

For the second night in a row, Kate and I stayed up past midnight. Before retiring, we put the fire to bed, extinguished the lights, and checked on the kitchen, where Dick often left a gas burner lit or something cooking in the oven. We found that his "lady friend," Virginia Harrington, had baked a gigantic chocolate layer cake. Kate insisted I take a slice, from which she scraped off a mouthful of icing with her index finger. Walking upstairs, I thought about all the personal stories Kate had imparted in the last few days and the urgency with which she shared them.

It occurred to me that most of the people in the professional stories she had told me were either dead or dying; and while she had scores of good acquaintances and millions of fans, she had few intimate friends outside her family with whom she could share things. I also believed that because of her injured foot, Kate was slowing down for the first time in her life, and all the time and energy that she formerly had to run around was being directed inward, forcing her to remember and to ruminate. "You and I see the world the same way," she said as we were turning down my bed.

And then she looked me soberly in the eye and said, "You are me." (Just like that, the way Emily Brontë's Cathy said, "I am Heathcliff.") I took it as a compliment, thinking she meant we both approached life with optimism . . . or, at least, that we laughed at the same things. With a kiss on my cheek and a "Night, night," she was gone.

By the next morning we had developed our routine. She had already enjoyed her swim, newspaper, and breakfast before I joined her. A pink grapefruit, prepared by the Lady of the House herself, always sat on my tray in the kitchen, and a discussion of the news awaited upstairs. Then Phyllis would magically appear, with a clipboard and pad, to make notes on our day's agenda and menus. This particular Sunday was drizzly, with heavy storms forecast well into the night. I asked Kate if she had slept all right, in light of the tenderness of our conversation the night before. She said she always slept well, though we would have to stop staying up that late.

Far from embarrassed by our conversation, Kate was eager to complete it. After her brother's death, she said, she had stopped attending the Oxford School, the sister school of Kingswood, and was tutored at home. She succeeded in being admitted to Bryn Mawr College, though during her first year she stuck mostly to herself. She occasionally ate with the other young women; but one day, as she approached a table, she heard one of her schoolmates say, "Self-conscious beauty." Kate easily accepted the "self-conscious" part but puzzled over the rest. She never returned to the dining room again, eating her meals in town.

Over the next three years, Katie Hepburn gradually came out of her shell, appearing in a succession of plays on campus. She had no reservations about taking the male leads, as she blossomed into a strong, striking-looking woman. Making little effort to find intramural friends, she cultivated a social life for herself off campus. While most of the students cloistered themselves within Bryn Mawr's neo-Gothic walls, Kate made friends with several men on the outside. The young woman who seemed to stride through town living by her own rules had become like catnip. At a dance she met a graduate art student named Bob McKnight and went so far as to pose nude for him. (The figurines on the mantelpiece in New York!) Both were smitten but too consumed with their respective budding artistic aspirations for much more of a relationship.

Senior year Kate befriended a townie named Jack Clarke, whose house literally shared a lawn with the campus. "He wasn't some parlor snake," Kate told me, though he was one of the many young men along Philadelphia's Main Line who had enough money not to have to worry about what she called "the mechanics of life"—men of ease, with apartments in New York City, and limited ambition. Clarke shared another property, a small country farmhouse on twenty acres, with his best friend, a similarly well-fixed young man named Ludlow Ogden Smith.

Kate often went out to the farm, sometimes allowing a few friends from Bryn Mawr to tag along. Unchaperoned, the young ladies flirted with a little danger. One afternoon, when Kate was alone with the two men, she went so far as to pose for some nude photographs. (She was proud of them at the time but wished she knew whatever happened to the set of blowups they sent her. "Long after I'm dead and gone," she said, "I'm afraid somebody's going to find them and say, 'Good God, that's Katharine Hepburn!'")

At a luncheon that same year, at the home of the dean of Bryn Mawr, Kate met a well-known poet, H. Phelps Putnam. Although a married man, Putnam's reputation as a rake was superseding his reputation as a writer. "Having such a man on the Bryn Mawr campus was like having a fox in the henhouse," Kate later admitted. "And I found him utterly fascinating." She used to climb down the vine outside her second-story tower room to take midnight strolls with him. But Kate maintained her virtue; "and I think I drove him wild," she said, laughing.

Barely twenty, she became the inspiration of his poem *The Daughters of the Sun.*

> *. . . She was the living anarchy of love,*
> *She was the unexplained, the end of love . . .*
> *She was my nourishment, my sister and my child,*
> *My lust, my liberty, my discipline,*
> *And she laid fair, awkward hands upon my head.*
> *She was discourteous as life and death*
> *And kindly as a dry white wine is kind*
> *On a blowzy summer day . . .*
> *For beyond space she was my quality,*
> *She was the very mask of my desire . . .*

By the time Kate graduated from Bryn Mawr College in June 1928, she had a pack of men pursuing her. But by then, this model of "the living anarchy of love" had set her sights on a career.

She depended on the kindness of suitors. Jack Clarke had some show-business connections, including a man named Edwin Knopf, who ran a theater company in Baltimore. Clarke wrote him on Kate's behalf, and upon graduation she appeared at the theater and was hired on the spot—evidently on looks and personality alone. She got a small part in *The Czarina*, with Mary Boland, a well-known actress of the day; and everything came easily to her. She learned lines and blocking quickly; and Miss Boland took her under her wing, teaching her how to apply makeup and how to make an entrance—"a rapid walk and a slow discovery of the audience."

After her second play, Knopf decided to include Kate in a production that he was taking to New York, a work called *The Big Pond.* The leading man, Kenneth MacKenna, recognized her talent but also her shortcomings. He strongly supported her inclusion but urged her to invest whatever money she made in voice lessons. He even wrote a letter of introduction to the best vocal teacher in show business, one Frances Robinson-Duff, who could boast that she coached two of Broadway's foremost actresses, Ina Claire and Ruth Chatterton.

"Duff" took Kate on as her pupil, forcing her to perform all sorts of Henry Higgins–like exercises—blowing out candles, speaking with marbles in her mouth, reciting phrases that emphasized certain sounds and syllables. To Hepburn's final days, it pained her to hear people pronounce the word "horrible" as though it were "whore-ible." She would interject with the Robinson-Duff corrective exercise, "Ha-ha horrible." (Similarly, "chocolate" was always "chock-lit," never "chalk-lit.") She never mastered breath control from the diaphragm, which, she claimed, caused her voice's premature rasp.

Neither of Kate's parents thought much of her career choice. Her father thought acting was just plain silly, a foolish way to spend a life; and her mother had practically no interest in the theater at all. But Kit Hepburn saw it as a way for her daughter to avoid the kitchen and nursery, to advance herself, to lead a life of her own. Despite his misgivings, so did Dr. Hepburn. He grubstaked her.

Kate moved to New York, only to discover what a small town it was. "Manhattan was really like an enchanted island," she said, "cut off from the rest of the world except for a few bridges." The theater world was even smaller, with everyone connected to everyone else. Her friend "Phelpie" Putnam, as she called him, was apartment-sitting for his friend Russell Davenport, an editor at *Time* and

Fortune; and Kate simply moved in with him. Suddenly, she was showing up at fashionable parties, meeting the likes of Robert Benchley and the rest of the Algonquin set, and turning heads.

Her virtue remained safe with Putnam, Kate later reported, as it seemed good enough for him just to be known to be living with a beautiful young actress. After a while, in fact, it was she who became miffed that Putnam did not even make a pass at her. Only later did she learn that her father had permitted this highly progressive living arrangement only after having privately confronted the poet. "Now listen, Put," he had said to this sophisticated "older man," "my daughter is like a young bull about to charge and she will do everything she can to seduce you, but if you lay a hand on her, I'll shoot you." Putnam soon decided to house-sit elsewhere, alone.

Of all Hepburn's suitors, Ludlow Smith was the most persistent. He was also the most convenient—with the mobility to keep up with Kate's desires, socially and otherwise. In addition to business interests that allowed him to work in New York, he had his own car, in which he drove Kate to Fenwick for weekends. He had very little ego and enough self-confidence to let hers run wild. She was often petulant and always impatient; but nothing ever seemed to faze him. More than once he raised the subject of marriage, of leading a long, comfortable life together outside of Philadelphia. But she refused, surrendering only her virginity—one afternoon when they were alone in Jack Clarke's apartment. She felt a kind of love for him— "What else could I call my gratitude for his constant devotion?" she asked me. "I think the Greeks called it 'philos,'" I said, "—a deep affection without passion." Where she had felt lust but little respect toward Phelps Putnam, she found it was the exact opposite with Ludlow Smith. She knew she was using him; and the only thing that made her behavior acceptable in her mind was that he knew it as well. She never veiled her ambition.

Eddie Knopf's production of *The Big Pond* went into rehearsal in New York, with Kate understudying the lead, who was suddenly dismissed at the last minute. And there in the wings stood Kate, a fireball of self-confidence. Not two months in the theater and she was already a star—"or at least I thought I was," she later reported. "I certainly acted as though I was." She was so carried away with her own pre-Broadway opening-night performance at the Great Neck Theatre on Long Island that she raced through the play, forgetting every lesson Frances Robinson-Duff had taught her. The next day, she was fired.

Although fished out of *The Big Pond*, she had made a splash. Two prominent Broadway producers made offers to her that week. One came from J. J. Shubert, who suggested a five-year contract at very good pay. She refused, not wishing to commit herself for that long a period and having to appear in plays she might not like. The other came from Arthur Hopkins, who had been associated with several prestigious productions and who wanted Kate to play a supporting role in a modest play he was opening. She accepted; and the play closed after three performances. But "Hoppy," as she called him, wanted her to learn lines immediately for another play that was about to premiere—Philip Barry's *Holiday*. He wanted Miss Hepburn to understudy the lead, Miss Hope Williams.

While Kate's career was not advancing as rapidly as she had egotistically imagined, she liked Hoppy and she liked the play. She agreed to take the part and figured she would simply hope against Hope. "Isn't it awful?" she said. "I used to pray for her to get sick." Just two weeks into the run, Kate herself got sick—of waiting. In a fit of impatience, she accepted Luddy's proposal of marriage.

While wedding so solid a citizen as Ludlow Smith was as much as any parent could wish for a daughter in the late twenties, Dr. and Mrs. Hepburn were shocked at the conventionality of it all. For them, their eldest daughter's impulsive marriage was an act of rebellion, a way for her to assert herself without having to rely on them any longer. All they knew was that Kate was still attempting to figure out who she was and who she intended to become. It was a trying time for Kate—"I felt I was just stepping out on a high wire," she later admitted. "Luddy was my safety net."

She told Arthur Hopkins that she was withdrawing from *Holiday;* and on December 12, 1928, Katharine Hepburn married Ludlow Ogden Smith in her parents' house at 201 Bloomfield Avenue in West Hartford. Her paternal grandfather, the Reverend Sewell Snowden Hepburn, presided before their collective families. After a short honeymoon in Bermuda, the newlyweds returned to Philadelphia to find a house where they could settle down.

Thus, after only six months in show business, Mrs. Ludlow Smith rang down the curtain on her career.

IV

Morning Glory

T ake off your pants!" Katharine Hepburn barked at me, as I
stood in the entry hall at Fenwick.

It was an early Sunday afternoon in April 1983—cold, windy, and
rainy—and I had to return to New York City for a dinner
engagement with a woman who over the preceding years had
become one of my closest friends, Irene Mayer Selznick. Only a few
hours earlier, Kate's brother Bob had arrived from Hartford with his
wife, Sue; and in the few seconds it had taken them to get from their
car to the front door, they had gotten drenched.

While I had been enjoying myself with the charming doctor—
"the sweetest man alive," Kate often gushed, "an angel!"—and his
well-read wife, I announced that I had to hit the road. After
unsuccessfully arguing how "idiotic" it was for me to make the trip
under such conditions, Kate said I should at least have the brains to
take off my pants, then dash to the end of the driveway where my
car was parked, and move the car to the garage . . . which I could
then re-enter through the house after I had put on the pair of
trousers that had been kept dry.

"I don't think that's necessary," I said. "I'll run with a large umbrella."

"But your pants," Kate pointed out. "With the wind, they'll get
soaked." I assured her that my plan was satisfactory. "Besides," I said,
"I'm waterproof."

"You may be," she snorted. "But your pants aren't!"

Of course, in the moment when I sprinted from the door to the car, the rain came down in sheets . . . and I could hear Kate howling with laughter. She met me at the back door to the garage with towels and said, "Now you've *got* to take off your pants, because you can't drive for two hours in them."

I sheepishly explained that this was the only pair of pants I had brought up for the weekend. Kate kindly said that would be no problem. She sent Phyllis on a mission to find a dry pair. "Go to Dick," she said. "Or go to my closet. And if you can't find anything there, bring him one of your dresses."

"I'm not driving into New York wearing one of Phyllis's dresses," I said.

"Oh, you might have to," she said, delighting herself. "And there's nothing wrong with that. Phyllis has some lovely things, don't you, dear?"

"Oh yes," said Phyllis, perfectly oblivious to the fact that Kate was now pulling our legs. "But I don't think he'd fit into any of my things. Too tall."

"Phyllis," I begged, "would you please try to find me a pair of pants?"

"You know," Kate began to reminisce, "the first time Spence came up here, we had exactly the same situation, and he made a run for his car."

"And?" I asked.

"And I don't *think* he had to put on a dress."

Phyllis returned with a pair of faded yellow sweatpants that belonged to Dick, far more conservative than anything I imagined Dick owning, which I gratefully accepted. As I started to go upstairs to change, Kate said, "Oh Christ, just take off your pants right here." Before I could even protest, she assured me, "Dad used to walk around the house without any clothes at all!"

"But he was your fa—" I started to sputter, when I suddenly realized that was even worse. When in Rome, I figured . . . and so I turned my back to my hostess and changed pants. "And you should probably change your shirt," she added. I didn't even argue, pulling a dry one from my bag.

"Now," she said with a big smile, "you're ready to go. Dinner tomorrow? Drinks at six." She leaned over for a hug and my hearty thanks for the weekend. While I was saying goodbye to Phyllis and Bob and Sue, she called out for Dick, who descended from upstairs, wearing a pair of long underwear and a red nightcap. His ethereal friend Virginia Harrington followed.

"The horn," Kate said. "Don't forget to honk the horn on your car—after you've left the driveway and you can see the front of the house. Two times long, three short. One, two, one-two-three. Have you got that? One, two, one-two-three."

"I've got it, but why?"

"Because that's what we do here," she replied, as though I had asked the stupidest question in the world. Then she explained it was a ritual for coming and going, a code that she and Howard had devised years earlier. I said my farewells and drove off. And as I turned left out of the driveway, I beeped the old "one, two, one-two-three," and looked to the front of the house. Through the rain I saw them all standing in the doorway, waving goodbye, Kate's hands reaching out wide, reminding me of the last shot of her in *Summertime*.

The drive into the city took longer than usual because of the weather, but I used the time to replay in my mind the many scenes from the weekend, moments that seemed to come right out of *You Can't Take It with You*, *Hay Fever*, and, on occasion, *Long Day's Journey into Night*. I returned my rental car, and went to the Upper–West Side brownstone of my former editor Thomas Congdon, and his wife, Connie, friends who had become a second family to me. Tom handed me a batch of phone messages—Myrna Loy, Sylvia Sidney, Joan Bennett, all of whom were consenting to interviews about Goldwyn. "And a Mrs. Lieberson," he said. "You're slipping," he added. "I haven't heard of her."

"No," I said, "but she'd interest you the most, because you love ballet, and Mrs. Lieberson is none other than Vera Zorina," the former star of the New York City Ballet and a former wife of George Balanchine. "And not only that," I said, "Sam Goldwyn was madly in love with her."

Connie was more interested in my pants. "Where did you get *those*?" she asked.

"Don't ask. I'll tell you later." I showered and changed and ran off to dinner. "And don't wait up," I suggested, "because I know I'll be late." I took a cab to the Hotel Pierre on Fifth Avenue at Sixty-first Street. The elevator operator brought me to the tenth floor, and at exactly seven, I walked to the door at the end of the corridor on the left, apartment 1007-10, and rang the doorbell.

Although nobody embodied as much Hollywood history as she, Irene Mayer Selznick was not too grand to answer her own door. The daughter of legendary film mogul Louis B. Mayer—the former junk dealer who soon parlayed his New England distributorship of films into Metro-Goldwyn-Mayer, the mightiest film studio in history—and the wife of David O. Selznick—the son of one of Mayer's archrivals in the early movie business, a young studio mogul himself who quickly became the most celebrated producer of his day, forever remembered for *Gone With the Wind*—was a longtime resident of the hotel. Some years earlier, she had bought up several suites and combined them into one luxurious apartment overlooking Central Park. I don't think she was more than five feet tall—with short dark hair in bangs and the shrewdest pair of eyes I have ever seen; and I know she was one of the most powerful presences I have ever beheld.

As if her lineage were not impressive enough, upon divorcing Selznick, Irene moved to New York and hung out her shingle as a theatrical producer. Her first effort was the landmark production of

A Streetcar Named Desire, for which she harnessed the talents of Tennessee Williams, Elia Kazan, and a young Marlon Brando. She subsequently produced such hits as *The Chalk Garden* and *Bell, Book and Candle.* It would be less than precise to call Mrs. Selznick an extremely difficult person, but she was easily the most challenging I have ever met. One never let down one's guard with Irene, unless looking to be knocked out or thrown out. Emotional, volatile, and analytical, she took nothing at face value, probing layers beneath layers in even the simplest matters.

I had by this evening known Irene Mayer Selznick for about five years. At the start of my research on *Goldwyn,* Sam Goldwyn, Jr., had said the most perceptive person I could possibly speak to about his father would be Irene Selznick; and, he added, she probably wouldn't speak to me. So warned, I didn't approach her until I had been researching for more than a year and could ask questions in an informed manner. Then I sent her a letter outlining my goals and included a copy of *Max Perkins.* A second letter announced that I would be coming to New York in the near future and if she could spare a few minutes it would be helpful to meet her. Several weeks passed before she called me in Los Angeles one night, after ten.

She was working on her memoirs, she said, and she had a few technical questions about "the merger" in 1924 of the Metro and Goldwyn companies. Could I possibly straighten out some of the dates for her and direct her to any documentation? We talked for more than an hour; and the next day I sent by overnight mail Xeroxes of a few relevant documents—providing answers I believed she already knew. The following night, at eleven, she telephoned again, inviting me to call upon her the next time I was in New York. Many long calls over the next few months ensued, during which time she had been diagnosed with cancer of the nose.

Before I arrived in New York, I heard from a mutual acquaintance that Mrs. Selznick was seeing nobody, having just undergone an operation in which half her nose was removed, as was some skin from her forehead to fashion a new one. I called her anyway, to wish her well, and she apologized for her inability to receive visitors. Five minutes later, she called back to say she had not seen anybody in ages, and as I didn't know what she had looked like previously, I would not be shocked by any disfigurement. She clearly wanted company; and I seemed the perfect visitor—a friendly stranger. Could I see her after dinner that night? I packed a notepad in my jacket breast pocket.

Upon arriving at her apartment, she ushered me into a small library, where the lights had been turned down. I could still see fine, raw red marks between her eyebrows and down the bridge of her nose. She asked how I was getting along with the Goldwyn family, then slowly—and in a voice so low I had to strain to hear—she spewed details of the feud between her father and Sam Goldwyn. I sat there spellbound, too mesmerized to take notes. Once or twice I instinctively reached for my pen, but I hesitated before drawing it. A little after one in the morning, I said, "Mrs. Selznick, I feel you should be getting some rest." She showed me to the door and said, "It's a good thing you didn't write anything down. If you come back for dinner tomorrow, I'll let you take that pad out of your pocket."

Over the next decade, we spent countless hours together—in person, when I was in New York, and on the telephone, when I was in Los Angeles, usually after her city had gone to sleep. Her insights about Goldwyn and Hollywood and even the world were invaluable; but she came to exert an even greater influence on me, leading me to dig constantly for deeper meanings. Her years undergoing professional analysis—to say nothing of her own insightful mind— and living with two of the most compulsive men in a community of severe personality disorders had taught her to look for the truths that lay beneath all the falsities of Hollywood. Everything had a subtext, Irene believed, an inner truth more interesting than anything the naked eye could see. She was always more interested in that which was unspoken, in all that was not said. For her, little was ever stated directly; every sentence was fraught with cryptic messages.

As a result, conversations were like chess matches—in which Irene was always thinking two moves ahead. During one of our midnight phone conversations, for example, her second phone rang. She said she had to take the call and would call me back. When she did call— a little after three in the morning in New York—she started by saying, "No, your name didn't come up." I was immediately meant to deduce that she had only one friend who called her at that hour— William S. Paley, whom I had recently interviewed. Another time, when I was in the midst of writing, she asked how the book was going. As I prepared to describe the "delicate stage" I was at, she simply asked, "Fenestration?" I didn't quite grasp what she was saying, so I proceeded to explain how I had finished laying down the entire story, and had gone through it a second time, stuffing in as many facts as possible, and that I was about to go through it again, this time taking things out, letting in air, opening up windows. "Ah," she said after my two-minute description, "fenestration."

In the middle of one extremely intense late-night conversation in apartment 1007, a siren outside sounded, and she saw my eyes move toward the window and hold there one beat too long. "Well," she said, "I just lost you. You were gone. We'll pick up this story next time."

It took me two days to figure out what she meant when she described a beautiful chorus girl her father had been attracted to as a "double-gater"—someone who swings both ways.

She had a wicked laugh, over which she would occasionally lose control; and nothing ever got past her. Her response to anything new, shocking, or hard to believe was, "You go to hell, go right to hell!"

"So, how did you get on with that brother?" Irene asked that wet Sunday night, not four hours after I had left Fenwick. We went into the cozy library, where we ritually sat for drinks. I went to the rear closet, next to an exquisite picture of a little girl by Mary Cassatt, and fetched a canister of thin wheat crackers, while she pulled from the refrigerator a crockery jar of herring and a chilled bottle. "Cary's aquavit," she always called it, a rare brand her longtime friend Mr. Grant had introduced to Irene years earlier. Because it apparently could not be obtained outside Sweden, he always kept her stocked with a case of it. "Oh, the chemistry," she never failed to say in response to the initial reaction in our mouths of the herring with the wheat and the aquavit. After a few gentle moans of ecstasy, and a toast to Cary, she said, "You never told me you knew my friend Kate."

I explained that until a week prior I had not known Katharine Hepburn but that over the last few days a friendship had instantly unfolded. I also told Irene that I knew that people in her position were often approached by writers in their efforts to get to more famous people; and though I knew of the close relationship between the two women, I never wanted Irene to think for a minute that that was why I had been spending so much time with her. (She had, for example, recently befriended a man whom she unmasked as someone who really wanted to meet Kitty Carlisle, the widow of Moss Hart.) Similarly, it had not been until my second day at Fenwick that I had told Kate of my friendship with Irene. This information had clearly prompted a call upon my departure, one that came after fifty years of ups and downs between them, a complex relationship in which each clearly admired the other despite diametrically opposed approaches to life.

After talking about Kate all through dinner and into the early morning, I realized I was about to become a Ping-Pong ball in a game of two experts who played hard and fast. Toward two, Irene got up from her chair, clasped my shoulder (rather melodramatically, I thought at first), and said, "You must go to her."

I realized she was dead serious and, as always with Irene, obviously meant more than the literal. I'm sure I looked puzzled at her remark.

"Kate has nobody," Irene said, with a touch of pity in her voice, "nobody she can really talk to. She has spent so many years keeping people away, now nobody really comes around." I said that sounded a little extreme, that she seemed to have an active social life, with people calling and knocking on her door all the time. "But nobody she can talk to," said Irene, "certainly not that insane brother. Who's still alive who knew George Cukor? Who knows who Grady Sutton is? Lowell Sherman? Dorothy Arzner? Everyone's either dead or doesn't know who they were when they were alive."

In a low voice, she said that she loved Kate—"Sister Kate," she signed her letters to Irene, referring to more than a popular song from their youths—and that the greatest favor she could now do for her friend was to present me to her. I said that I did not see the need for taking sides, that we were all friends here. But Irene said that Kate was quickly going to become even more insistent about her friendship with me, and that I must not fail her, that on those occasions when both would be calling, and I could respond to but one of them, I must "always be there for Kate." Boy, I thought, sitting in her vast living room—with a stunning Matisse (looking all too much, I thought, like Jennifer Jones, David Selznick's second wife)—there's a lot written between these lines. As Irene showed me to the front door, she repeated, "Go to her."

I did—the next night, for dinner . . . and the next few nights after that. The drill was generally the same, with Phyllis sitting with us through the meal, occasionally chiming in with some funny observation, then discreetly disappearing so that Kate and I could talk alone. The only part of the dinner routine at Hepburn's that I didn't enjoy was that she ate so fast. Sometimes I'd just be finishing my soup while she was impatiently waiting to move on to dessert. In an aside, I once quietly commented to Phyllis that I had heard that many people didn't like dining at Schönbrunn Palace with the Emperor Franz Josef because he ate so fast, and the half-eaten servings of the guests were cleared as soon as the emperor had finished each course. "What are you two muttering over there?" Kate asked, never wanting to be excluded from any conversation. "Oh," Phyllis explained, "Mr. Berg was just saying that he thinks of us as royalty." To this day, I'm not sure how clever Phyllis was.

Periodically, I would draw Phyllis into the conversation by asking about her background, and Kate would spur her on, insisting, "She has some of the greatest stories in the world, and she'll take them all to her grave."

Indeed, Phyllis Wilbourn was born in England shortly after the turn of the century and trained as a nurse. Sometime in the twenties, the English actress Constance Collier, who was diabetic, decided to settle in America, and she wanted to take a full-time nurse to provide her daily injections of insulin. Phyllis took the job; and through Miss Collier got to know the entire British movie colony in Hollywood—including Ronald Colman, Noël Coward, and, most especially, Charlie Chaplin. Miss Collier—as Phyllis always referred to her—died in 1955. She left Phyllis some pieces of jewelry and furniture and some money, but not enough to insure the future of a middle-aged woman. "Miss Garbo wanted me to look after her," Phyllis cheerily told me one night, "but then Miss Hepburn stepped in and swept me away, thank goodness." I asked Phyllis what would have been wrong with looking after Greta Garbo, and Kate interrupted to say, "Oh Christ, I'm much more fun than Garbo."

"Oh yes," Phyllis concurred, "I hear Miss Garbo just sits in that gloomy apartment and stares at the East River all day. Not that I wouldn't mind a few days of rest here and there."

"You'll have plenty of time to rest, dearie," said Kate, "when you're dead."

"Oh yes," said Phyllis, in one of those moments when she seemed to turn into Nigel Bruce to Hepburn's Basil Rathbone, "I suppose I will."

In time, I came to regard my dinners with Kate and Phyllis as my own personal production of *Arsenic and Old Lace*. These "two old spinsters"—Kate's phrase, not mine—constantly bickered and amused each other, each looking out for the other in a way that was most touching. I can hardly recall an evening in which Kate did not comment—often in Phyllis's presence—on how indispensable "Miss Phyllis" was to her existence, how she was a "blessing," an "angel," a "Godsend." Periodically Kate reminded me to "speak up—because Phyllis is turning as deaf as a post." Just as often, if Phyllis found me alone, she would tactfully suggest that I talk a little louder, as "Miss Hepburn is losing her hearing." In truth, I didn't really find it to be the case with either of them.

Despite their employer-employee relationship—"Phyllis is richer than all of us!" Kate would often say. "God knows what she does with her money!"—Kate and Phyllis were like an old married couple, completely on to each other's foibles and idiosyncrasies, and always mindful of each other's needs. Although many people over the years have made certain assumptions about Miss Hepburn and her "companion," there was nothing even vaguely sexual about their alliance. They simply cared for each other, even loved each other . . . and every night, Phyllis hopped onto a bus or (entering her eighties) popped into a cab and went to her own nicely furnished apartment uptown.

In some ways, however, their relationship hardly differed from Kate's marriage to Luddy. It was all in service of Kate. For the Ludlow Ogden Smiths, the honeymoon was over within two weeks, when she realized she was happier standing by in the wings of a full house

72

on Broadway than sitting in an empty manor house in Pennsylvania. At her urging, they moved into a small apartment Luddy kept at 146 East Thirty-ninth Street. There she insisted he change his name to S. Ogden Ludlow—just so that she would not be Kate Smith. The name was simply too plain, she insisted, to say nothing of its being that of a popular, overweight singer. Mr. Smith obliged; and once settled in Manhattan, Katharine Hepburn Ludlow went hat in hand to Arthur Hopkins. He said he had been expecting her and that her old job awaited.

One night, and one night only, the understudy did get to go on for Hope Williams in *Holiday.* That performance made her realize just how wonderful the star was. While Kate had previously enjoyed what Miss Williams had done with the role of Linda Seton (the unconventional daughter in an upper-class family who falls in love with her sister's unconventional suitor), those two hours onstage made her positively worshipful. While she felt she had performed the part well enough, she now realized that Williams had played it "brilliantly," always making the aggressive character extremely attractive.

Hepburn liked Williams's portrayal enough to start imitating aspects of it and incorporating them into her own persona—nuances that softened some of her youthful stridency. Where Hepburn had a pushy, overeager walk, for example, Hope Williams had a sophisticated, arm-swinging stride . . . and always a light touch instead of a heavy hand, insouciance instead of arrogance, a sense of fun. A genuine New York socialite who wore her hair bobbed and parted on one side, she was, Hepburn described, "half boy, half woman." No performer had a greater influence on the young actress; and Kate stayed in touch with her for the rest of her life, into Williams's nineties. "Without Hope Williams," Kate said many times, "Katharine Hepburn would not have gone very far."

Hepburn's theatrical career over the next two years made that very point. Choosing not to have an agent, she would sit in producers' offices and get parts for herself—giving charming interviews and readings. More than once the jobs were as understudies to the female leads, and more than once she got fired. She was clearly a powerful presence—a different look and sound—one to which people reacted strongly, favorably or otherwise. She had all the makings of a star; the mixture just hadn't yet come to a full boil.

Even after several more plays, including a season of summer stock at the Berkshire Playhouse in Stockbridge, Massachusetts, and another with the Ivoryton Players (in a charming theater in Ivoryton, Connecticut, a short drive from Fenwick), Katharine Hepburn was still getting fired almost as often as she was hired. The problem was not, as was often suspected, her know-it-all attitude and troublesome stubbornness. It was rather, as playwright Philip Barry told her when he suggested she be replaced before opening in the lead role in his play *The Animal Kingdom,* because she was "simply no good."

Undaunted, Kate continued to make the rounds, acquiring contacts and becoming known. She made fast friends with a fellow student of Miss Robinson-Duff named Laura Harding, with whom she costarred in Stockbridge. Laura was the perky daughter of a financier and later an heiress to the American Express fortune. Living in a Fifth Avenue mansion, Laura had the kind of wealth the public later ascribed to Hepburn. In truth, Kate credited Laura for introducing her to such grandeur. "Laura thought I was fascinating, as fascinating as I thought she was," Kate recalled, "and I think we brought out the best in each other." After playing together in the summer of 1930, they carried their friendship into the city, where they staked out producers' offices together.

One day they heard about a theatrical troupe being formed that was holding an organizational meeting that very night—The Group Theatre. Kate and Laura went to hear Harold Clurman, Lee Strasberg, and Cheryl Crawford talk about this exciting new venture.

The two novices were fired up by all the enthusiasm in the room, until Strasberg said, "And we will do all kinds of plays and play all kinds of parts. And everybody will be equal. One week you'll be the star, and in the next play you'll carry a spear." That was all Kate needed to hear. She stood up, said, "Not me," and walked out of the hall.

In early 1932 a leading role fell from the skies into her lap, in a play called *The Warrior's Husband*. The author, Julian Thompson, had already written a one-act version of the love affair between Theseus and Antiope, the sister of the Queen of the Amazons; and after a successful production at The Comedy Club in New York, he expanded the work into a full-length play. Hope Williams had originally starred as Antiope, and the playwright hoped she would reprise the role. By the time the new play was finished, however, she had a prior commitment she would not break. The producers naturally turned to her recent understudy, the athletic Miss Hepburn, who would be required to make her entrance bounding down stairs, three at a time, carrying a stag over her shoulder. A few anxious weeks for Hepburn passed while the producers sought bigger names for the part. In the end they settled on her.

"I knew it was a great role for me," Kate told me one night after dinner, "—very showy." She got to wear a dazzling costume—a metallic tunic with a spiraled cone over each breast, an ornate helmet, and silver leather shin guards "that would make anybody's legs look good." And her entrance, which concluded with her throwing the stag to the ground then collapsing to one knee, brought the house down every night. The play received mixed notices, but Hepburn received raves and became the talk of the town. It was only a matter of time before Hollywood would knock on her door.

"Here's the moment I really got lucky," Hepburn would later pinpoint, "—right place at the right time." At that moment, she explained, David O. Selznick, then head of production for RKO in

Hollywood, was preparing a film version of a Clemence Dane play called *A Bill of Divorcement* for John Barrymore, the greatest actor of the day. Selznick and the director, George Cukor, were consciously looking to create a new movie star by casting a first-time film actress in the ingenue role, Barrymore's daughter—a part that had made a star of Katharine Cornell a decade earlier.

Hepburn's timing was more exquisite than that. Hollywood was just coming out of the tailspin it had entered five years earlier when *The Jazz Singer* opened and introduced talking pictures. The careers of most of the great silent stars had dissipated, some overnight, and the producers had become desperate to fill the vacuum. They combed legitimate theaters across the country for promising new directors, playwrights, and, most especially, actors. It was no longer enough for actors to have faces the public liked. They also needed good voices.

Although most of the silent-screen stars with foreign accents were the first to plummet to oblivion—Vilma Banky, Pola Negri, Nazimova, to name but a handful—the mysterious young actress from Sweden became one of the last to subject her voice to public scrutiny and was greeted with even greater applause. In becoming the greatest of the silent-screen stars to make the leap to talking film stardom, Greta Garbo also changed the public's attitudes toward beauty. Before Garbo, most leading ladies were rounder of face and fleshier of body, more curves than angles. As Irene Selznick had reminded me that first night we talked about Hepburn, "Producers were desperate to find an American Garbo—somebody with her looks but an all-American attitude."

From a friend in New York, Selznick's executive assistant Merian Cooper had received a photograph of the young actress in *The Warrior's Husband*. "What legs!" Irene Selznick gasped to her husband when she saw the publicity still; and he ordered his East Coast staff to make a screen test. Hepburn welcomed the opportunity, but when it came time to shoot the test, she refused to play the scene they handed her. She said she preferred to perform a scene from *Holiday*, a part she had honed and which would show her off to better advantage, rather than one she was stepping into cold. She asked her friend Alan Campbell, a handsome actor who would later marry Dorothy Parker, to play in the scene with her.

The test did not bowl over either George Cukor (a recent transplant from a theater company in Rochester, New York) or David Selznick. There was something jerky about Hepburn's movements and jarring about her voice. But Cukor liked one particular moment, when she lowered a glass and set it on the floor, a moment he found real and theatrical and graceful at the same time. "Original," weighed in Irene Selznick upon seeing the test.

David Selznick offered the twenty-five-year-old untried film actress a respectable $500-a-week contract, which Hepburn refused. He kept returning in $250 increments, until he had climbed to three times his starting offer. (Actually, he offered her $1,250 with a four-week guarantee; but Hepburn said she preferred three weeks at $1,500, thus setting her rate higher than she had any right to.) The producer agreed. Luddy was prepared to go west with his wife and stay throughout the filming; but Kate asked him to remain in New York. On July 1, 1932, she boarded the Twentieth Century with her friend Laura Harding instead. They changed trains in Chicago, catching the Super Chief to Los Angeles.

Excited about the journey, Kate found the journey passing quickly until the first night on the Super Chief, when she went back to the observation car for some fresh air and a glimpse of the moon. As she opened the rear door of the last car and walked onto the platform, something flew into her left eye. Each blink made it feel worse. Rushing to a mirror, she saw the sclera turning crimson. She suffered through the rest of the trip, hoping to see an eye doctor upon her arrival. Her eyelids began to swell.

Attached to their train was the private railway car of Florenz Ziegfeld, then fatally ill, traveling with his wife, Billie Burke. Unbeknownst to Kate, Miss Burke—who would later become best known for her role as Glinda, the Good Witch of the North, in *The Wizard of Oz*—was coming to Hollywood as well, to play Hepburn's mother in *A Bill of Divorcement*. (The job, Kate would soon learn, was just another example of George Cukor's legendary generosity toward his friends.) Before pulling into the Pasadena station, Kate— then in considerable pain to say nothing of dismay over her appearance—changed into the special outfit she had bought for her July fourth arrival, the latest design from Elizabeth Hawes, the most expensive couturier in New York.

"Anybody who went to Elizabeth Hawes," Irene Selznick later remarked, "was out to make a statement." What a statement this was! Hepburn wore a gray silk suit, an extremely tailored, collarless tailcoat and almost ankle-length skirt with a ruffled turtleneck blouse; her gloves, pumps, and purse were navy blue. The crowning touch was a straw toque hat, one she later remarked that "made me look like I was wearing a beanbag on my head." Said Mrs. Selznick, "This was an outfit that cried out, 'I'm different. I'm special. Watch out!'"

Waiting for Hollywood's latest arrivals were two men who had become Kate's West Coast agents, Leland Hayward and Myron Selznick, David's brother. Laura Harding immediately recognized the former, one of the most urbane men in show business, a handsome swain she had known from her debutante days in Manhattan. The other was long considered one of Hollywood's liveliest characters, not the handsomest man in town but certainly one of the most amusing. Kate delighted in retelling what she later heard he had said when she stepped off the train: "Jesus, they're paying fifteen hundred dollars a week for that!"

Before Kate could explain her swollen red eye enough for them to see the urgency in getting her to a doctor, they whisked her away in a Rolls-Royce to the RKO studios. *A Bill of Divorcement* was to start shooting in five days, and there was not a moment to lose, what with costume fittings, makeup tests, and rehearsals. She was immediately introduced to George Cukor, an excitable dynamo, who wasted no time in bringing out sketches of her wardrobe, which was already being run up. Determined to take on Hollywood on her own strict terms, the untried ingenue sniffed at the drawings and said, "No well-bred English girl would wear these clothes." Without missing a beat, Cukor asked, "What do you think of what you're wearing?" Hepburn knew her outfit was "pretty goddamn queer-looking," but said, "I think it's very smart." Cukor said, "Well, I think it's ludicrous." Touché. She liked him already.

As hairdressers and assistants and makeup artists popped in and out of the director's office, Kate kept trying to ask for a doctor. Then arrived "The Great Profile" himself—at that point in his career, as famous for his alcoholism and lechery as he was for his acting—to pay his respects and look over his young leading lady. With so many people milling about, Barrymore asked Miss Hepburn if they might speak privately. In the hall, he took her hands and spoke of her screen test. "My dear," he enounced in his most actorly tones, "you're going to be a big star." Then staring into her bloodshot eye and reaching into his coat pocket, he handed her a small vial and said, "I have the same problem. Take this. Two drops in each eye." Kate protested that she was not hungover and insisted that she had something in her eye. With a wink and a smile, Barrymore said, "Yes, of course you do, my dear . . . that's two drops in each eye."

Not until the end of the day was Kate able to get medical attention. A doctor pulled three steel filings from her eye, prescribed some painkillers, and gave her an eyepatch. When she dutifully appeared at the studio the next morning, still in pain and wearing her patch, Cukor took one look at her and asked, "What do you think we're making here? A pirate picture?"

The filming of *A Bill of Divorcement* began on July 9, 1932, and Kate took to the process immediately. "From the very beginning," she said, "I found it a fascinating, romantic medium." By the time she appeared before the cameras, her eye had healed. Other than trimming her hair and streamlining her eyebrows, the studio bosses ordered no changes in her appearance, though they suggested she tone down her voice to soften its metallic quality. The most drastic adjustment she made was one small but painful cosmetic operation she performed on herself. Two nights before shooting, she plucked all the hairs from her nose.

While Hepburn argued every possible reading of every line with George Cukor, she realized that she and her director were, in fact, generally of the same mind. When they were not, she saw that film allowed them the possibility of performing a different interpretation in each take. Stage actors who made films and talked about their "craft" and the difficulties adjusting their gestures and voices to the more intimate sets on soundstages would forever bore Hepburn. "It's pretty obvious you don't have to project if there's a camera three feet away and a microphone over your head."

Strangely, she felt that John Barrymore, a twenty-year veteran of motion pictures, was not making any such adjustments. She had enough respect for the head of the American theater's royal family not to say anything; but she felt he knew he was overacting and that she was underreacting to his performance. He often asked Cukor if he could redo a scene; and, Hepburn later reflected, she thought a lot of those retakes were because "he somehow didn't want to disappoint me."

Barrymore was out to make a good impression on everybody— especially the ingenue. "He was," remembered Kate, "utterly incapable of letting a girl walk by without grabbing some part of her anatomy." A simple slap on the wrist was generally enough to get his mind back to business. On one occasion, however, he would not settle down, and the novice became extremely distracted. "I'll never play another scene with you!" she screamed at him. To which the great Barrymore replied, "But, my dear, you never have." A few days later, he asked if she might come to discuss another scene in his dressing room, a swank bachelor's apartment he had been given on the lot. She knocked on the door and upon entering discovered John Barrymore lying on the couch—which was made up with sheets and a blanket—his head propped on the armrest. He was stark naked.

By the end of the picture, Hepburn felt the pathos of Barrymore's performance in the film matched that of his life. She thought he was as brilliant and charming an actor as she would ever meet, and just as tortured—a sad, lonely man. She found his portrayal of Hillary Fairfield, a shell shock victim who escapes from an insane asylum only to find his wife about to remarry, "really touching."

Alongside his melodramatic school of acting, Hepburn's more naturalistic performance as his engaged daughter—who, fearing future insane children of her own, dismisses her fiancé so that she might care for her father—has a quality that is at once both green and evergreen. George Cukor said she was like "a colt finding her legs" during the first weeks of the movie. By the end, he said, she had proved that she was "a thoroughbred."

Hepburn's determination to succeed kept her focused on her work; and, at first, she eschewed any kind of social life in Hollywood. "I felt I had my own thing to do," she said, "and I didn't want to compromise that." She and Laura Harding rented a comfortable house up in Franklin Canyon that one of Laura's society friends had found for them. Another of his friends, a conservatively dressed Mrs. Fairbanks, called on them one day, inviting the two young women to dinner. Kate begged off, insisting that she never went out to dinner while she was in the middle of production. After Mrs. Fairbanks left, an appalled Laura Harding said, "Don't you know who you just snubbed?"

"Mrs. Fairbanks," said Kate. "She didn't look very interesting to me. We're well out of it."

"Maybe *you* are," said Laura. "But that was Mary Pickford, and I would love to have dinner with her and Mr. Fairbanks!"

Fortunately, a second invitation to Pickfair arrived, which the Hollywood newcomers accepted. Kate got to sit next to Douglas Fairbanks and found him "completely charming"; Pickford proved to be even more interesting, downright shrewd, with "a real nose for business"; and dinner was every bit as grand as she imagined dinner with royalty was. The hosts ran a film afterward, and Kate was already looking forward to a return visit to the town's most prestigious address. "Oh, I thought I was absolutely fascinating that night," Kate recalled, "chattering about this and that, and full of opinions on every subject." Mrs. Fairbanks, evidently, didn't find Miss Hepburn remotely interesting. She never called again.

"For some reason or other," Kate also remembered, "I was asked to visit the Hearst ranch—which would have been fascinating—and I said, 'No.' Can you imagine anyone as dumb as that?"

Upon completion of photography of *A Bill of Divorcement*, Kate returned to New York. Then she and her husband embarked on a second honeymoon to Europe. "We traveled well together," she recalled, in a way that suggested there was more politeness in the marriage than passion. *A Bill of Divorcement* was released little more than two months after shooting began—while Mr. and Mrs. Ludlow were in Austria—and it proved to be a great success for everybody involved. Many critics commented on the strangeness of both Hepburn's voice and appearance, but in the end most found her extremely appealing, different but attractive. For that, Hepburn credited one man.

"George Cukor *presented* me," she said, practically every time the subject of her first movie came up. "He knew I was an odd creature to most audiences and that I would take some getting used to. And so, he *presented* me." After her character first appears in the film—making a showy entrance, skittering down a set of stairs and dancing off in a man's arms—Cukor inserted a few shots that did nothing whatever to advance the story nor to deepen character. They were simply lingering shots of Hepburn, moments in which the audience could adjust to her and get acquainted with her. "So few modern directors have any theatrical background," Hepburn said, "and so they have no sense of entrance, the importance of introducing somebody to the audience. Thank God George did. I don't think I'd've had a career without those few shots, just those few extra seconds of screen time."

The studio publicity department certainly did its part to help promote her. But, as Hepburn later noted, "I bucked all that publicity stuff. I came back and started to read all these stories about myself, with quotations of things I never said, and, well, frankly, I just didn't give a damn. Since then I've never really taken any interest in what anybody writes about me." From the start, she entered a false birthdate for herself into the public record—November eighth, her brother Tom's birthday; and she shaved two years off her age.

Kate returned to Hollywood alone, with RKO lining up one project after another for her to star in. The first was a film, based on a novel, called *Christopher Strong*. The material was extremely melodramatic, but several elements of the project appealed to her. She would play a fiercely independent aviatrix—not unlike Amelia Earhart, who was one of Hepburn's heroes, not just for her accomplishments but also for her style and attitude. The lady flyer falls in love with a married man, becomes pregnant, and then—according to the social dictates of the day—meets her death trying to break a world altitude record.

Another reason to appear in the film was the director— Dorothy Arzner, for all intents and purposes, the only female director in the business. Hepburn never completely understood why there were so few women directing; there were, after all, many women writing scenarios and editing film. For that, she did not blame the men who ran the studios so much as the women who chose not to challenge them. "It never occurred to me that I was a second-class citizen in Hollywood," Hepburn later recounted, "—nor that women had to be."

While *Christopher Strong* rather quickly crashed and burned, Hepburn garnered wonderful notices, securing her position as a headliner. That, the new star just as quickly realized, carried certain responsibilities. With even the smaller studios cranking out movies every month, some as many as two a week, Hepburn realized that if she wanted to remain at the head of the pack of actors, she would have to take charge of her career—to the extent of scouting and securing the best possible material for herself.

"I usually don't look through people's desks," Hepburn told me one afternoon—somewhat disingenuously, I thought—"but one day I saw this thing on Pan Berman's desk." The thing was a script called *Morning Glory,* which was based on a play by a popular writer named Zoë Akins, and Pandro S. Berman was a twenty-seven-year-old assistant to David Selznick, then starting his own prestigious career as a motion-picture producer. Hepburn had taken an immediate shine to him and simply walked off with the script, telling Berman's secretary that she would be back for her appointment with the producer.

"This must have been written for me," she said to Berman when she returned to his office not two hours later. Few could deny her appropriateness for the part—that of a stagestruck girl from New England who comes to New York in quest of an acting career, stringing along a lover or two, then becoming an overnight sensation when she takes over for the star of a play who has walked out on opening night. No, Berman told her, it had been written, in fact, for Constance Bennett, a silent-screen actress who had just made a "comeback" at the age of twenty-seven in *What Price Hollywood?* (which George Cukor had directed just before *A Bill of Divorcement*). This film was to be directed by her costar, Lowell Sherman (who had successfully appeared as an actor in another work by Zoë Akins). "Hollywood was an even smaller town than Broadway," Miss Hepburn realized. She spent the next several days meeting everybody connected to this production, talking up this "thrilling" screenplay . . . until she convinced them that she was "born to play this part."

The company rehearsed for a week, then shot the entire film in seventeen days. And, Hepburn recalled, director Lowell Sherman never appeared on the set before nine-fifteen or after five-thirty. Although he was alcoholic and dying of cancer of the throat, Sherman put everything he had into this picture, keeping the entire cast (which included such veterans as C. Aubrey Smith and Adolphe Menjou) constantly engaged and amused. Hepburn's young romantic interest in the film was Douglas Fairbanks, Jr., with whom she became close friends. Although it was ultimately cut from the picture, Hepburn and Fairbanks, Jr., performed the balcony scene from *Romeo and Juliet,* filming it before a small audience that included Doug's father and stepmother, the Fairbankses. Kate confessed it was one of the few times in her life that she had stage fright.

Hepburn gave a remarkable performance in *Morning Glory,* one praised for revealing new dimensions as an actress and for bringing originality to potentially trite material. In truth, Hepburn would confess, she had borrowed heavily from another actor in delineating her role. Ruth Gordon had appeared in a play called *A Church Mouse,* in which she spoke in a monotone at a fast clip, conveying both eagerness and nervousness. Hepburn "copied her totally" in playing this heroine, Eva Lovelace—who was determined to become "the finest actress in the world." Stolen acting tricks or not, Hepburn proved completely winning and became one of the studio's prime assets.

Meantime, David Selznick—who had a penchant for translating classic works of literature into motion pictures—had been developing a pet project, one featuring another Yankee with artistic yearnings, *Little Women*. He had been through several bad versions of the Louisa May Alcott novel about the four March sisters growing up in Concord, Massachusetts, before he assigned a husband-and-wife team to tackle it anew. In four weeks Sarah Y. Mason and Victor Heerman wrote a shooting script, one with a role that seemed to be written for the new queen of the RKO lot.

"I would defy anyone to be as good as I was in *Little Women*," Kate Hepburn would say of her portrayal of Jo March. "They just couldn't be, they really couldn't be, because I came from the same general atmosphere, enjoyed the same things. And I'm sure Louisa May Alcott was writing about herself and that kind of behavior that was encouraged in a New England girl; and I understood those things. I was enough of a tomboy myself; and my personality was like hers. I could say, 'Christopher Columbus! What richness!' and believe it totally. I have enough of that old-fashioned personality in myself. Coming from a big family, in which I had always been very dramatic, this part suited my exaggerated sense of things." David Selznick agreed, and he recruited George Cukor to direct Hepburn a second time.

Based on the earlier scripts, Cukor had resisted the project, thinking the material was frilly and sentimental. Selznick insisted that he read the Alcott novel, with all its hardships of the Civil War era playing in the background of the lives of the March women. Cukor later told me, as I reported to Kate during one of our dinners, that reading the source material had completely turned him around. "Oh, that's such bunk!" she said. "I'm telling you that man never read that book." I replied that he told me she would say exactly that;

and she said, "So, he didn't deny it. I'm telling you George Cukor never read that book. But that didn't matter. We had a wonderful script to work with, one that was really true to the spirit of the novel."

Director and star bickered throughout the production—never about personal matters, only the material—in a collegial manner that brought them closer together. More often than not, Kate would get her way by either throwing her own New England background in his face or by reminding him, "You haven't read the book." The only time Cukor genuinely got mad at her on the set was the day she had to run up a flight of stairs carrying some ice cream while wearing a costume for which they had no duplicate. He repeatedly urged her to be careful not to spill on the dress, and finally said, "I'll kill you if you do." As though preordained, she did—and Kate burst into laughter. Cukor slapped her across the face and screamed, "You amateur!" running her off the set. She spent the rest of the day vomiting.

Hepburn enjoyed playing with her entire cast—which included Spring Byington as "Marmee" and the great character actress Edna May Oliver as Aunt March. Kate's "sisters" included Frances Dee as Meg, Jean Parker as Beth, and Joan Bennett as Amy, her costumes having to be redesigned to conceal her pregnancy. But from that luminous cast, it was Hepburn's portrayal as Jo that shone in the public eye. In less than a year she had become more than a Hollywood leading lady. She was a star.

At a time when the Depression was hardening Hollywood's edge—with movies about gangsters and tap-dancing gold-diggers—RKO suddenly had a big hit on its hands with this modest piece of counter-programming, a family drama full of family values. The film had its share of pain and reality, but its success sprang from the lives of characters the audience cared about. When the six-year-old Academy of Motion Picture Arts and Sciences announced its best pictures of the year, *Little Women* was among the ten nominations. Katharine Hepburn was nominated as Best Actress—though not for the same picture. She got shortlisted for *Morning Glory.*

Hepburn forever believed she was nominated for the wrong movie, that her work in *Morning Glory* was "very good" but that it was "tricked up, charming, mugging." In *Little Women,* however, she said, "I gave what I call the main-course performance, not a dessert." After much consideration, Hepburn chose not to attend the award ceremony, in the Fiesta Room of the Ambassador Hotel on the night of March 16, 1934. That night Will Rogers presented all the golden statuettes, whose new nickname of Oscar was starting to spread beyond the industry. After announcing that *Cavalcade* was the Best Picture and Charles Laughton was Best Actor, Rogers pronounced Katharine Hepburn that year's Best Actress.

The Academy Awards conflicted Hepburn from the very outset of her career, beginning with her believing that somebody so young and new to the game couldn't possibly win. There was more to it than that. Indeed, even after she was told she had won, Hepburn said she wanted to release a statement saying she did not believe in awards— "or some asinine answer like that." In truth, she later admitted, "mine was really bogus humility, because I was genuinely thrilled to win."

From that first nomination, Hepburn vowed never to attend the Academy Awards ceremony, a vow she was not proud of. "I think it is very noble for the people who go and lose, and I think it is very ignoble of me to be unwilling to go and lose," she confessed. "My father said that his children were so shy because they were afraid they were going to a party and they were not going to be either the bride or the corpse. And he may be right. I can't think of a single, logical defense of someone who occupies a position in the industry that they refuse to go to the biggest celebration that that industry has to offer. I think it's unpardonable, but I do it. . . . I have no defense."

At the same time, Hepburn added, she believed the industry and the public at large exaggerated the importance of the prize. A lot of it, she insisted, is luck and timing. "If you have a very good part," she said, "you have a very good opportunity . . . and sometimes you can shine in a dull year. But honestly," she added, "if you give an award-worthy performance, you know it. And I do think I'm terribly self-indulgent in refusing to appear." When I asked Kate in 1982 where her Oscars were, she could not say, other than that she had given them to a museum in the Empire State Building. "I mean, if I don't go to the ceremony," she explained, "I can't very well put them on my mantelpiece, can I? I simply have no right to."

Having risen to the top of her new profession in little more than a year, Hepburn still felt she had plenty to prove. Triumphant on the West Coast, she told her studio bosses that she wanted to return to New York, to the theater. She thought she could take Manhattan by storm by appearing in a new play called *The Lake*. RKO would not release her, unless she agreed to make one more picture before leaving. Star and studio found themselves stalemated, until Kate had the nerve to say she would appear in a movie called *Spitfire*. Feeling capable of anything, she said she would star as the heroine—an uneducated, barefooted tomboy, an Ozarks faith healer named Trigger Hicks. She demanded $50,000 for four weeks of work plus $10,000 for each day beyond that. Hepburn gave it her all (and collected $60,000 for her efforts) and had banked enough good will with the critics to escape virtually unscathed.

The few who ever saw *Spitfire* rank it among the worst movies Katharine Hepburn ever made. The star felt the same, later chastising herself by saying, "The few times I did something for the money, it was mediocre material, and I did mediocre work." While Kate kept few photographs of herself on display around any of her homes, a picture of her as Trigger Hicks remained for years in a place of prominence just outside her bedroom at Fenwick. "A reminder," she told me with an arch of an eyebrow. "Trigger keeps me humble."

Besides the theater, Hepburn had another reason for returning east. Her marriage. Few in Hollywood even realized that Katharine Hepburn had a husband back in New York, in the business world. It appeared that Kate herself had forgotten all about him. Although she continued to live quietly in the hills with Laura Harding (fueling speculation of a lesbian relationship), Kate was occasionally seen in the company of attractive men.

She went on a few dates with Douglas Fairbanks, Jr., but the nights always ended earlier than he would have liked. She spent her sunniest days off work that year with a young actor raised in Southern California, Joel McCrea—"so good-looking, so charming." They would drive up the coast, then picnic and swim at Zuma Beach; their friendship also remained platonic. Increasingly, she was secretly spending her nights at the Franklin Canyon house with her agent, the urbane Leland Hayward. Like her, he was married; and *their* friendship became something more than that.

Hayward was virtually a singular presence in show business—as handsome and debonair as many actors, extremely tasteful, and intelligent in matters of business. He had already created a presence for himself in Hollywood and on Broadway. He was known at the time as Hollywood's only "Princeton man," which was accurate if one counted his single year there. His passion was women—the more challenging the better. In his aloof new star, suddenly considered the most sophisticated presence in movies, he had met his match.

While Hepburn was outdoorsy, athletic, and liked to be in bed early, Hayward's most active sport was late-night club-hopping. Despite their conflicting clocks and calendars, Kate said, "We were really mad for each other"; and they constantly scrambled to make time to be together. They enjoyed a sexually charged affair, in which it was difficult to ascertain who had the upper hand. Equally infatuated with one another, he suggested that he would divorce his wife, an adventurous Texas beauty named Lola Gibbs, if Kate would divorce Luddy. Returning to New York would keep Hayward in mad pursuit.

There was yet another reason lurking behind Hepburn's leaving Los Angeles—a man she would later call "hands-down the most diabolical person I have ever met." His name was Jed Harris; and in the colorful theater world of the 1920s and '30s, nobody was as revered and reviled (at the same time) as much as he. The brilliant producer and director, largely responsible for such highly regarded hits as *The Royal Family, The Front Page,* and, later, *Our Town* (also the man on whom Laurence Olivier would later model his performance of Richard III, evil incarnate), Harris had fallen into a slump in his career. He was trying to climb out by mounting a production called *The Lake.*

Sinister in looks and satanic in ambition, Harris was extremely seductive—especially to actresses, who found themselves vulnerable to his promises of artistic success. He had already captivated Ruth Gordon, fathering and abandoning a child with her; and he had lured Margaret Sullavan away from her husband, a budding actor, Henry Fonda. In this case, however, it was not the fox who went after another hen, but Hepburn who approached Harris. Flush with success, the young Hollywood star dared to pick up a telephone and call him directly.

The Lake was the story of a woman desperate to marry; on her wedding day, she skids the car in which she is driving her husband into the lake, killing him. Hepburn later confessed that she was simply so consumed with the notion of working with Harris that she did not know whether the play was even any good or not. Her motivation, she claimed, was "to help restore him to his throne . . . and I felt powerful enough to do that. Crazy! What was I thinking?"

Only years later did she realize that she wasn't thinking at all, that it was sheer hubris that drove her to believe her sudden status as a movie star was enough to meet the challenge. Helen Hayes, whom Hepburn barely knew, sent her a note out of the blue, warning her not to work with Harris. But after "conquering Hollywood," Hepburn was vain enough not even to consider this enterprise a contest. Alas, she didn't realize that Harris was sociopathic, and her munificent gesture of riding to his rescue (if that's what it was) only angered him even more, making him hell-bent on doing her harm.

She showed her vulnerability at the start, agreeing to a much smaller salary than a star, to say nothing of a movie star, was entitled to. Then, at the first rehearsal, Harris set about breaking her. He stopped her every few moments, correcting every move, generally insisting she do the exact opposite. At last, in a scene that required her to play the piano—or at least fake playing the piano—she could not position her hands to match the music that was being piped in and say her lines at the same time. He made her play the scene again and again, delighting in her failure to improve. When she finally protested, he said, "Helen Hayes learned to play the piano for me!" That knocked whatever confidence she retained out from under her. As a result of this relentless torture, she felt her performance becoming robotic.

The Lake previewed in Washington, D.C., where there was a huge advance sale. The crowd was enthusiastic. "There really is nothing as generous as an American audience," Hepburn long maintained, "especially for a movie star trying to stretch. I'm always amazed that more movie stars, especially those actresses who hit their forties and fifties and complain that Hollywood isn't writing any parts for them anymore, don't take to the stage. If Broadway is too scary, there are hundreds of wonderful theaters all over the country who would be thrilled to have them. Actors should act." But Hepburn herself was not pleased with her performance. Feeling she was "a bore" in these preview performances, she looked forward to some new direction from Harris and a chance to rehearse further.

After seeing the advance ticket sales in New York, however, Harris chose not to give the play another thought. He simply brought the company into town and opened it. "I felt as though I were sleepwalking through a nightmare," Hepburn said of the experience, "and I kept hoping I would wake up." She claimed never to read reviews, but after this play opened, she knew perfectly well that the critics had a field day with her. Very proudly, she recited to me Dorothy Parker's famous review of sixty years earlier, one of the legendary wit's most famous quips: "Go to the Martin Beck and see Katharine Hepburn run the gamut of emotion from A to B." Kate pronounced the word "gam-MUTT," saying, "That's what I was— a great big mutt." After a few weeks, the crowds dwindled, but not quickly enough for the star, who was locked into a run-of-the-play contract. She just wanted out.

But Jed Harris was not done with her. Even though neither the play nor the star was very good, he realized Hepburn's name on a marquee was enough to draw people in for a few weeks in any city in which they opened. With Hepburn preparing to jump ship the moment the show closed in New York, where it had made its investment back, Harris announced they were moving to Chicago and then onward across the country. At last, she put her foot down, asking why he would continue with this play in which neither he nor the public had much interest. "My dear," he said, "the only interest I have in you is the money I can make out of you."

She respected the honesty of the answer and came right back to him, asking how much she would have to pay to see the show close. "How much have you got?" he replied. She grabbed her bankbook and read him the balance, some thirteen thousand dollars. He said, "I'll take it." The check arrived in the morning, and the show closed in New York after a few more performances. Except for a chance meeting of no consequence in a theater years later, by which time Harris had become a broken man, Hepburn never saw him again.

Leland Hayward encountered Harris years later. "You know," said the producer, by then completely washed-up, reflecting on *The Lake*, "I tried to destroy Katharine Hepburn." Hayward was dumbfounded by the revelation. At last, he mustered wits enough to say, "You failed, didn't you?"

By the start of 1934, however, Jed Harris had come close to getting his wish. For one of the few times in her life, Katharine Hepburn's confidence in herself was terribly shaken. *Spitfire* opened and raised doubts about her future in Hollywood; and her marriage, at last, was no longer proving to be even one of convenience. For $100 a month, the "Ludlows" had moved into the Turtle Bay house on East Forty-ninth Street; and Luddy had relocated his business—a corporate payroll system for big companies, which Kate never completely understood—to New York. At the same time, she knew that she had better hurry back to Hollywood, to continue her climb up the career ladder, and that Luddy was excess baggage. He was willing to move to Hollywood, even to stay in New York and keep the home fires burning. But by then, Hepburn was feeling more romantic toward Leland Hayward than toward her own husband, and she couldn't bear the thought of "using" him more than she already had. Though Luddy moved out of the Turtle Bay house, he was content to remain in marital limbo. At last, however, Kate decided, "I should perform one act of generosity for my husband—divorce him." In April 1934, she flew to Mérida, in the Yucatán, accompanied by Laura Harding, and filed for a Mexican divorce.

Some fifty years later, while she and I were tidying up the kitchen before going up to bed, I asked why she had bothered to marry Luddy—whom I never met—in the first place. After giving the counter a final swipe of the sponge, she looked me right in the eye and, without thinking twice, said, "Because I was a pig."

After having practically every dinner with Hepburn that week after my first visit to Fenwick, I had to return to Los Angeles. The bulk of my Goldwyn research was there, and I had to pull together the interview with her that I was preparing for *Esquire*. As she walked down the stairs to send me off that Thursday night, she took me into the kitchen, where she pulled a key out of the table drawer. "Now, look," she said, pressing it into my hand, "you're obviously coming back to New York, and you'll need a place to stay; and hotels are so damned expensive, and they're so cold and impersonal. And, well, you know the way here now. So, dinner is always at seven, drinks at six, and if you're eating with us, let us know by three. There's always a bed upstairs."

She opened the door and followed me to the little black iron gate at the sidewalk, looking up and down Forty-ninth Street. I wondered if she wanted to be seen or not. "Let us know when you're coming back," she yelled, when I was a few doors away; and I turned back to see that several passersby, recognizing the voice, had, in fact, stopped and stared at her.

She was smiling.

V

Katharine of Arrogance

C an you hear this?" the voice of Katharine Hepburn asked over my telephone a few days later, clinking a spoon against a glass dish. "I am just finishing the most delicious hot-fudge sundae I have ever eaten. Dick has added exactly the right amount of coffee into the fudge and created the perfect sundae—over coffee ice cream. It's an absolutely perfect spring day, and the sunlight is absolutely brilliant. Did you send me that arrangement of flowers in New York—all sorts of lilies and irises?"

"Yes, they're from me."

"You must forgive me for not thanking you sooner. The card was signed, 'Your Parcheesi partner,' and so I called Marion, because we played Parcheesi every day when I was recovering up there, and she was always my partner. And she said she didn't send any flowers, and then I realized it must be you. And I thought you really are quite silly, because you are completely hopeless at Parcheesi, truly incompetent, and I will not play that game with you ever again."

"May I hold you to that promise?"

We talked on the telephone for several minutes. I could tell that she didn't want to hang up—not that I wanted her to—that she was strangely content just to make small talk. She had told me early on that she felt her social life had been "very boxed" for most of her adult years—living in the same house and getting to know few people. And while Fenwick had long been her retreat to sanity, with few callers, I realized that her activity since her accident had slowed down radically. There was more forced quietude to her life than she liked. She suggested that I call her frequently—"Because who knows?" she said. "The next time you call, I may be dead!"

Over the next fifteen years, I called regularly. If more than a week ever went by, she usually greeted me with, "I thought you died." She always asked when I was visiting New York next and how my work was progressing.

In fact, our work together—the interview for *Esquire*'s fiftieth-anniversary issue—took an odd turn. In the fortnight after my return to Los Angeles from our initial meeting, I learned, by chance, that *Esquire* had, in fact, commissioned a number of pieces on other Hollywood personalities, designating such stars as Gary Cooper and John Wayne as among the "Fifty People Who Have Made a Difference." I didn't necessarily disagree with their choices, but—as I promptly reminded the magazine editors—my chief argument in coaxing Miss Hepburn into our interview had been *Esquire*'s assurance that she would be the only Hollywood figure represented. "Don't tell her," suggested the editor in chief.

I told him that was unacceptable. What was more, I reminded him, I had not yet received either a contract or any money for the piece—so, legally speaking, I could just walk away from the assignment. "That's terribly unprofessional," the editor insisted. "I think it's more unprofessional for you to break a promise you made to a writer and one of your honorees," I replied.

On my next visit to New York a few weeks later, I explained the situation to Miss Hepburn. "But if you don't turn it in," she worried, "you won't get paid." I assured her that the money they were offering was not enough even to factor into the decision. "Well," she said, "it's not as if I need it for my career." That settled that.

When I reported the verdict to the editors at *Esquire,* they were furious. They quickly turned their indignation into invention. As the forty-nine other authors were turning in their assignments, they evidently received an unpublishable piece from Truman Capote. Desperate to have his name on their cover, and now just as eager to have a piece on Hepburn, they asked him to write about her. He didn't know her but said he had an anecdote in which he stepped on her foot at the theater one night. "I told you they were slick," Hepburn said to me when I brought her a copy of the final product. "Who knew they were morons?" As a result of the incident, my stock with Kate soared.

I returned to my Goldwyn book more dedicated than ever. I was visiting New York to interview supporting players in his life five or six times a year, thus allowing me to see Hepburn often. She always wanted to hear about my latest interview or conversations with anyone from "the old days."

With the number of her own projects decreasing, Hepburn delighted in dabbling in mine. Over the next several years, she consistently asked how she might help. In retrospect, it occurs to me that all her largesse—the time we shared, the meals, lodging, intimate conversation, and lots of dark chocolate ("the best in the world," she insisted, came from a small shop on upper Broadway called Mondel's—turtles, almond bark, and breakup)—had always been given freely, before I even had to ask. I never made a single request of her . . . with one exception. After conducting literally scores of interviews for my book, only one important source kept evading me; and I thought Kate—who prided herself on pulling rabbits out of hats—might be able to help.

Irving Berlin had been one of Samuel Goldwyn's closest friends. Well into his nineties when I began my project, I had written America's composer laureate several times in hopes of arranging an interview. His eldest daughter had put in a good word for me, as had Goldwyn's son. Irene Selznick suggested I use her name in one of my entreaties; and even Berlin's private secretary of many years, with whom I had spoken several times, said she would take up my cause.

I had heard stories that Berlin had become senile and was living in his pajamas on the top floor of his town house on Beekman Place, watching television all day and talking to nobody. Then one day he telephoned—to say (with the television blaring in the background) that he could not see me, that it was too exhausting even to think about all those games of gin rummy at which he caught Sam Goldwyn cheating. Before I could even try to engage him in a conversation, he hung up. I figured it was time to play my trump card.

"You're always asking if you can help me," I said to Kate during one of my weeks in New York. "Well, maybe there is. Can you think of any way I might get to Irving Berlin?" For a moment, Kate warmed up to the challenge, then a cold, worried expression came across her face. "I hear he's become Garbo," she said, "and that he sees nobody. And I haven't seen him since RKO"—which meant the mid-thirties. "I understand," I said. "But if you have any suggestions . . ."

The next night I returned for dinner from my rounds in New York and found Kate sitting in her chair with a big smile pasted across her face. Her clothes were less casual than usual. She was even wearing a little makeup and some perfume. "Well, I had a most interesting day," she said, all Cheshire-catlike.

"Really?"

Yes, she said. After lunch she had walked to 17 Beekman Place, a five-story Georgian brick house, which is practically around the corner, and rang the bell. A maid answered, and Kate said she didn't wish to disturb Mr. Berlin, but she wanted to leave a note for him. The maid asked if she cared to come in, and she said no. She just wanted to know that Mr. Berlin was all right. Then, as Hepburn related the story, a clear voice from several floors above sang out, "Kate, is that you?" And she replied, "Yes, Irving, is that you?" He told her to wait a moment, that he would be right down.

American River College Library

"He looked quite wonderful," she said. "Especially for a man close to a hundred."

"At one hundred," I responded, "whatever you look like looks wonderful."

No, she continued, he looked healthy and was well-groomed and nicely dressed. They sat in the living room, and she explained her mission, that she was calling on my behalf, hoping he might see me. He replied that his stomach got so churned up just thinking about Sam Goldwyn (a common malady, even among Goldwyn's friends), he couldn't think of sitting down with a biographer and dredging it all up. But surely, he told Kate, she could stay for tea. Stay she did . . . for more than three hours! "And," Kate recounted to me that night, "he was wonderful—full of stories and full of life and full of memories. We talked about RKO and remembered things I hadn't thought of since the thirties. And it was one of the most wonderful afternoons I've ever had. And he absolutely refuses to see you."

"Oh," I said. "I'm glad I was able to provide you with a good time. Did you at least ask him anything about Sam Goldwyn?"

"Oh yes," she assured me. "He told me several stories about old Sam, and they were very funny, just killingly funny . . . and I was having such a good time I don't remember a goddamned one of them."

The next night at dinner, I found Kate again sitting with another big, smug smile. "Well—I had a most interesting day," she said. So enchanted was she by Mr. Berlin's hospitality, she dropped by that afternoon with a bouquet of flowers and a thank-you note. Again, the door was opened and the voice from on high called, "Kate, is that you?" And down came Irving again, and she stayed for another three hours, these more intoxicating than the last. "And," she said with a huge laugh, "he still refuses to see you. But I must say, he's most delightful."

"Thanks a lot."

Irving Berlin aside, some one hundred fifty people did speak to me about Sam Goldwyn; and Hepburn, after more than fifty years in motion pictures, knew most of them. She especially perked up the week I told her that I had just visited with Joel McCrea, a former Goldwyn leading man. She said she would love to see him again and asked if I would invite him to visit the next time he was in New York. I said I would pass along the invitation, but I was under the impression that he and his wife, Frances Dee, seldom left California. "My God," she said, "I think those two have been married for fifty years. They were an adorable couple."

"They still are," I assured her, having seen her recently when I went to interview him at his ranch. "She's got a terrific figure, and the two of them seem very happy together." Hepburn recalled McCrea's saying that he always wanted to be a rancher—"and that he was using his acting just to get there. And it's funny, because I really think he was the most underrated actor of his day. He could do everything. Look at him in that Hitchcock thing [*Foreign Correspondent*] and then in *The Most Dangerous Game* . . . and all those comedies—the George Stevens picture [*The More the Merrier*] and the Preston Sturges pictures [*Sullivan's Travels* and *The Palm Beach Story*]. And he looked great on a horse. But the problem [and this was one of those words she made all her own, landing on each syllable with equal emphasis] was, he never really had a studio behind him. Nobody to present him . . . to develop him. And that was so important in those early days. With the big studios grooming big stars, you needed that kind of push. That's what Gable had and Crawford. They weren't great actors, but they were great personalities, and the big studios got completely behind them.

"Now who are the big male stars today?" she asked me.

"Pacino, Hoffman, De Niro, Stallone—"

"Exactly," she interrupted. "That's the prob-lem. Now those old boys—Gable and Cooper and Jimmy and Bogie and Spence, well—

they looked good riding a horse . . . or in white-tie and tails. Now who can you name today who can do that?"

"Who else have you seen?" Kate would ask whenever there was a lull in a conversation. There was always a trace of yearning in her voice. I felt she wanted to know not just whom I was seeing but which of her contemporaries was still alive and working. She enjoyed providing thumbnail sketches, bits of background for the book, which I always found enlightening and entertaining. "Joel put me on to Barbara Stanwyck," I said.

"Well, they really had the same prob-lem, didn't they. I mean, she was a freelance actor, a kind of gun for hire, and in the beginning didn't really have the backing of a big studio. I mean she had a broad range of things she could do—not the classics, but certainly heavy drama and light comedy. She could make you laugh, and she could make you cry. Chaplin, of course, could make you do both at the same time."

Garbo forever remained Hepburn's favorite movie star. "I think she was a great actress. But even more than that, she carried so much mystery with her. From the moment she walked on the screen, you simply couldn't take your eyes off her, you wanted to know everything about her, and you knew she wasn't going to give it to you. That's a movie star. And that's what we all wanted to be," she said of the thousands of girls who took trains and buses to Hollywood to be discovered.

In the spring of 1934, Katharine Hepburn returned to Hollywood. She was, for that moment, at least, a star with a six-picture contract with RKO—then considered the liveliest studio in town. The most minor of the major studios, RKO prided itself on low budgets, fresh talent, and original material, coming up with such recent hits as the early Fred Astaire–Ginger Rogers musicals ("Fred gave Ginger class;

Ginger gave Fred sex appeal," Hepburn famously observed), *Little Women,* and *King Kong.* She was also returning to Leland Hayward, her "beau" (her word), one of the most dashing men in town. Her theatrical experience with Jed Harris only doubled the intensity with which she reapproached her work on the screen. Hepburn was back, with a vengeance—which, unfortunately, occasionally showed.

In an attempt to replicate her triumph in *Little Women,* RKO promptly cast Hepburn in *The Little Minister.* Like the former film, this was based on a nineteenth-century literary favorite, a novel and play by Sir James M. Barrie. With the notable exception of Richard Wallace, a journeyman director standing in for George Cukor, most of the former crewmembers reassembled to craft this project. As before, the Heermans produced the final draft of the screenplay— the love story of Lady Babbie, who often escaped from her guardian's manor house dressed as a gypsy so that she could walk among the struggling weavers of the Auld Licht Kirk in Scotland, only to fall in love with the kirk's new minister.

The film was a mild success, not as big as the studio had hoped or expected or—as Hepburn said—"it should have been." She believed George Cukor's presence might have made a great difference; but he had been involved in the making of a genuine classic that year, *David Copperfield.* The star herself ultimately took the blame for *The Little Minister's* failure—largely because, she later admitted, she hadn't really wanted the part in the first place. "The main reason I did it," she confessed, "was that I had heard that Ginger Rogers really wanted to play it; and I knew the studio wanted me more and that I could do it better. What an IG-noble reason. I'm still quite disgusted with myself."

Still, she believed a strong director would have curbed what she called "a rather fancy performance." Looking back, she said, "I thought I had discovered what magnificent hands I had; and I remember that they became the most important part of my performance. Most peculiar." Viewing the film today, one sees the accuracy of Hepburn's memory. In almost every scene her hands appear self-consciously folded or clasped or flapping or floating. Beyond that distraction, the part calls for whimsy, an almost otherworldly elfin quality; and, Hepburn admitted, "I think I'm probably just too down-to-earth for that." Adopting a Scottish burr— which came and went from scene to scene—forced her voice into its highest registers, often proving irritating for both the actress and her audience.

She proceeded immediately to her next picture, a deservedly forgotten modern romance called *Break of Hearts*. It was intended as another vehicle for Hepburn and John Barrymore—she as an aspiring composer, he as an alcoholic conductor. This time, however, she would have the star billing. But Barrymore turned down the sentimental melodrama, and it fell to Charles Boyer, one of the few French actors to achieve leading-man status in American films and one of Hollywood's great lovers—on screen and off. Rumors immediately spread that she and Boyer were intimately involved. Kate later denied them, insisting that it was not for her lack of trying. She called the film, which garnered her worst reviews to date and fared poorly at the box office, "a mistake," one she explained away by saying, "I felt I was sitting out there in Hollywood, and my career was such that if I wasn't moving ahead, I was falling behind. And so I did the picture out of a kind of desperation. Never a wise move."

Just as she was about to overstay her welcome with the public, one of the most appealing screen roles ever written came her way. While she was finishing *Break of Hearts*, RKO was adapting Booth Tarkington's *Alice Adams*, which had already been a successful silent film. The eponymous heroine, a socially ambitious, middle-class girl in the Midwest who falls for a handsome man above her station, was, in Hepburn's words, "a big plum—a sweet and juicy role. I had read Tarkington growing up and always thought he was a wonderful writer, a great social observer with a lot of heart. And I thought the script captured Alice's desperation to be more than she was or than she could be. . . . She was in a race that she couldn't win. And, of course, that's great fun to play because she doesn't know it's hopeless and the audience does. So the harder Alice works at it, the more heartbreaking she becomes."

What appealed to Hepburn most about the part, and what she believed she could bring to the role more than any of her competition in Hollywood, was the gentle humor. To ensure its place in the film, she insisted on a director with a comic bent. The studio was about to sign William Wyler, a promising young man just coming into his own as Samuel Goldwyn's prize director, primarily of social dramas. But Hepburn had reservations and kept stalling. Then her friend Eddie Killy, who had served as assistant director on practically all of her RKO pictures, recommended a young director named George Stevens. He had broken in under Hal Roach, the king of two-reel comedies, and had recently directed an episode in a popular comedy series featuring two different families, the Cohens and the Kellys. Hepburn asked to meet him.

"I thought he was a really odd duck," she said of Stevens, a big man with a weathered face and an aloof air. "He hardly spoke. And at first I wasn't sure if he was just plain dumb or so smart that he was busy analyzing everybody else." Whether or not to let him direct *Alice Adams* virtually came down to the toss of a coin. Producer Pan Berman flipped a quarter, and when it came up heads—Wyler—he and Hepburn looked at each other. He asked if they should flip again, and Hepburn said yes. "I just felt George was strong and fun. We signed him up, mostly on my hunch, I would say, which, in this case, proved to be very good."

Her hunch was not entirely professional. Although she still told herself that her future with Leland Hayward was advancing— possibly toward the altar—she still found herself attracted to a growing number of men, especially directors. The inherent drama between the man calling the shots and the woman who had to perform created a sexual tension that most people never thought existed on the sets of Katharine Hepburn movies. But during the course of shooting *Alice Adams,* it became apparent to those around them that Stevens and Hepburn were having an affair.

It was an intense love match—real, emotional duels as opposed to the more jocular jousting on George Cukor's sets. "We were both incredibly strong-willed," Kate said of her first picture with George Stevens. "I seemed to have the upper hand because I was the bigger star; and I had been largely responsible for his being hired. But George had the upper hand because he was, after all, the director, and a very tough director at that. He would not budge. And he made us do one scene [with her handsome, easygoing leading man, Fred MacMurray] close to eighty times."

For Stevens, these battles were more than simple lovers' quarrels. "Now George Stevens was a really brilliant director," Kate averred many times. "And this was not just some personal conquest on his part. I think he felt he really had something to offer me. I had had some success, but I was still pretty new to the movie game. And he believed he could direct me to become better. Not necessarily different than I had been, but somehow more than I had been."

That was never more evident than in one of the film's most famous scenes: Alice has just returned from a society dance, which proved to be a series of slights and humiliations for her from start to finish. Throughout the night she has maintained her pluck and dignity. Only after she returns from the party in the rain, raps on her parents' door to let them know she's home, and goes into her own bedroom, does she allow herself to cry. In playing the scene, Hepburn intended to throw herself onto her bed and sob into her pillow.

Stevens had what he thought was a better idea. Using one of his trademark shots, a huge screen-filling close-up, he thought Alice should walk to the window and look out into the rain, so that the drops running down the pane would accentuate the tears running down her cheeks. Hepburn liked the idea. But when she had to perform the scene, the tears would not flow. She claimed, at the time, that cold water had dripped through the leaky set window and frozen her up. She attempted the scene repeatedly, but to no avail. Then, instead of admitting that she was having a technical acting problem, she insisted the problem was in the staging, that throwing herself on the bed was not only the way she had envisioned playing the scene but that it was truer to Alice's character, that Alice would stifle her crying.

Director and actress crossed swords. He insisted that Alice could not possibly keep herself from crying in the scene, that the one who would stifle her tears was Katharine Hepburn! At last, her illogic fractured his normally calm facade, and he flew into a rage, the sheer force of which terrified her into playing the scene one more time—at the window, with tears flowing. "It's a wonderful moment," Kate recalled half a century later, "but it occurred only because I thought he was going to kill me."

Alice Adams became a big hit and one of Hepburn's personal favorites. Both she and the picture were nominated for Academy Awards. *Mutiny on the Bounty* won Best Picture that year; and Bette Davis was named Best Actress for *Dangerous*. More important, appearing in practically every scene in this successful, critically acclaimed film seemed to ensure Hepburn's place in the public's heart and her position as a star. Feeling the rush himself, RKO producer Pandro Berman told her she had only to name her next project.

Hepburn's pal George Cukor—coming off three consecutive blockbuster hits—had become infatuated with a novel by Compton Mackenzie called *The Early Life and Adventures of Sylvia Scarlett*. It was a peculiar picaresque story about a girl who masquerades as a boy, so that she can accompany her father, a crook on the lam. In their travels, they meet up with an odd lot of characters, including a cockney rogue. Hepburn thought it was "a brilliant book," but she never really saw its cinematic possibilities. Cukor had enough enthusiasm for two. Full of themselves, they told Pandro Berman this was the project they wanted to work on next. The producer could hardly deny them.

The story, with its androgynous sexual interplay, was unlike anything else on the screen; and it was another showy part for Hepburn—for which her hair was cut like a boy's. But as she later admitted, "Just because something is different doesn't necessarily mean it's good." She felt only one member of the cast really made something of his role, and that was the young actor who played the cockney—Cary Grant. The former Archibald Leach had, in fact, already appeared in some twenty films in his first three years in Hollywood, but he still had not fully developed his screen persona yet. He was handsome but slightly pudgy in this picture; and instead of the clipped English tones for which he would become famous and widely mimicked, he spoke "flawless" cockney, which was, in fact, more akin to his mother tongue. Hepburn had never had so much fun on a movie set with an actor; and she became fast friends with this former "acrobatic dancer" from Bristol, England, who had the know-how to parlay his charm and looks into respectability. Indeed, he would soon become a twentieth-century icon of suavity and breeding.

Sylvia Scarlett was, in the star's opinion, "awful." Even before the film opened, all involved knew they had "a big flop" on their hands. After a preview in nearby Huntington Park, Pan Berman came to George Cukor's house to commiserate with his director and star. They urged him to forget about this film, assuring him that they would both do another for him for free. "Please," said Berman, "don't bother."

Although they remained bosom buddies, Hepburn steered clear of George Cukor for a while, at least professionally. She made her next three pictures with more rough-and-tumble directors, none of whom, as it happened, was especially happily married. John Ford—one of Hollywood's most brilliant filmmakers, who had just taken the town by storm with *The Informer*—was hired to direct *Mary of Scotland,* a successful Maxwell Anderson play, which had starred Helen Hayes on Broadway, about the Stuart heir trying to claim the throne of England from Elizabeth I.

Again, Hepburn was not crazy about her part, the title role. "I thought she was an ass," she said, "and I would have rather played Elizabeth, who, after all, was the powerful one." But she knew it was a great vehicle for a star, and she welcomed the opportunity to work with Jack Ford, whom she had known slightly over the past few years. Frederic March, one of Hollywood's most versatile leading men, played her husband and protector, the Earl of Bothwell—James Hepburn, who was, in fact, a distant ancestor.

It proved difficult to cast the antagonist of the play, Elizabeth. Bette Davis wanted the role, but Warner Brothers made a practice of never loaning her out. She would limn her own indelible version of the formidable monarch for the studio just three years later. Even Ginger Rogers, forever trying to prove to her studio bosses that she could play serious drama, threw her hat into the ring. "Can you imagine?" Kate said one night, striking a pose of shock. "The Virgin Queen!"

At one point, Hepburn—whom some wags in town had by then dubbed "Katharine of Arrogance"—suggested that she play both roles. "But if you played both queens," asked John Carradine, a favorite Ford player who had a supporting role in the film, "how would you know which one to upstage?" Hepburn found nothing amusing about the comment at the time. Years later she roared with laughter telling it.

Long before shooting finished, Ford lost interest in the project. The sets, staging, and photography were unusually good, but he offered no support in fleshing out the characters, all but reducing the actors—including March's real wife, Florence Eldridge, as Elizabeth—to pageanteers. One day Ford walked off the set in despair and told Hepburn to direct the scene herself. Said Kate of the final product, "It laid a great big egg."

But Ford—born Sean Aloysius O'Fearna—never lost interest in his leading lady. A big, red-haired, melancholy Irishman, who had problems with his wife and with the bottle, he loved nothing more than getting out to sea on his ketch, the *Araner*, usually with some salty chums and some fun-loving young women and plenty of booze.

He found Katharine Hepburn even more intoxicating. When he wasn't lording over her on the set, he privately allowed himself to turn submissive, succumbing to her energy, excitement, and enthusiasm for life. She called him Sean, and found him a slightly tragic figure, full of demons—which he seemed to elude on the water. She often went out on the *Araner* with him. Although he generally concluded each picture with a long, drunken voyage somewhere, after shooting *Mary of Scotland*, he hied off with Kate on a healthier retreat to Fenwick. A romance ripened.

Hepburn followed *Mary of Scotland*, a flop, with *A Woman Rebels*, a Victorian costume drama in which her character defies the conventions of her class by having a child out of wedlock and editing a progressive women's magazine. Mark Sandrich, who had been directing Astaire and Rogers musicals, proved unusually clumsy in this particular outing. The film ended up a "mistake," said Hepburn, "a complete error on everyone's part, mostly mine for doing it in the first place."

She followed that with "a disaster," another attempt at recovering some of the charm of *Little Women*—a second Barrie play called *Quality Street*. Under George Stevens's characteristic direction, it also proved to be a labored attempt at whimsy, to nobody's credit. "That made four skunks in a row," Hepburn recounted, "and I felt I had to get out of town for a while."

It was not just her recent track record that sent her running. Thinking she had the best of both worlds—living with one man yet having occasional love affairs with others—Hepburn realized she had been living in a fool's paradise. "You might say I lived like a man," Kate recalled, until she suddenly found herself being dumped by her near-fiancé. Leland Hayward had spent a great deal of time in New York that year, tending to his client Edna Ferber, who had written a big hit play with George S. Kaufman called *Stage Door*. It starred Margaret Sullavan, an incandescent rising film star who had already blazed through marriages to Henry Fonda and William Wyler, to say nothing of her flaming affair with Jed Harris. "Well, Ferber and Kaufman were the toast of Broadway, and Margaret Sullavan was the toast of Broadway," Kate said, "and Leland—well, he always liked toasts." Despite the seemingly excessive amounts of time he spent on the East Coast that year, he spoke often of his desire to marry Hepburn.

During one of his absences, in November 1936, Kate was dining at George Cukor's house when she heard over the radio that Leland Hayward had just married Margaret Sullavan. A telegram followed. She was distraught—until her mother made her realize that only her pride was wounded, and that she was not really smarting from any genuine matrimonial plans of her own being scrubbed. Kate sent the newlyweds a congratulatory telegram; and in her next face-to-face conversation with her erstwhile agent, she learned that the bride had been pregnant at her wedding. "It was really quite simple," Kate explained to me. "She trapped him."

Over the years, Kate spoke of Leland Hayward only in affectionate tones. He treated her similarly. His enduring feelings for her were corroborated by Hayward's third wife, the former Pamela Churchill, whom I got to know when she was later married to Ambassador Averell Harriman, a friend of Sam Goldwyn. She told me—as had Kate—that when Leland Hayward was on his deathbed, she called Hepburn and said, "He loved you the most. He's dying. Will you come to see him?" Hepburn did.

Kate believed Pamela Digby Churchill Hayward Harriman had overstated her dying second husband's feelings in order to get her to make a deathbed appearance. "I think that was the secret to her success; she knew how to please men, and she would do anything for her husband," Kate explained, quickly amending, "husbands!" Kate did not undervalue her relationship with Leland Hayward. She knew it had been a golden time for him as well, one with no rules and little reality. "We were two helium balloons," she said, "who popped."

While she wanted to get out of Hollywood for a while, Hepburn knew that she had become "a joke" on Broadway. The stench from *The Lake* still lingered. She found safe harbor in a group called the Theatre Guild, one of whose founders, Theresa Helburn, wanted to star Hepburn in a production of *Jane Eyre*. She liked the company; and though she had some concerns about the play, she thought they could be worked out on tour. After playing Boston and Chicago, however, Hepburn and the producers found that the playwright refused to make the necessary changes. If Hepburn had learned anything in the last two years, it was that she should not play in anything she instinctively felt was not right. Unable to afford another fat mistake, she decided against taking the show to Broadway.

Hepburn had painted herself into a corner. She had established her career in such a way that she could only appear in starring roles. But in the last year, the public had shown little interest in the leading characters she had portrayed. She had nobody but herself to blame for the flops in her past; and she had no venues or vehicles lined up for the future.

Under such circumstances, most studios would have been through with her. But Pandro Berman convinced RKO to make one more attempt at reviving Hepburn's career. The studio had just purchased a property that he thought might do the trick, mostly because she would not have to carry it alone—*Stage Door*. For Hepburn, playing in this film was like rubbing salt into her wounds. It was bad enough being cast in the very part that had been created by Margaret Sullavan. It was worse that the play was an ensemble piece, a group of struggling actresses all living at the Footlights Club. In fact, RKO's primary purpose in making the movie was to elevate its other star Ginger Rogers—"who was on the up and up"—at least as much as it was to rescue Hepburn—"because I was on the down and down." The latter's role was that of Terry Randall, a snooty society girl who moves into the boarding house as a way of experiencing what it's like to be an actress, only to feel some of their suffering, thus becoming an actress along the way.

Gregory La Cava, who had a drinking problem, had become that year's hottest talent because of his urbane comedy *My Man Godfrey*. Under his direction, RKO packed *Stage Door* with young talent— Lucille Ball, Eve Arden, Ann Miller, and Gail Patrick. Constance Collier played the tragicomic role of the Footlights Club den mother (a role she began to assume in Hepburn's life). Adolphe Menjou was cast as a Broadway producer, in an attempt to re-create some of the rapport he had with Hepburn in *Morning Glory*. The very touching Andrea Leeds—whose character's demise would allow the amateur Terry Randall to go on with the show—was borrowed from Samuel Goldwyn. Although they were all working from the basic Kaufman-Ferber text, which had been transposed to the screen by Morrie Ryskind and Anthony Veiller, La Cava liked to work by throwing out the script and improvising upon it every day.

For the first two weeks of the shoot, Hepburn felt that she was just standing around, watching other actresses steal scenes. At last she went to Pan Berman and said, "What am I supposed to do? I don't know what my part is or anything about it." Berman said, "Listen, Kate, you're lucky to be playing a bit part in a successful picture. Just shut up for once, and do what you're told." She knew he was right . . . but was not ready to acquiesce altogether.

She went to La Cava—whose drinking frightened her at first, until she came to feel it was part of what made him "a very talented, artistic man"—and asked, "Who am I? This character, Gregory, who is she? I don't know who she's supposed to be." La Cava said, "Kate, she's the human question mark." Hepburn nodded knowingly and walked away. A moment later, she came back and asked him, "What the hell does that mean?"

"Kate," he replied, "I'm damned if I know."

All Kate really knew was that this was probably her last chance at maintaining her position as a star. Sufficiently humbled, she held her tongue and she held back her performance, letting those around her shine. After a few weeks of watching Hepburn's moodiness on the set, La Cava was able to answer the actress's question about her character's identity. He used Hepburn's own feelings of self-pity and exclusion to turn the character around. He enhanced her role—as Terry Randall blossoms into an inspired actress, an artist passionate enough to deliver an anthemlike curtain speech that reaches out to the others in her sorority. Kate later admitted that it had been "terrifying" working on a set in which so much was improvised every day, even more so because the part mirrored so much of her own life.

To help Hepburn confront some of her career frustrations, La Cava decided that the play within the film, in which Terry Randall ultimately triumphs, should be Hepburn's old bête noire, *The Lake*. "It was a brilliant idea," Kate realized the moment he suggested it, "because it allowed me to take my most miserable moment in the theater and turn it into something fun." As a result of La Cava's instincts, audiences would forever remember Hepburn fondly, not foolishly, for uttering, "The calla lilies are in bloom again. . . ."

The film was nominated for a Best Picture Academy Award and still plays like gangbusters, but it was a box-office disappointment—

financially successful, but only barely so. For the small profit margin, industry pundits blamed Hepburn. Believing she had at least bounced back from intense unpopularity, RKO figured the way to keep reversing the trend was to make her even bouncier. They cast her in a farce called *Bringing Up Baby.*

Like most "screwball comedies," the plot to this wisecracking, nonsensical love story crossed the traditional lines of social class and sexual roles. In this case, a persistent heiress sets her madcap on a paleontologist, losing an important dinosaur bone and gaining a pet leopard named Baby along the way. Howard Hawks, who had theretofore been making his name with action-packed dramas, turned to producing as well as directing with this comedy, creating the template for most of the best pictures of his career. He liked his comedic leading men to be good-looking and good-natured and his leading ladies to be fast-talking and slightly androgynous, able to wear the pants in the picture. He kept every scene galloping at a breakneck pace to a finish in which all the disparate pieces of plot fall into place.

"Now I had a very strong body," Kate said of herself, "and that allowed me to play broad, physical comedy very well, because I had complete confidence in my moves. And I was haughty enough in the mind of the public that it would be funny for them to see me roll in the mud or have the back of my dress ripped off." Cary Grant, who had become Hollywood's number-one romantic comedy star upon the release of *The Awful Truth,* was an obvious choice for David Huxley, a Harold Lloyd–like professor. "We were very good together," Kate observed, "because it looked as though we were having a great deal of fun together, which we were."

For all the wonderful moments in the film—including scenes with such familiar character actors as Charles Ruggles, Walter Catlett, and Fritz Feld—*Bringing Up Baby* fizzled at the box office. Some have argued that it came at the tail-end of the "screwball" cycle, when a Depression-weary public was tired of watching silly escapades of the rich. But several classics of the genre, in fact, would appear over the next three years. The awful truth seemed to have been the public's genuine disinterest in the star.

So thought one Harry Brandt, president of the Independent Theatre Owners of America. Speaking on behalf of the hundreds of businessmen whose movie houses were not part of the big studio chains, he published a list of actresses he claimed were "box-office poison"—including Greta Garbo, Marlene Dietrich, Joan Crawford, and Katharine Hepburn. He even posted their names on big one-sheets, which he had pasted around town. Those actresses didn't draw patrons into theaters, Brandt claimed, and he asked the moguls to stop hitching their vehicles to such dim stars.

Nobody at RKO could disagree. Two or three big hits out of fifteen pictures were not enough to warrant greater investment; and Hepburn had already survived five years as a star, the standard run for all but the sacred few. The studio had clearly lost interest in her, offering her an obviously inferior "B" picture called *Mother Carey's Chickens*. Refusing to pull the trigger on her own career, Hepburn bought up the rest of her RKO contract for some $200,000. That her father had been prudently investing her hefty paychecks over the years made her bold move affordable.

George Cukor stepped in with an offer that even made it desirable. Columbia Studios, the poor cousin to the more established majors, had recently bought a parcel of old scripts from RKO, including the rights to *Holiday* (which had been filmed in 1930 with Ann Harding). Columbia head Harry Cohn hired Cukor to direct the film, figuring they could get Irene Dunne to play Linda Seton, the spunky girl who attracts her socialite sister's impractical fiancé. Cukor vigorously argued that the roles were ideal for Hepburn and Grant. Again, Cukor's enthusiasm carried the day. "I knew that Harry Cohn was legendary as the biggest pig in town," Kate said, "but except for some coarse language, he was never anything but a gentleman with me. More than that, he took a chance on me. He knew how bad my track record had been, and he stuck by me anyway."

Kate thought *Holiday* displayed some of her best acting, and definitely her best work with Cary Grant. After two pictures together, their acting rhythms were in complete synch with one another. And, like their characters, they both found amusement in pretentiousness. "This," Kate liked to remind me, "was before Cary got too rich, while he still had to work for a living and had fun doing it." Ten years after she had understudied Hope Williams in the role of Linda Seton, Hepburn made the part indelibly her own, committing to celluloid a performance that is at once moving and comic, complete with her executing double somersaults with Cary Grant. Donald Ogden Stewart, who had acted in the Broadway production, had adapted the play into a fast-clipped scenario; and George Cukor made Hepburn look more glamorous than she ever had before. The film flopped.

The star girded her loins to fight yet another round in Hollywood, when she received a script from MGM with an offer of $10,000—a lower fee than she received when she first landed in Hollywood. She didn't need anyone to tell her it was time to get out of town. In the summer of 1938, Katharine Hepburn retreated to Fenwick with absolutely no prospects for a future in show business.

"I always liked that poem by Robert Frost," Kate said, referring to *The Death of the Hired Man*—"Home is the place where, when you have to go there, they have to take you in." (It was the only line of poetry I ever heard her recite.) She knew a summer by the sea, with her family and a few select friends, playing tennis and golf, would help her find her bearings. While Hartford was where she came from and New York was where she lived, Fenwick was the place that felt like home, the place she loved most, her family haven for the last twenty-five years.

Most of the Hartford crowd had left Fenwick by mid-September, but the big wooden Hepburn house, built on brick piles, was more than a summer cottage. Kate intended to stay there indefinitely—until the afternoon of the twenty-first, when a hurricane, which had been threatening the eastern seaboard all week, gusted northward, heading right for the Connecticut River. Kate swam and golfed that morning, but by the afternoon, the waters had turned ferocious, swamping the lawn and pounding against the house. After the chimneys toppled, the windows imploded, and a wing of the house snapped off, Kate, her mother, her brother Dick, and the cook fled to higher ground. They looked back and saw their uprooted house wash out to sea.

"I think," said Kate looking back on that entire year, "God was trying to tell me something."

VI

In Bloom Again

In 1929 book editor Maxwell Perkins joined Ernest Hemingway in Key West for eight days of fishing. Toward the end of his visit, the editor looked at the panorama of life there in the Gulf Stream and asked his author why he didn't write about it. Just then a big, clumsy bird flew by. "I might someday but not yet," Hemingway said. "Take that pelican. I don't know yet what he is in the scheme of things here."

During the ten years I worked on my biography of Samuel Goldwyn, I thought of Katharine Hepburn as my "pelican"—this unusual creature that was so much a part of the Hollywood landscape but somehow always flapping above it. I used my understanding of her role in the motion-picture community to measure when I was ready to stop researching and begin writing.

She proved to be a good yardstick. Although she never worked with Samuel Goldwyn, her name surfaced practically every day, either in a document or during an interview. In fact, she provided a most pungent comment about Sam and Frances Goldwyn herself, observing, "You always knew where your career in Hollywood stood by where you sat at the Goldwyn table." For somebody who considered herself a Hollywood outsider, she left lasting impressions there over six decades.

Lucille Ball (who broke in as a "Goldwyn Girl" before attaining costar status in *Stage Door*) remembered Hepburn with adoration and admiration. "We all wanted to be Katharine," she said, thinking mostly of Kate's self-assuredness. "Even Ginger. No, *especially* Ginger." Joan Bennett from *Little Women* (who had first worked for Goldwyn as a child in silent pictures) said, "Kate was always the star, there was no mistake about that. But she was always busy giving everybody advice. But it was good advice." Joseph L. Mankiewicz (who directed *Guys and Dolls* for Goldwyn) was talking about Hollywood's bringing out the best and the worst in people when her name entered the conversation. "You know," he said, to illustrate his point, "Katharine Hepburn actually spat at me." As I was wondering whether he was describing the worst being brought out in him or in her, he sheepishly added, "I had it coming."

By the time I met Edith Mayer Goetz, she had not spoken to her sister, Irene Selznick, for about a decade. ("We fought over who was top dog, socially, in town," said Irene dismissively, from which I was to infer that there had been seventy years of sibling rivalry, the causes of which Edie was too superficial to understand.) When I interviewed her, Mrs. Goetz brought up Hepburn's name, bragging how she and Spencer Tracy used to come to her magnificent art-filled house in Holmby Hills. "Oh, the vulgarity," Irene groaned of the boast when I told her, "and the falsity." I was surprised myself at the claim, as Kate had told me she and Tracy saw few people as a couple, and the Goetzes were hardly on their social roster.

I asked Mrs. Goetz about their "friendship." Without missing a beat, Edie produced the guest lists of every one of her fabled parties, and there, indeed, were Katharine Hepburn and Spencer Tracy attending a party for the newlyweds Frank Sinatra and Mia Farrow. ("I never really cared for Frank," Kate later told me, "and you must never ask me about the girl." I later learned that she considered Mia Farrow's father, an Australian-born writer-director named John, so "depraved" that there was "no way that girl could have any moral structure to her life.") "But Spence and Frank were friends, and he liked to go out, and so we went to that 'wedding party'—in separate cars. But, honestly, I don't remember seeing the inside of the Goetz house more than twice in my life.") As I was leaving my interview with Mrs. Goetz, her butler (whom, she proudly told me, she had lured from Buckingham Palace) had evidently fallen asleep on the job and was nowhere to be found. My hostess herself walked me to the door, where I had trouble figuring out the unusual handle. "Mrs. Goetz," I said, after fumbling for a few seconds, "can you help me get this door open?"

"No," she replied. "Doors have always been opened for me." (Irene howled about that for years . . . and trotted out the line almost every time I left her apartment.)

Of course, no conversation with George Cukor was complete without some reference to Kate, with whom I think he had more fun than anybody on earth. And yet Kate had always felt she played second fiddle in his life. They worked together nearly a dozen times, he was her landlord for years, and she was the only person licensed to walk into his house unannounced—whether it was a weeknight dinner party ("He always seated me below the salt, usually at the very end of the table with Irene Selznick"), Saturday garden parties where, decade after decade, the other great actresses could let down their hair and pick up acting pointers . . . or even the private Sunday pool parties for men only. But Kate knew the leading lady in George's life was Sam Goldwyn's wife, Frances.

As theater novices in upstate New York, they had lived in the same boardinghouses and had become instant friends. Something of an outcast, he found a great admirer in Frances, who appreciated this "angel," a generous soul who took her under wing and shared his wealth of artistic ideas. For his part, he enjoyed having a Galatea who was such a quick and appreciative study, an icy beauty. Their friendship deepened over the next fifty years, during which time "George's harem," as Frances Goldwyn often referred to his coterie of famous Hollywood women, widened. Even with Cukor's constant devotion, from the 1930s on, Frances found herself admitting, "I'm really his second favorite. Kate's his first." In her mind, she invented a rivalry for his affections.

Kate found such talk ludicrous. "George and I adored each other," she said. "But whenever things got personal, I'm sure he went to Frances first. He and I had a wonderful rapport . . . but they had a history together. Trust. A deep trust." While Mrs. Goldwyn and Miss Hepburn never became friends, they were always cordial with each other. Upon Sam Goldwyn's death in 1974, his son learned that there was an extra crypt in the family plot for George Cukor. When the younger Goldwyn raised this subject with his mother, Frances laughed gently and said, "Well . . . at least Kate won't get him there."

In her first fifteen months of widowhood, Frances suffered from a fast-metastasizing cancer of the nose and trachea, which invaded her brain. Kate fondly remembered the special attention George paid to her during that period. She entertained them for dinner on several occasions, and every time the weakening Frances's nose would run or a little bit of food would dribble from the side of her mouth, George was there to dab her face with a handkerchief. Frances died in 1976 and was buried alongside her husband.

On January 24, 1983—just a few months before I had met Hepburn—George Cukor died at the age of eighty-three. Kate had no idea that in the hours after his death, Samuel Goldwyn, Jr., had immediately informed Cukor's executor that Frances had pre-arranged for George's burial. The executor found as much in Cukor's will, and those wishes were observed. He rests eternally alongside the Goldwyns (and Frances's batty mother) in the unmarked Little Garden of Constancy, a large private plot within the walled Garden of Honor, which sits behind two locked iron doors, accessible only by private key, at Forest Lawn Memorial Park in Glendale. The day I researched the site for *Goldwyn,* I noticed the grave of Spencer Tracy, only a few gardens away. "How fascinating!" Kate said upon learning this information. "I never knew . . . and I've never been there. . . . You say you need a key to get in? How extraordinary!" Then, with the catchphrase she always used to express that there was nothing more to say on a subject, she added a world-weary, "Life, life, life."

Immediately after the hurricane of 1938 had blown past Fenwick, the Hepburns began reconstructing their house. "We learned a lesson from 'The Three Little Pigs,'" said Kate, "and built with brick this time." Choosing the same site, they raised the property by three feet. With the passage of another half-century, Kate realized they had woefully undercalculated, as future storms periodically pushed waters through the ground floor of the house and washed away a little more of their beach each year. In the days following the great hurricane, Kate combed the sand and recovered a dozen of her mother's silver place settings and her complete tea service. After all the upheaval of 1938, two other important pieces of her life remained.

For almost three years, Katharine Hepburn had been keeping company with another beau, far and away the most exciting and complicated of them all—Howard Hughes. The heir to the Hughes Tool Company, a motion-picture producer, a celebrated aviator, and a notorious playboy, the tall and handsome Hughes had been smitten with Katharine Hepburn since she first appeared on the screen. Orphaned as a teenager, he followed his Uncle Rupert, a hugely successful writer (for Goldwyn) to Hollywood. He dallied with movie stars, falling in love with the silent-screen queen Billie Dove, who was five years his senior. By 1935, however, his eyes had turned toward Katharine Hepburn.

In early 1936, while she was filming *Sylvia Scarlet* just above Trancas Beach, Kate and George Cukor used to have their staffs prepare picnic lunches for them and selected members of the cast and crew. One day during their break, a small plane circled overhead, zeroed in on them, then landed but a short walk away. Kate suddenly noticed Cary Grant looking sheepish. "That's my friend Howard Hughes," he said.

Hepburn had heard that Hughes was eager to meet her, and she was put out with her friend Cary for springing their introduction on her this way. "I'm sure the boys thought, 'Oh, this will be a cute meet,' all very romantic and irresistible. But Howard and I met, and we shook hands, and it was all too self-conscious. So staged. False. There was nothing spontaneous about it. I was so angry I ate my lunch without looking at either one of them."

A short time later, Kate was playing golf at the Bel-Air Country Club, when Hughes performed a similar stunt, this time landing right on the seventh fairway. "Out of his plane he hopped, carrying a golf bag," Kate said, "and he finished the nine with my instructor and me. And he was quite a good golfer. But what gall! But you see, Howard was a man of action and not words, and I think this was simply the best way he could think of expressing his feelings."

Hughes was a practical dreamer, prone to planned "impulsiveness." He liked to act on the spur of the moment, but only after he had thought through the details of his action. In this instance, he suddenly found his plane sitting in the middle of a golf course—which had provided enough room to land but not enough to take off again. Hughes had thought that through as well. "There were few problems a little of his money could not solve," Kate pointed out. "He simply had some mechanics come and dismantle the plane and cart it off. As for getting himself home, he'd just assumed I'd cart *him* off. What gall! God, he was exciting. Great fun."

Hepburn gave Hughes a lift to the Beverly Hills Hotel. In almost no time, she learned that after having produced *Hell's Angels, The Front Page,* and *Scarface,* he had really had no great passion for picture-making: "He was a brilliant man," said Kate, "and not as silly as that." But he did have a passion for movie stars.

In 1936, when Hepburn toured with *Jane Eyre*, Hughes would suddenly arrive before her performances in Boston, and then Chicago. In time, she got caught up in the rush and surrendered. "I think we were both thrill-seekers, you might say," Kate suggested. "I always liked to go, go, go; and Howard was always up for adventure. Now, he always liked to think things through, and I was always more instinctive. But we had a lot of common interests."

Not the least of these interests, Kate admitted, was "courting fame." She said, "When I met Howard, the man he admired most was Lindbergh—not just for what he accomplished but for all the acclaim. Howard was determined to set new records in aviation, but I think that was largely because he really wanted the big parade. And, you see, I too wanted to be a star, desperately wanted to be a star." Paradoxically, neither Hepburn nor Hughes liked crowds. In fact, they expended much of their energy evading the public, craving privacy. They were always on the run, from newsreel cameras and popping flashbulbs.

"I think that was part of the fun for the two of us," said Kate, "that we could indulge in this game with the public together. It was definitely more fun together. And, in a way, that was the basis for our relationship. We were both famous and came from comfortable backgrounds. We understood each other. I think we felt we were right for each other, and secretly I think we felt the public thought we were somehow right for each other. Going around together enhanced both our reputations. But there was a basic problem. . . . I am, by nature, a loner, and that's not a very good basis for a serious relationship."

But it was obviously pleasurable for these two enormously attractive people. I never heard Kate talk about anybody with more of a glint in her eye, making it very clear that this was the lustiest relationship of her life. It was not the most profound, but it was definitely the one built most on plain physical attraction. Eros.

During their time together, Kate increasingly found Hughes to be a loner as well. Losing his parents as a teenager was one apparent cause for that; but she believed there was another, equally strong. "People simply don't understand how deaf Howard was," she explained, "—from the age of fifteen. And I think this contributed to everything that happened to him in his life, for both good and bad. It made him terribly detached and a real self-starter. But it also started him down an endlessly lonely path, really cut off from people."

In my experience, Kate always expected one to speak clearly, concisely, and audibly. If one rambled on too long in her presence, she'd interrupt to ask, "What's your point?" If one mumbled, she'd interrupt to say, "I don't understand you," or "Speak up, I can't hear you." That, she said, was something Howard Hughes never did; and that failure condemned him to isolation. The deafness, she explained, was not his great weakness so much as his failing to acknowledge it in public, thus forcing him to miss parts of conversations and often to misunderstand those parts that he had heard. Quite simply, Kate said, "It ruined his life."

"I mean, what does that do to a person?" she wondered out loud decades later. "It forced Howard into a world of his own, one in which he dwelt more and more on himself, becoming obsessed with the details of his own life. From the time we first started going around, he was concerned about germs and disease. He washed his hands a lot and he took a lot of showers, and nobody else was allowed to use the same shower. It had to be disinfected after each use. Now a lot of that just makes common sense. Doctors tell us today that it's good to wash your hands a lot to keep them from spreading germs. And I always took a lot of showers. But in his loneliness—and I think there was a well of loneliness within

Howard—he gradually crossed the line, that line between peculiar behavior and what I guess one would call 'neurotic.' Then you must remember his upbringing, which left him virtually alone in the world. . . . And then years later, you know, he suffered terribly after an airplane accident and got hooked on 'hard stuff'—morphine. And, then again, there was his deafness. I know he heard ringing in his ears; and I'm sure he heard voices in his head for years and years. So, you see, we really are extremely fragile creatures . . . because here was this absolutely *brilliant* man, I mean *brilliant* in everything he attempted, and yet he was never more than an inch away from crossing that line into the land of cuckoo."

Their time alone together was, for the most part, a great romp. They were, Kate insisted, "in love—at least with the *idea* of each other." They flew together—with Hepburn once taking off in a seaplane under the Fifty-ninth Street Bridge. They skinny-dipped in the Long Island Sound, diving off the wing of his plane. They golfed in Fenwick—where they were often joined by Luddy, who always seemed to have a movie camera in his hand. Once, while golfing with Kate and her father, Hughes objected not only to Luddy's omnipresence but to the invasion of his privacy with the camera clicking away. "Howard," Dr. Hepburn interjected, "Luddy has been taking pictures of all of us for years before you got here, and he'll be taking them years after you've gone. He's part of this family. Now drive."

Hughes never felt comfortable with the Hepburns . . . or, Kate pointed out, with anyone else's family. "It's hard to understand what it's like to be really close to your family," Kate said, "unless you come from a close family yourself. You get that," she said to me, knowing I was close to my parents and three brothers, "and I get that. But Howard never did."

Left to themselves, Hepburn and Hughes "played house"— sharing some tranquil domesticity in his large, Monterey-style house on Muirfield Road, which bordered the Wilshire Country Club. "Golf balls," Kate said, "used to fly into our backyard." On quiet days—which they both cherished—they'd crawl under the fence and play nine holes there themselves. Meantime, they pursued their careers—Hughes becoming increasingly potent in aviation, just as Hepburn was becoming "poison" in the movie business.

The more time Hughes spent with Hepburn, the more he wanted to marry her. Thinking that her career slump might make her more open to the suggestion of sharing their lives, he proposed to her— more than once. Hughes had read her wrong. The downturn in Hepburn's career only made her more ferocious about her independence, more determined to prove herself on her own. "Now look," Kate said to me one afternoon, "I think Howard really was in love with me, and I really loved being with him. But honestly, what kind of marriage would that have been? I was trying to put my career together again. I was thinking all about me, me, me. And even if my career had been in another place, I don't think I ever would have married him. I was always straight with him about that. But Howard just didn't hear me."

"Maybe," I suggested, "he couldn't hear you."

"Howard heard," she amended, "what he wanted to hear."

She had already refused Hughes's offer when he took off on an around-the-world flight in July 1938—a record-setting journey of three days, nineteen hours, and seventeen minutes, for which he received his ticker-tape parade through Broadway's "Canyon of Heroes." The tabloid-reading public buzzed nonetheless about his pending nuptials to Katharine Hepburn.

In fact, Hepburn was entertaining another suitor that summer, who arrived with an offer far more tempting than marriage. Her old friend Philip Barry, whose career was in a slump of its own, called from Maine one day and invited himself to tea. "I was surprised," Kate said, "because the last time I had heard from him was when he got me fired from *The Animal Kingdom* as the understudy"—eight years prior. On the pier at Fenwick, he described two stories he was hatching, plays in which he kept hearing her voice. One was a father-daughter story called *Second Threshold*. The other centered on a society wedding on Philadelphia's Main Line, where a rich, young divorcée was about to marry again, this time to a boring self-made man who was "marrying up." The proceedings would be disrupted by her raffish first husband, who lingers in her life, Luddy-like. Looking out at some sailboats on the sea, Barry and Hepburn talked about the heroine, who, in her first marriage, had proved not to be "yare," a nautical term meaning easy to handle, quick to the helm. Kate voted for the latter play because it sounded "more fun." Within weeks, she was reading pages of the first act of *The Philadelphia Story.*

Then came the hurricane of 1938. Hughes sent a pilot to Fenwick that week with huge bottles of fresh water. Upon hearing about this life preserver Barry was throwing to her, he also gave her some advice—to purchase the motion-picture rights of this new play even before it opened. If *The Philadelphia Story* was that good, he reasoned, it could prove to be her vehicle back to Hollywood; and if it did not pan out, an investment this early in the game would hardly be that great. Hughes went so far as to buy the rights as a present for her, withholding a percentage as an investment for himself. While he would soon move on to business ventures and romantic adventures with other partners, Hepburn and Hughes would forever be bound by their joint interest in *The Philadelphia Story.*

While Barry was finishing his play, Hepburn set about getting it produced. She felt beholden to the Theatre Guild because they had let her both star in and leave its production of *Jane Eyre.* Barry had had a bad experience with the Guild and wanted to go elsewhere; and neither he nor Hepburn knew that the company was then practically bankrupt. Meantime, the Theatre Guild didn't know that Hepburn had been banished from Hollywood. "We were all washed up," Kate said, "and nobody knew the whole truth about the other. Hopeless."

In the end, they all came together, as Hughes and Hepburn each put up a quarter of the production costs, thus becoming profit participants. Under the direction of Robert B. Sinclair, who had recently triumphed with Clare Boothe Luce's *The Women,* they assembled a remarkable supporting cast, while Barry struggled with the play's final act.

From the Mercury Theatre, they grabbed Joseph Cotten to play C. K. Dexter Haven, Tracy's first husband; and from *A Woman Rebels,* Kate remembered the virile performance of her costar Van Heflin, who was cast as Macauley Connor, the cynical reporter assigned to cover the Philadelphia wedding. Shirley Booth was cast as his photographer sidekick, and Kate thought her performance was "brilliant," because she found much more in the part than had appeared on the page. They lucked out further with the discovery of a remarkable ten-year-old named Lenore Lonergan—"a real caution," said Kate—to play the heroine Tracy Lord's wisecracking kid sister. After one of the out-of-town performances, Lawrence Langner came backstage and said, "Kate, I think the girl is copying you—all your movements, your gestures, your delivery."

"You've got it all wrong," she told Langner, dead serious. "I'm copying her."

At last Barry finished the play, and from that moment on, Kate said, "It smelled like a hit." Pleasing her as much as the elegance of the comedy—"there was nothing cheap about any of it, just real humor that grew from the character"—was the construction of the drama. "People don't realize how ingenious Phil Barry's play is," she said, "how he drew three different men, all from different social positions. And up until the last moment of the play, there's a good argument to be made for Tracy to marry any one of them. In the end, I think the play draws the truest . . . and most romantic conclusion." As if that were not enough, the entire work was tailored to showcase Hepburn—allowing her to rattle off passages of witty dialogue while men fell at her feet. "An actress doesn't get many of those in a lifetime," Kate said of her role in *The Philadelphia Story.* "And she doesn't need many."

For yet another reason, the timing of Tracy Lord's entrance into Hepburn's life could not have been timelier. Like most film actresses in the late thirties, she felt she had just lost the role of a lifetime— Scarlett O'Hara—a role that she thought, for a moment, might be hers. A few years earlier, Katharine Hepburn believed she had been the first actress to receive a set of the galley proofs of *Gone With the Wind,* at the behest of the author, Margaret Mitchell. She adored the part and immediately saw herself in it. Pandro Berman's assistant read the book for him; and after hearing the story, Berman felt Hepburn was wrong for Scarlett. RKO passed on bidding for the project, though they could probably have bought the film rights for a song.

A few weekends later, Hepburn and George Cukor went to visit Myron Selznick at his vacation house at Lake Arrowhead. David Selznick answered the door, carrying the galleys of the book. Hepburn said to him, "Don't bother reading it, David. Just buy it. It's sensational." Selznick didn't need convincing. He immediately grasped its immense possibilities and purchased the film rights for $50,000. George Cukor was to direct; and Selznick said he wanted Hepburn for the role . . . at first.

Over the next few months, Selznick heard from every important actress (and her agent) in Hollywood. While much has been said over the years about how Selznick ultimately believed Clark Gable as Rhett Butler would never go through years of the war lusting after Katharine Hepburn, it was, in fact, the actress's greatest supporter who first dissuaded the producer from casting her. George Cukor, as Kate herself related, "felt that it was unsuitable for me, that I was a heroine and Scarlett was this wicked sort of sexual creature." That Cukor, who was the director of the film from its earliest days of preproduction to its first days of filming, felt so strongly about Kate's unsuitability gave Selznick license to keep widening his search.

The longer Selznick delayed in casting his lead, the larger his problem became, as the "search for Scarlett" became an international treasure hunt, one of great interest among moviegoers. As the date by which they had to start filming approached, Hepburn went to Selznick and said, "David, you've got to have an unknown girl in the part. You've made this big thing now, and you have to deliver. You can't cast me or anyone else who is well known because audiences would walk in with certain expectations." At the same time, she still dreamed of playing the role. So she made one last-ditch play. "Look," she said, "you've got Walter Plunkett doing the clothes, and Walter knows me backwards. He could do five costumes in one night for me and would. So, if you're stuck, you can just let me know twenty-four hours before it's too late." Hepburn didn't like being in a second (or possibly tenth) position like that, but she knew her only prayer at getting the role lay in some desperate act of midnight casting. Hardly a week later, Selznick met Vivien Leigh—and the contest was over.

While *Gone With the Wind* was being filmed, most of the other leading ladies in Hollywood were busy appearing in what would prove to be signature roles, contributing to what would become the most glorious year in Hollywood history—1939. Garbo was in *Ninotchka;* Crawford played her first important unsympathetic "bitch" role in *The Women,* alongside Norma Shearer, Rosalind Russell, Paulette Goddard, and Joan Fontaine. Greer Garson debuted in *Goodbye, Mr. Chips;* Bette Davis was in *The Private Lives of Elizabeth and Essex, Dark Victory, The Old Maid* (opposite Miriam Hopkins), and *Juarez* (as the Empress Carlotta); Jean Arthur was in *Mr. Smith Goes to Washington* with Jimmy Stewart, and *Only Angels*

Have Wings with Cary Grant; Irene Dunne made *Love Affair* with Charles Boyer; Ginger Rogers was twirling with Fred Astaire (in *The Story of Vernon and Irene Castle*); Judy Garland went over the rainbow in *The Wizard of Oz*; and even Snow White got to cavort with seven dwarfs.

Katharine Hepburn—after fifteen motion pictures in six years— was nowhere to be seen on the screen that year. She was, instead, trodding the boards in Wilmington, Washington, Boston, and the title city in *The Philadelphia Story*. For five weeks out of town, she and the play received rave notices, and the star begged the producers to keep the show on the road as long as possible, building up good word of mouth before coming into Broadway. "The critics are funny about me," she tried to explain to Philip Barry and the Theatre Guild, her financial partners in the venture, "they'll just land on me." Despite the vehemence of her protest, they outvoted her, and *The Philadelphia Story* opened at the Shubert Theatre on March 29, 1939.

The play was a "huge hit"—Kate's assessment—critically and financially. But it took a while before it performed the trick she hoped it would—providing the opportunity to reprise the role on film. She employed an agent named Harold Freedman—who represented playwrights and a handful of actors (such as the Lunts)—but forbade him from telling anybody that she controlled the film rights. Indeed, all the major studios called, hoping to buy the source material for their biggest stars; but upon his client's instructions, Freedman stalled them. Meantime, Hepburn carried on to nightly acclaim, playing more than four hundred performances on Broadway. (She would later play in another two hundred fifty performances on the road.) In the end, Hepburn made close to a half million dollars in salary and profits. More important, the play had warmed up enough audiences nationwide to rekindle her career.

After the play had packed houses for a year, Howard Hughes approached the studios on behalf of the film rights' co-owner.

Because he kept a private office for himself on the Samuel Goldwyn lot, he started there. Goldwyn was interested enough to send his number-one director, William Wyler, to New York to convince Hepburn that they were the best team for the project. Sitting in the garden in Turtle Bay, she told the director exactly what she had told Goldwyn herself, that she would make a deal on the spot if they could deliver Gary Cooper to play C. K. Dexter Haven. She explained that this was not any kind of ploy for more money; it was simply that she had left Hollywood as "box-office poison" and she was smart enough to know that she needed a strong man or two by her side as antidotes. Although Cooper was under contract to Goldwyn at the time, he would not agree to play opposite Hepburn.

Warner Brothers was willing to take a chance with her, offering a lot of money, the opportunity to produce the picture, and Errol Flynn. Hepburn was considering the deal when she got the call she had hoped for, from the biggest man in movies, Louis B. Mayer himself. He came to see *The Philadelphia Story* in New York, with Norma Shearer on his arm, and went backstage to offer his congratulations. The next day he called to say he wanted to come speak to her about the film. "Oh, no, Mr. Mayer," she said, remembering the way her mother used to influence the local powers in Hartford, "I'll come to you."

In his New York office, L. B. Mayer said everything he could to wheedle the rights away from Hepburn so that Shearer might play the part. At last Hepburn said, "Mr. Mayer, you are deliberately charming me, and I know it, but the remarkable thing is that I'm charmed. Now, you're a real artist. But this property is not about making money for me. I'll sell it to you for exactly what I paid for it, without a dime of profit. It's quite simply about getting a good part for me, and I want only what would be a reasonable salary for myself. But what I really want from you are two stars." Mayer asked which two.

"Gable and Tracy," she said, aiming for the top. Mayer said he doubted either of them would accept the offer but that he would try them both. He promptly reported that one wasn't free (Tracy, she learned) and the other didn't want to do it. (Despite Gable's star-power, she was, in truth, just as happy not to get him, because she thought he was "wrong for both parts, though he could have played the newspaperman—which is the part Spencer should have played.") Then Mayer said, "I can give you Jimmy Stewart [who did not yet have much control over his roles] . . . and I'll give you $150,000 to get anyone else you can get." That was a lot of money, Hepburn thought—enough to allow her to call upon her friend Cary Grant. He was delighted with the offer, selected the role of C. K. Dexter Haven, and ultimately contributed his three weeks of salary to the British War Relief Fund. Mayer assigned Joseph L. Mankiewicz—one of the most formidable talents in Hollywood—to produce the picture.

Permitted to choose her director, Hepburn considered nobody but George Cukor. "George saw the show in Chicago," Kate remembered, "and he thought it was awful, just plain awful—not the play itself, which he liked, but the direction. Of course, that's partly because he didn't get to direct it. Now, I don't think he was being self-important in not liking it. It's more that George was a brilliant director, who knew how to keep things moving all the time. He didn't believe in fussy business or lots of mannerisms, but he knew each character had to keep things moving at all times, that a good play had to be like a solar system, in which all the planets are spinning in their orbits at all times. He felt our director [Bob Sinclair] hadn't done that. And, of course," she added, "George really knew *me*, and he wanted to ensure that the film would be a great showcase for me."

By then, Hepburn and Cukor spoke the same language. "And so when it came time to make the movie," Kate explained, "I said,

'Look, I don't want to make a grand entrance in this picture. Moviegoers haven't seen me in over a year, and they already made it clear that they think I'm too la-di-da or something. A lot of people want to see me fall flat on my face.'"

"Or your ass," Cukor corrected.

From that suggestion, Donald Stewart, the screenwriter who was adapting the play, devised what Hepburn considered an "ingenious" opening for the film. While Cukor had done "a brilliant job" in "presenting" Katharine Hepburn in *A Bill of Divorcement,* he would prove equally invaluable in "re-creating Katharine Hepburn" in *The Philadelphia Story.* In the opening scene, Tracy Lord is throwing her husband, C. K. Dexter Haven, out of the house, golf clubs and all. When she cracks one of the clubs over her bended knee, she has gone too far. He comes back to push her in the face, knocking her right on her backside. "Oh, I loved it," Kate said. "Just what Tracy—and I—needed."

The last time moviegoers had seen her, Katharine Hepburn was running off with Cary Grant at the end of *Holiday.* So she thought this scene would be as much fun for her fans as for those who didn't like her—"Although I must tell you," she said, "I truly believed that everybody still adored me, that it was nothing but bad material that had made me 'box-office poison.'" In some ways, Kate said, "The opening of this picture showed that running off with me could be fun and exciting, but that living with me was clearly no holiday. Life imitating art!" she said, laughing hard.

While Hepburn had never complained about the production values of her pictures at RKO and Columbia, she saw how they paled alongside the work of the legendary MGM production team in full force. Everything there was, as she said, "top drawer." Joseph Ruttenberg, who had just won the first of his four Academy Awards for *The Great Waltz,* was the director of photography; Cedric Gibbons, who would win seven of those golden statuettes, which he had designed in the first place, was the art director; and Adrian—who designed clothes for Garbo—created the costumes, each one of Hepburn's outfits a vision. Franz Waxman wrote one of his most sophisticated scores. Every supporting player delivered a star turn—including Henry Daniell, Roland Young, and Ruth Hussey in the Shirley Booth role. And Kate said, "we got lucky again with the girl—this time little Virginia Weidler, who had me in stitches. She was so terrifyingly funny I truly had a difficult time doing scenes with her. Honestly, I couldn't look at her, she was so funny." John Halliday, a veteran of the stage and silent screen, had the small but pivotal role of Seth Lord. He had the responsibility of delivering perhaps the play's most touching moment, a father summing up his daughter's wonderful attributes but feeling compelled to add, "You have everything it takes to make a lovely woman except the one essential—an understanding heart. And without that, you might just as well be made of bronze."

It is, of course, the stars of *The Philadelphia Story* who carry the day. Hepburn had never looked more glamorous nor been more commanding. She was an utterly contemporary woman, full of herself. Cukor closely monitored her performance, allowing the audience to laugh at her enough so that they would ultimately sympathize with her. While many critics praised her for the originality of her performance and spoke of the emergence of "a new Hepburn," she knew that she was, in fact, reverting to a former idol for inspiration. "I kept thinking of Hope Williams," she confessed. "I kept thinking how Hope could make everything so attractive, and how I must use all her tricks to keep Tracy from becoming a deplorable snob."

While Cary Grant was at his most charming, full of humor and insouciance, Jimmy Stewart proved to be the revelation in the picture. In a role that got beefed up from the play because of the deletion of another character, that of Tracy's brother, Macauley

"Mike" Connor was more cynical than any Stewart had played before. And, Kate noted, "Jimmy had always been attractive, but for the first time, I think, he was very sexy. He was known, you know, as one of the great bachelors around town, but people outside the business just thought of him as this nice boy next door. Without danger." That quality, Kate said, led to one of Cukor's "brilliant" pieces of direction.

Stewart had attempted his crucial speech in the film several times, the one in which he professes his love for the heroine—"You've got fires banked down in you . . ."—without nailing it. At last Cukor pulled him aside and said, "Now listen, Jim—just forget that you are that young boy running away to the circus. And play this scene absolutely straight." Kate said people never really understand what it is that a director can give an actor. That quick tip, she said, was a great example—"divine inspiration."

Veteran Oscar-watchers often assert that Jimmy Stewart's winning the Academy Award that year—over such contenders as Laurence Olivier in *Rebecca* and Henry Fonda in *The Grapes of Wrath*— was a consolation prize for his having failed to win the year before for *Mr. Smith Goes to Washington*. Hepburn disagreed. "I think Jimmy's absolutely brilliant in *Philadelphia Story* and completely unexpected. And I think it was his big speech that put him over the top." Hepburn in her signature role lost the Oscar that year to Ginger Rogers in *Kitty Foyle*. Publicly, she said Ginger Rogers deserved to win. Privately, Kate said, "It's a silly part in a silly soap opera. And I'm still glad I turned the part down."

The roaring success of *The Philadelphia Story* (almost $600,000 in six weeks at the Radio City Music Hall alone)—put Hepburn on top again, especially in the eyes of the moguls. "Dad worshiped Kate. It's that simple," Irene Mayer Selznick told me of her father. "She represented everything that he thought was good about America. She had a tight-knit family, she had a first-class education, she had elegance—class without airs. And she had a good business head on her shoulders. She talked straight, without ever compromising her femininity."

More than once Mr. Mayer called upon Hepburn to help "straighten out" one of his studio wunderkinds, Judy Garland. She had been desperately attempting to work her way out of a vortex studio doctors had created in which they had subjected her to amphetamines to help her lose weight and barbiturates to help her sleep. Mayer suggested to Hepburn that the young singing star's problem was a lack of character, one which Kate could help her overcome simply by being there for her, standing by as a good example. George Cukor later told me that "Judy worshiped Kate, as did most of the women on the MGM lot." But it wasn't until years later that Hepburn realized to what extent the studio had been the agent of Garland's drug-addicted demise. "When I met Judy," Kate explained, "I didn't know what was wrong with her. And by the time I learned the source of her problems, it was too late for me to do anything about it." There was little either star could do but admire each other's talent.

In the early forties, when Louis B. Mayer sat front-row-center in the famous team photograph of his contract players—the one displaying "More stars than there are in all the heavens"—he insisted on Hepburn's sitting to his right. (Greer Garson was the other rose to flank the thorny Mayer.)

Irene easily understood her father's adoration of Kate, though she found it crazy-making. So much of what L.B. admired in Hepburn he kept his own children from enjoying. Irene had a first-rate mind, for example, but was prohibited from attending college—because it would make her "too smart to get a husband." Where Dr. Hepburn had thrust independence upon his children, Mayer had subjected his daughters to countless rules, all in service of his own whims and needs. Much of Kate's forthrightness in the Hollywood community stemmed from the fact that she was there virtually on her own. Unlike a great number of actresses, whose mothers accompanied them as chaperones and managers, Hepburn slipped in and out of town alone, without the protection of a husband or even, at that point, an agent. Irene's father, on the other hand, ranted nightly about his twenty-something daughters being unmarried, banging on the dining-room table as he boomed, "It isn't enough that I'm L. B. Mayer?"

For several years, in fact, Irene and David Selznick had longed to marry, but Mayer had refused permission until her older sister, Edie, was married. Only one month after a producer named William Goetz ("a schlep with the filthiest mouth in town," said Irene) walked Edie down the aisle in one of the grandest weddings in Hollywood history, Irene and David married quietly. During one of my late nights at the Pierre, after several shots of "Cary's aquavit," Irene suddenly burst into tears, describing how she had secretly engineered the entire courtship of Goetz and Edie. She confessed to making up positive remarks each had allegedly said about the other, and making suggestions to her father that might advance Goetz's career. "But," I said appeasingly, "the ends justified the means. The Goetzes had a long marriage—certainly by Hollywood standards; and Edie said they were very happy. In fact, she even bragged that Bill was more successful than your father."

"Doesn't that just tell you everything?" Irene said. "It's the thing I feel guiltiest about. But I had no choice."

All the Mayers feuded the rest of their lives. Irene and Edie went decades without speaking to each other; Irene was always at odds with one of her two sons; and upon his death, L.B. left nothing to Edie or any of her children. But in business, Kate said, "he was the most honest man I ever met in Hollywood. A straight shooter. We closed our deals with a handshake in his office. Then I would go to Benjamin K. Thau [vice president of Loews, Inc., which owned

MGM] to discuss the details. And when the contracts were drawn, I'd go to Mr. Mayer and say, 'Look, I don't have a lawyer, and I know you wouldn't cheat me, so would you please give this to one of your lawyers to look over for me?'" He would and did. "I think that's what Dad liked most about Kate," Irene said in the end, "—the trust. She brought out the very best in him."

"Oh, these men—the Mayers and Goldwyns and the rest—make no mistake about it, they were pirates, real buccaneers," Hepburn said. "But they were also romantics and gamblers, and they weren't afraid to express their opinions and put their money where their mouths were. Because they believed in the movies. The movies were *their* dreams. And I—and Greer and Joan [Crawford] and Garbo—were all part of those dreams."

After the triumph of *The Philadelphia Story,* Hepburn and Mayer were determined to work together again. The studio head even urged the star to become a director or producer. "I was a one-track Charlie," Kate used to tell him. "I was too interested in being a star to get bogged down in the details of the rest of the production." But she always made her voice heard on even the most minute points of every production, whether they affected her directly or not. She and Mayer did work together ten more times over the next fifteen years—on successive three-year contracts loose enough to amount to her working on an ad hoc basis.

Upon filming *The Philadelphia Story,* Kate honored her commitment to the Theatre Guild by returning to the road, completing the tour of the show. (She knew it could only create buzz for the upcoming release of the movie.) Not until the film's premiere did the producers close the play, appropriately, in Philadelphia. On February 15, 1941, just before going on the stage of the Forrest Theatre for the final performance, Hepburn went to the stage manager and said, "If I give you a sign at the end of the show, don't pull the curtain down. Let there be a pause." At each big moment in the play that night, the star realized from the reactions that practically everyone in the theater had seen the play before and that she was playing to "a real fan audience." By the curtain calls, the crowd had gone "absolutely mad." So Hepburn stepped forward for her final bow, coming out of Joseph Cotten's arms, thinking what a terrible moment it is when a play has to come to an end. She signaled to the stage manager, quieted the audience, and said to them, "The curtain will never be rung down on this play." With that, the cast simply walked off the stage; and as the audience left the theater for the streets of Philadelphia, the crew set out the worklights and dismantled the set.

A few weeks later Kate heard that Helen Hayes—"The First Lady of the American Theater," whom she admired greatly—had said to a friend, "That goddamned Kate, resorting to that cheap little piece of business, when there are a million actors with a lot more hits. I can't believe I never thought of that." Commented Kate in the end, with an enormous cackle: "I really should have been disgusted with myself."

At the start of the new decade, however, she was feeling too good for that. Hepburn was in demand again. In 1940 Franklin D. Roosevelt invited her to Hyde Park, where she pledged support of a third term for the President in a radio broadcast. A few months later, Eleanor Roosevelt asked Hepburn to narrate an Office of War Information documentary called *Women in Defense*. Back in Hollywood, not only was L. B. Mayer pushing to make another picture with her, but writers were once again composing scripts with Hepburn in mind.

Ring Lardner, Jr., for example, was fashioning a story about a prominent newspaper columnist, modeled on Dorothy Thompson, who falls in love with her paper's sportswriter. It was a natural setup for a witty battle of the sexes, rife with the comic possibilities imposed by the attraction of opposites. A centerpiece of the story would be the couple's attending a baseball game together—turf that was as foreign to her as global affairs were to him. Lardner gave the story idea to his friend Garson Kanin—a young writer in Hollywood, who was married to Ruth Gordon and was friendly with Hepburn—in hopes of drafting the script together. Hepburn liked Kanin and thought he was "extremely clever," though she often found him "quite full of himself." He was a good fifteen years younger than his wife, and that always made Hepburn a little wary of him as well. "Princes," she said of spoiled men married to much older women, "—looking for Mother." All that aside, she liked this new idea. Kanin worked on the treatment with Lardner before enlisting in the armed services as the nation approached war. Then he suggested his younger brother might fill his boots in cowriting the script.

The two fledgling writers, Michael Kanin and Lardner, wrote several drafts, tailoring the character of Tess Harding for Hepburn. Just as important, Hepburn made clear from the start, was that the sportswriter, Sam Craig, be skewed toward attracting the one actor with whom she most wanted to work—Spencer Tracy. Kate would later insist that she had no personal designs on Tracy in baiting this trap, only professional ones. She felt, quite simply, that "he was the best movie actor there was."

In 1940, that was a widely held opinion. Spencer Tracy had, by then, appeared in more than forty pictures, playing everything from gangsters to priests and winning back-to-back Oscars for his performances as Manuel the Portuguese fisherman in *Captains Courageous* and Father Flanagan in *Boys Town*. He had become something more than an actor or even a successful movie star. With his unaffected delivery, Tracy had become a national icon, appearing over and over as a kind of truth-teller in movies, the solid American. He was, Kate suggested in an incautious moment, "completely male."

And he was not afraid to turn that trait to sentimental use, maintaining a gruff exterior to disguise an obviously emotional inner life. She thought his performance in Fritz Lang's *Fury*—playing an Everyman who stands up to a mob—was "one of the greatest ever put on film. Absolutely thrilling in its simplicity." And, she told me one night, "I've watched *Captains Courageous* at least seven times, and I've never seen the end of it, because I'm always in tears once Spence dies without letting the boy know he's lost his legs."

When Hepburn thought Kanin and Lardner's extensive treatment was ready for the marketplace, she sent it to Joe Mankiewicz—without the writers' names on the pages. She gave him twenty-four hours to respond—not only to its quality but also to its ability to entice Tracy. "I want him or no dice with MGM," she insisted. When Mankiewicz called to say it scored on both counts, she left for Los Angeles to meet with Mr. Mayer.

As with *The Philadelphia Story,* Hepburn controlled the material. Mayer asked how much she wanted for the story and who wrote it. She requested $125,000 for herself and as much again for the writers. She refused to name them, knowing novices could not demand that high a figure. When Mayer kept insisting on hearing their names, Hepburn sensed his vanity was about to get in the way of his negotiating a deal. Again she remembered her mother with the elders in Hartford and how she never let her own ego detract from her causes. "Just pour the tea, Kath," Kate told herself. So before Mayer was forced into making a decision about buying the script, Hepburn quickly added that she had not come that day to close a deal, merely to see if MGM and Spencer Tracy were interested. Clearly Mayer was, enough for Hepburn to encourage her writers to polish the script. Tracy, unfortunately, was booked up, filming Marjorie Kinnan Rawlings's classic tale *The Yearling* in Florida.

Hepburn didn't know at the time that *The Yearling* had been plagued from the start with bad weather and bugs, which were not only eating the actors alive but also swarming around the camera, rendering much of the footage unusable. Providentially, the film soon shut down (and would not recommence for another five years—then starring Gregory Peck); and Spencer Tracy was looking for a new picture. "The boys," as Kate called young Kanin and Lardner, completed their script posthaste. Tracy liked it and committed to appear in it.

In early August of 1941, Hepburn was walking out of the Thalberg Building on the MGM lot when she saw Joe Mankiewicz walking with Spencer Tracy on their way to lunch. Although the two stars worked for the same studio, they had never met. They approached each other, and Mankiewicz made the unnecessary introductions. Kate held out her hand and sized up her new leading man from head to toe. Then she made a comment about her high heels and coquettishly remarked, "Mr. Tracy, you're not as tall as I expected."

"Don't worry, Kate," Mankiewicz interjected, "he'll cut you down to size."

VII

Yare

How is your friend Irene?" Kate invariably asked at some point in every telephone conversation or visit. It was a loaded question, fraught with baggage—great interest tinged with melancholy.

Katharine Hepburn and Irene Mayer Selznick had, after all, been friends for more than fifty years. Kate had known Irene through most of her fifteen-year roller-coaster ride of a marriage to Benzedrine-fueled David Selznick; and they became closer in its aftermath, when the divorced Irene reinvented herself as a major force on Broadway. For her part, Irene had been ringside for Kate's arrival in Hollywood, her exile, and then her comeback, as well as the five successful decades that followed. She had also observed Kate's serial love affairs of the thirties yield to the one serious romance that consumed her for the next twenty-five years. With one Selznick son or the other almost always on the outs with his mother—sometimes Jeffrey and Danny were "in the doghouse" at the same time—"Sister Kate" became a favorite "aunt" to them. Despite all that shared history, by the end of the 1980s, the two women had all but stopped speaking to each other. But I can hardly remember a single telephone conversation or visit in which Irene did not ask, "How is your friend Kate?"

They had experienced less of a rift than a drift, two seemingly parallel lives that gradually arced in different directions. Born a month apart, each entered her eighties differently. Irene, a lifelong hypochondriac (the only way to get attention growing up alongside a sickly sister), was proud of her age. While often complaining of undiagnosable aches and pains, she bragged that she had "all her marbles," and she worked steadily on a book of memoirs. Kate never said boo about her foot, which refused to heal properly; she stoically applied ice packs and stuck to her physical regimen as best she could; and she continued to entertain offers to work. She complained only that she couldn't remember things so well as she used to. For years, I had been suggesting that she commit episodes of her life to paper— something I learned she had already quietly been doing; but their actual publication struck her as a kind of death knell to her acting career. She didn't celebrate birthdays, though every year—usually on the wrong date that she had disseminated for publicity purposes back in 1932—the press ballyhooed the occasion. In May of 1989—her eighty-second birthday—one newspaper announced that she had just turned seventy-nine. "It's bad enough that I have to get older every year," Irene dashed off in a note she mailed to Kate. "But do you have to keep getting younger?" Irene never received a reply. "The Kate I used to know would have called up and laughed," Irene told me a few nights later at dinner.

Without ever saying a word directly on the subject, to each other or to me, their life-paths seemed bound never to recross. For one, Irene didn't get around much anymore. While she was still "full of piss and vinegar" (as she used to say) on almost any topic, from politics to Broadway to her children, her social life was shrinking to long telephone conversations with her intimates—Kitty Carlisle Hart, Leonora Hornblow, Jean Kerr, and Mr. Paley chief among them—and dinners for two in her apartment. Every now and then, she would say to me, "I've got to have that bean soup at the Post House" or "I've got to have some Chinese food tonight"; and without a moment's thought, we'd tear down to Chinatown and eat five or six courses, each in a different restaurant—one specializing in dim sum, another in Szechuan soup, another in Peking duck. Such nights became rarer, and with each visit to the Hotel Pierre, I found her a little less willing to venture out.

Kate, Irene claimed, was "growing old disgracefully." After years of privacy and discretion, she appeared to be ubiquitous—needlessly grabbing headlines. There had been the performance she attended of *Candide* at which the audience had to sit on benches so uncomfortable that she felt impelled to seat herself in a more comfortable chair—on the stage! While attending a play written by her niece Katharine Houghton, Kate fainted to the floor—through no fault of her own, really: the paint fumes from the still-wet scenery simply knocked her out cold. She attended a Michael Jackson concert at Madison Square Garden as the artist's special guest; and she was appearing in a string of what Irene called "horrible little" television movies. "Dad always said Garbo had the right idea. Get off the screen while they still love you," Irene would add to underscore her point.

Perhaps hardest for Irene was that Hepburn seemed to be chugging along with a new train of friends, mostly younger. Anthony Harvey, who had directed her in *The Lion in Winter,* was proving himself as caring a friend as he had been her director—in many ways replacing George Cukor in her life. Laura Fratti, who had coached Kate in faking her piano-playing in movies and onstage, came around with her intellectual husband and their daughter. Sally Lapiduss, who had been a stage manager while Kate was performing *The West Side Waltz* on the road, accompanied her back to New York as a personal assistant and became a friend of Kate's, prior to becoming a successful television writer-producer.

"I remember when that phone number was a state secret and only a few of us had it," Irene recalled one night, somewhat wistfully. "Now everybody does." Mrs. Selznick, on the other hand, was in the phone book. ("If you really don't want to be found," she once told me, "list yourself in the Manhattan directory.") Somehow, Irene kept current on everybody who came in and out of Kate's life—through Norah, I always suspected, whom she liked a great deal and who was always up for a good gab.

"And who's Cindy?" Irene asked me over the telephone late one night in 1983.

"I'll be honest with you," I replied, "I haven't met her yet."

"I think you better," said Irene, "because I think she's taken over your room at Two forty-four."

Cindy was, in fact, a young woman from Maine named Cynthia McFadden, who had worked her way from Bowdoin College to Manhattan, where she apprenticed to the legendary newsman Fred Friendly. She became executive producer of his Media and Society Seminars on Public Broadcasting, a stimulating series on moral, legal, and ethical issues, in which a law professor would hit fungo-like questions to a team of experts, batting them back and forth Socratic-style. A highly ambitious graduate of the Columbia University School of Law, Cynthia moved on to produce a show about books for Lewis Lapham.

Cynthia's introduction to Kate came through Hepburn's sister Marion, who arranged for her to meet Kathy Houghton and Kate herself. A deep friendship quickly developed. One night I called from Los Angeles and caught Kate in the middle of what sounded like a rousing dinner. "You should be here," she said. "I even have a dinner companion for you, a brilliant young girl. She has big beautiful eyes, beautiful skin, and she wears her hair—why, she wears her hair piled high and tied in a knot like—"

"Tell him," a young voice shouted across the room, "I look like you."

"Well, yes," said Kate, as though realizing it for the first time, "I suppose she does look like me."

On my next visit to New York, I met Cynthia at dinner and found her as attractive as Kate had said—though not quite the lookalike I had expected. Kate said she was sorry my room was currently occupied, would I mind using another? I had, in fact, already made arrangements to stay with another friend across town. Over the next few years, Cynthia's friendship with Kate blossomed, as did her career. She was extremely attentive to Kate, treating her with respect and tenderness. This infusion of young blood—a woman starting out on her career in Manhattan and making Kate's home her own—had an obviously tonic effect.

While Kate still preferred to arrange most of our dinners for just the two of us, we always had fun when Cynthia or Kathy Houghton or Tony Harvey came over. One night Kate and Cynthia and I went to the home of Nancy Hamilton, a longtime friend from the theater. We were celebrating Cynthia's having taken the New York bar exam that day. After dinner, Nancy—a songwriter, among many talents—wanted to play a record of Kirsten Flagstad singing Wagner. Kate could not have been less interested. She tried to get Nancy Hamilton to turn off the machine and return to conversation, but Nancy would not stop the music. Kate fired a desperate look my way, suggesting that I do something. At the close of an aria, I just sat down at the piano and started playing—making it impossible for our hostess to ignore me. The first song that came to mind was "Coco," a number Kate had performed several hundred times. After playing it from start to finish, Kate looked puzzled and said, "Play that again," which I did. Looking even more puzzled, she asked, "What is that song? I know I've heard it!"

I laughed until I realized she wasn't kidding. "Heard it!" I said. "You sang it four hundred times! It's 'Coco.'"

"Oh, Christ!" she said. "I knew there was a reason I couldn't remember it. I couldn't stand that song."

Cynthia was always interested in meeting new people; and she tended to make Kate more social, even less averse to appearing in public. Besides accepting the occasional dinner invitation, Hepburn increasingly found herself "on the town" during the day, occasionally performing unnecessary tasks. One day we had to find the perfect carrot peeler. Kate's driver took us to three different stores before we found an emporium selling kitchen utensils that had the exact size and model she wanted. I was fascinated to watch a dozen shoppers in that store near Union Square all suddenly develop an interest in carrot peelers and to see Kate's way of noticing them without being noticed.

While Kate and Phyllis went to the cash register to pay for the item—Kate never carried cash, just a checkbook; Phyllis was there to pull out a roll of bills from a change purse of household money—I lingered with the crowd. Eleven out of twelve shoppers bonded in excitement—"Is it really her? She still looks great. She's my grandmother's favorite; she's my mother's favorite. She's my favorite." One severely tailored, middle-aged matron said, "I always thought she overacted." I reported the results of my straw poll to Kate, who said I should always tell people she was my aunt, so they would be polite enough not to criticize her, at least in our presence.

Kate was back to seeing every show on Broadway; and she often asked if we might duck out to the movies, though little interested her there. She avoided action pictures and couldn't believe that Sylvester Stallone and Arnold Schwarzenegger were international stars. "I don't understand him," she said of the latter after we had seen a preview of one of his movies. As I tried to explain the worldwide appeal of the Austrian-born bodybuilder, she said, "No, I mean when he speaks—I don't understand him!" She found most of the Merchant-Ivory pictures "a bore," though she delighted in Vanessa Redgrave's performance in their production of *The Bostonians*—or any role she ever saw her in. She had flipped for John Travolta in *Saturday Night Fever,* and she greatly admired Sally Field in *Norma Rae* and *Places in the Heart.* She liked Harrison Ford in *The Mosquito Coast* and again in *Working Girl.* She said the new star of that picture, Melanie

Griffith, reminded her of Judy Holliday but feared her career would fade fast. "There's something lethargic about her," she explained, "where Judy was full of energy." She had zero tolerance for Woody Allen movies, though she thought *The Purple Rose of Cairo* captured the flavor of the RKO movies of her vintage. After seeing Julia Roberts in *Mystic Pizza,* she predicted her becoming "the next big movie star," the first she had "seen in years." Meryl Streep was her least favorite modern actress on screen—"Click, click, click," she said, referring to the wheels turning inside her head.

Glenn Close was her least favorite actress on stage. "She's got these big, fat, ugly feet," Hepburn told me upon returning from a matinee of Tom Stoppard's play *The Real Thing,* in which Close had opened on Broadway opposite Jeremy Irons. "And she goes around barefoot in the play and almost ruins the whole thing." She thought Irons gave a spectacular performance, though she didn't think he was a well-trained actor. "It's a personality performance," she said, "all tricked up with mannerisms and charm—like me." On the other hand, she admired Irons's wife, Sinead Cusack, who was in New York around that time performing with Derek Jacobi and the Royal Shakespeare Company in *Much Ado About Nothing* and *Cyrano de Bergerac.* Hepburn thought she was "the real McCoy—one of the most exciting actors I've ever seen."

Glenn Close's feet notwithstanding, Kate insisted I see *The Real Thing.* She thought Stoppard was a cold playwright but that this was the most emotional work he had written. She wangled two house seats for a Wednesday matinee, one for me and one for "your friend Irene." (Irene would later assert that Irons's performance was one of the three greatest performances she had ever seen, ranking alongside Brando's in *Streetcar.* The third great performance she would later cite was John Lithgow's in *Requiem for a Heavyweight,* which had been adapted from a Rod Serling teleplay for a short-lived Broadway run.)

In addition to the tickets, Kate invited us back to her house for dinner that night. The invitation thrilled Irene and led to an amusing evening. I sat back and listened as these two old friends hopscotched across a half century of show-business acquaintances, all the obvious Hollywood names plus some mutual Broadway friends—producer Hugh "Binky" Beaumont, agent Audrey Wood, Lillian Hellman, Tallulah Bankhead . . . "and do you remember how Myron was always betting on that goddamned horse named Malicious?" Irene asked. "Always a longshot and it paid off every time."

The next morning, Kate said it had been nice to see Irene, but "all she talks about are aches and pains and dead people." Irene said it had been nice to see Kate, but "you're the only one of her friends that I can stand." Although she hadn't met Cynthia McFadden, she didn't like the sound of her. She bristled at Kate's extreme interest in the young woman's career. She occasionally asked longingly about my visits to Fenwick, wondering, "Who makes the beds?" I said everyone seemed to make his or her own . . . and if I was ever slow about it, Kate would just march in and make it. "That's what I was afraid of," said Irene. She returned only once more in her life to 244 East Forty-ninth Street.

I finished my Goldwyn biography in the late spring of 1988, a rocky moment in the history of my publishers, Alfred A. Knopf. The firm's longtime standard-bearer, and my editor, Robert Gottlieb, had recently decided to leave the publishing house upon being offered the editorship of *The New Yorker*. A brilliant gentleman from London, Sonny Mehta, replaced him, and my book was assigned to one of Gottlieb's protégées to edit. I handed over the twelve hundred–page manuscript on which I had worked for some eight years and made a plea few editors ever hear: "Please," I begged, "cut anything you can out of this manuscript. I feel it's about four hundred pages too long, so if anything even makes you pause for a moment, please mark it as material I might cut."

Four months later the editor returned the manuscript to me—shorter by twelve pages. As she put the book into production, I sent this "edited" version to Irene. A day later she called to say, "You've sent me the wrong pages. I've got one of your rough drafts." After I explained that this was the edited version, Irene said that was unacceptable. She strongly felt that the material was all there but that much of it was out of proportion. If that was the best Knopf was going to do with my book, she said, she would just have to edit the book herself. For the next ten days, she did just that, working it over word by word. Twice a day she would call outraged by something. "Zsa Zsa Gabor's in your book, but no Pearl White!" she screamed one day, reminding me that I had left out the silent screen's most famous cliff-hanging heroine. Her edited version had marginalia everywhere—all perfectly precise. When she had reached a paragraph I had written about Jon Hall, the star of Goldwyn's production of *The Hurricane,* for example, she simply wrote in the margin: "Sonny Tufts," a reference to a second-string leading man who also didn't warrant much attention.

The Pierre was featuring a special chef that week she was playing editor, and Irene recommended that we sample his food one night in her apartment while discussing the manuscript. Over turbot with an intense lobster sauce, she pointed out stories that ran on for pages that should be condensed to paragraphs, paragraphs that should become sentences, and sentences that should be two-word mentions. When we reached the pages I had written about a terrible Goldwyn picture called *A Song is Born,* I spoke of simply cutting most of it. Upon hearing that, Irene grabbed a piece of bread out of my hand and mopped her plate clean of the remaining sauce. "What made that sauce so good?" she asked rhetorically. Before I could speak, she provided her own answer: "Reduction."

The next morning Irene called to say that she had just called "his nibs"—Bob Gottlieb, whom she looked upon as a third son—and "gave him hell." She suggested I rework the draft as quickly as possible and send the revised pages to him, even though he had already assumed his duties at *The New Yorker.*

Irene's comments helped me reduce the manuscript by three hundred pages. Then Bob Gottlieb moonlighted for a few days, living up to his legendary reputation and finding another hundred pages on top of that. With the book at last on the production schedule, I began searching for my next topic.

An editor at Knopf introduced me to the executrix of the Tennessee Williams estate—Maria Grenfell, Lady St. Just—who was then actively searching for a Williams biographer. This was a brass ring in nonfiction circles. Arguably America's greatest playwright, (the debate still rages between pro-Williams and pro-O'Neill camps), Williams left a massive collection of unpublished material; and a well-researched, well-written life story of the man had not yet appeared. The Lady St. Just was a colorful character—reputedly Williams's model for Maggie in *Cat on a Hot Tin Roof,* and a former actress who had married a Morgan Bank heir. Upon her longtime friend Tennessee's death, she was left to oversee his literary matters. "I remember when she was working the streets," Irene told me when I discussed my having dinner with her.

Our meeting was such a triumph that the next day the Lady St. Just literally pulled me by the hand to two different law offices to meet her co-executors and to arrange for my securing the necessary rights and permissions to the Williams archives. A lovely man and friend of mine named Lyle Leverich had been researching a Williams biography for years, working from authorization by Williams himself. But the Estate was trying to block him at every turn, including their ultimate threat that they would prohibit his quoting any Williams material. I figured I might be influential with the Estate in allowing Leverich to publish his work, knowing that I would have access to material he did not have and that my book would be published at least a decade later. After everything seemed to be arranged for me to write the official biography—all too quickly, I thought, especially after one of the attorneys showed me Leverich's authorization and commented, "it's not exactly the wine-soaked cocktail napkin Maria says it is"—I went to the Hotel Pierre bursting with my good news. "Congratulations!" Irene said upon learning of the offer. "Now run like hell."

I didn't have to sell the producer of *A Streetcar Named Desire* on the importance of my subject. But she felt compelled to tell me that my writing such a book would be like "entering a snake pit." She suggested that I would never survive working with "that woman"—Maria St. Just—and that Tennessee Williams's affairs were as big a "cesspool" after his death as they had been during his lifetime. I was happy to have somebody with whom I could discuss all aspects of the story before I signed a decade of my life away; and I made all the compelling counterarguments about the drama of Williams's life. Irene listened to my earnest oral argument, staring at me through her glasses. At last, she closed the debate by saying, "Lousy third act."

Before I left her that night, she urged me to discuss the subject with "your friend Kate." Hepburn had, after all, played two of Tennessee Williams's juiciest parts—Violet Venable and Amanda Wingfield; and he had written another, Hannah Jelkes in *Night of the Iguana,* for her. I stopped by 244 the next day. "I am afraid," Kate said, "Irene's right. Tennessee's life was a nightmare, a total nightmare; and I don't think you'll ever wake up. You really don't want to spend years with those people, his people." Kate had just read the finished manuscript of *Goldwyn*—for which she unsolicitedly called my publishers and gave them an advertising blurb—and said, "That man was a pirate, but there was lift to his life. I didn't much care when he died in real life, but I did when he died at the end of the book. I don't think you'll feel the same about

Tennessee. His life was one long suicide. He dragged people down in the gutter with him, and I'm afraid he'll drag you too."

I rethought. But even before I could express my doubts to anyone, the Lady St. Just—of whom many joked she was "none of the three"—suddenly announced that she was rescinding her offer because she had heard that I was "incompetent." Case closed. Once again, I was casting my net in the biographical waters.

At dinner one night Kate asked if I had any new prospects. I told her that three different publishers, who had heard of our friendship, said I should write about her. "Yes, you should," she said. "But not while I'm alive."

I continued to put feelers out, and told the editor I had been assigned at Knopf that I was actively looking for a subject, another great American cultural figure but—because I had written about Perkins and Goldwyn—not somebody from the worlds of publishing or film. When she suggested Italian film director Luchino Visconti, I felt free to roam.

At the urging of Phyllis Grann, then head of G. P. Putnam's Sons, I began to chase the rights to the papers of Charles Lindbergh. My pursuit took most of a year. Irene heard the idea and screamed, "Aaah, Goyishkeit!" But she saw all the dramatic possibilities of the story of the great hero who became a great victim and a great villain. "I don't like him," she said. "But I want to know more about him. And at my age, I can't say that about too many people."

Kate adored the idea before I could get it out of my mouth. "I can't wait to read it," she said. "It has everything—spectacle, tragedy, controversy, mystery, and a love story. You've got to do it." I explained that the rights were complicated, as Lindbergh had evidently died prohibiting anyone's entry to the papers for years after the death of his wife . . . and Anne Morrow Lindbergh was very much alive and well. I told Kate that I seemed to be making some inroads with the Lindbergh children, but Mrs. Lindbergh still held the key.

"Look," she said. "Get me her address, and I'll write her a letter. Do you think that would help?" I said I thought it might, but I wasn't sure. "Do you know her?" I asked. "No," said Kate, "but we had the same doctor for many years. And I think she knows who I am."

"Of course she knows who you are!" Phyllis interjected with her lovely way of stating the obvious. "Everybody knows who you are. Why, everybody in the world knows who you are."

"Yes, dearie. Of course they do. But this is a tricky situation. Think about it. I'll write a letter tomorrow, and you can decide then if I should send it."

I said that was a good idea, and a generous one at that . . . and that we must *all* keep mum on the subject. "Oh, don't worry about Phyllis," Kate assured me. "She's an absolute crypt. She's walking around with all sorts of secrets. Of course, she's losing her mind, so God only knows what she even remembers any longer."

"That's not true," Phyllis protested. "I remember everything I remember."

"Yes, of course, dear."

The next day Kate showed me her letter, which she had entrusted Cynthia to type. It was strong and concise; and we agreed it could only help. Just days after Kate mailed it, I learned that Mrs. Lindbergh was willing to meet me, the first sure sign that the permissions to write her late husband's biography might be mine. Weeks later, they were.

Suddenly, I had unique access to some two thousand boxes of papers, the bulk of which were in Sterling Memorial Library at Yale University in New Haven, about forty miles down the turnpike from Fenwick. The headquarters for my work for the next few years would become Connecticut, and the time I would get to spend with Kate would increase and intensify.

Hepburn continued to become more public than she had in the past. She agreed to show up at benefits for the Actors' Home in New

Jersey, to accept an occasional fashion award ("Are you sure they didn't mean Audrey?" I asked her while opening one such invitation, and she pushed an ice-cream cone in my face), and to be the guest of honor at the annual Planned Parenthood banquet, for which she wrote a long, moving speech. (I urged her to conclude her remarks with the statement, "I believe strongly in Planned Parenthood because I had the benefit of a mother and father who planned theirs." But she dismissed it as "too corny.") In 1990 she accepted one of the prestigious Kennedy Center Honors, having refused the decoration several times. When I asked why she had finally agreed to take part in the ceremonies that year, she explained that she just couldn't turn down George Stevens, Jr.—one of the founders of the award and the son of her former paramour—any longer. "And," she said, "I was waiting until the Reagans were out of the White House, because I wanted nothing to do with either of them."

She also began to allow documentary filmmakers into her life—into her houses and her history. She sometimes called the night before a shoot, ostensibly about something else but ultimately to discuss what she might talk about. Katharine Hepburn hardly needed coaching; but I think she was questioning the seemliness, at her age, of talking about her personal life, notably the one topic she had avoided most of her life—Spencer Tracy. The primary reason she had long held out was Tracy's widow. But Louise Tracy had died in 1983, and Kate had since come to meet their daughter, Susie. She took a real liking to her and repeatedly made a point of saying they were friends.

I gave one general piece of advice to Kate—that if she was about to discuss Spencer Tracy in an upcoming documentary, she should not be coy. Kate asked what I meant by that. I said that a lot of people for a long time had made certain assumptions about her relationship with him, but that until somebody heard something from her lips, it was hearsay. Only she, I said, knew her true feelings;

and if she planned to "go public," then she should be specific about them.

She asked how frank she should be. Coming from someone who had guarded her privacy so masterfully for so many decades, this question threw me. I could see that she was growing anxious—eager to impart but not to exploit. I suggested she make her comments more about herself than about Tracy, about how *she* felt. If you could, I asked, what would you say to him today? That, I explained, might show the audience what he meant to her, with twenty years of hindsight. That night she wrote a letter to Tracy, which allowed her to put some of her thoughts and feelings in perspective. To my amazement, she read it the next day—rather dramatically, as it turned out—on camera.

My friend Irene once said, "I liked Spence, but I never really understood him or what his life with Kate was about." In many ways, neither did Kate. Her open letter to him was largely a litany of questions—Why couldn't he sleep? What did he like to do? What were the demons he was battling? Why the "escape hatch" of alcoholism "to get away from the remarkable you? What was it, Spence?" Even more revealing, Kate added, "I meant to ask you."

Spencer Bonaventure Tracy was born in Milwaukee on April 5, 1900, the second son of Carrie Brown, a Protestant turned Christian Scientist, and John Tracy, a hard-drinking Irish Catholic whose parents had been refugees from the Great Potato Famine. In one generation, the Tracys had become middle-class, middle-of-the-road Midwesterners, as John worked his way up to becoming general sales manager of a trucking company. According to Kate, who never met him, "he worked hard and drank hard" and made his two sons toe the line. Spencer often fell short.

Possessed of seemingly ordinary intelligence and looks, he stumbled through his youth, getting kicked out of several schools and serving a hitch in the navy before completing high school and entering Ripon College. He didn't find himself until a dorm-mate introduced him to college dramatics. On the Ripon stage, Tracy proved to have a prodigious memory for dialogue and an utterly natural acting style. He suddenly had an identity on campus, doing something at which he excelled.

Road companies of Broadway hits often came to Milwaukee, and one provided Tracy his first glimpse of a professional theatrical production—Laurette Taylor in a wildly popular sentimental comedy, *Peg o' My Heart.* By the time the collegian saw the play, it had become Taylor's war-horse, a role she had played on and off for a decade. Kate noted, "Spence always said it was the most exciting piece of theater he ever saw in his life."

At the end of his first school year, Tracy leapt at an offer to join the Ripon debating team—because it meant a trip to New York City. There he not only saw more plays but he also auditioned for the American Academy of Dramatic Arts. Upon his acceptance, he dropped out of Ripon to study acting. His father's unexpected approval of the decision came no doubt because Spencer was self-supporting, receiving a monthly pension as a veteran. He shared a small room with a friend from Milwaukee who was also taking classes at the American Academy, Pat O'Brien. He quickly picked up bit parts—including a nonspeaking role as one of the robots in the Theatre Guild production of *R.U.R.*

In 1923, Tracy graduated from the Academy and went on to small roles in summer stock. In White Plains, New York, he met Louise Treadwell, the leading lady in his repertory company, which dissolved after one season. When she was offered a similar position in another troupe in Cincinnati, she accepted—on the condition that they hire Spencer Tracy as her leading man. That September, they married.

Nine and a half months later, their first child was born—a son, John, who, they realized a year later, was totally deaf. While the boy's condition remained a dark subject into which Hepburn herself seldom delved, she said, "Spencer felt responsible, for the rest of his life. It just didn't seem possible to him that God should have brought such an innocent creature into the world that way, and, so, it must be his fault. This was his cross to bear, and when he could take it no longer, he drank to forget about it." Kate's few descriptions to me of Tracy's marriage made it sound as though it had been based more on his gratitude toward his wife—for believing in him and his talent—than love, and that the Tracys' lives were bound together by his feelings of indebtedness and guilt.

For a few years, Tracy found little solace in his career. He got a promising part in a forgettable play called *A Royal Fandango,* starring Ethel Barrymore and featuring a young Edward G. Robinson; but it quickly closed. (A framed playbill listing the dramatis personae— Ethel Barrymore at the top of the list and Spencer Tracy at the very bottom—sat on a bookcase in Kate's bedroom.) When he sought comfort in bottles and brothels, his wife looked the other way.

After almost seven years of good enough performances in bad plays to keep getting cast again, Spencer Tracy received the lead role of Killer Mears in a prison drama called *The Last Mile.* It opened in February 1930, and the star became that year's "overnight sensation," receiving powerful notices in what became a hit play.

Hollywood noticed as well. John Ford was in New York scouting for actors for a prison movie called *Up the River,* which he was about to direct for Fox. Tracy took a six-week furlough from the play to appear in the film—alongside newcomer Humphrey Bogart. Then he returned to Broadway.

When *Up the River* proved to be a hit, Fox offered Tracy a five-year contract. The actor moved to Hollywood with his wife and son. He made two dozen films during that period, most of them forgettable. Unlike Katharine Hepburn, who became an instant star, Tracy followed the path of most studio players, who had to slog through scripts whose primary distinction was that they were ready to be filmed right away, thus fulfilling the studio-owned theaters' need for new product. Tracy continued to drown his sorrows and to find solace in one-night stands, becoming known as one of the biggest drunks and womanizers in town. Louise Tracy revealed her concern publicly only when one of her husband's affairs with a costar proved to be of greater significance. The Tracys separated, and he announced that he wanted to marry Loretta Young. Ultimately, she refused his offer, however, and Louise Tracy took her husband back.

His studio no longer felt the same. Despite Tracy's consistently strong performances—notably in Preston Sturges's production of *The Power and the Glory*—Fox wearied of his drunken escapades and resultant bad press. In one picture, he went missing so long that they had to replace him. In April 1935, Fox let his contract lapse.

MGM wasted no time in offering him a richer one. With it came better material and bigger costars. Within the next five years, Tracy had worked with Clark Gable twice (in *San Francisco* and *Test Pilot*) and won his back-to-back Oscars. He also made films—and had affairs—with Myrna Loy (during *Whipsaw*) and Joan Crawford (during *Mannequin*). Despite the endless gossip about Tracy's escapades, most people in Hollywood contended that he had become the finest actor in movies. Louise contented herself with her ceremonial role as Mrs. Spencer Tracy, which now included caring for their second child as well, the daughter named Louise whom they called Susie.

In 1941 Tracy reluctantly agreed to appear in an MGM remake of the classic story *Dr. Jekyll and Mr. Hyde*. He had hoped to play the dual role with a minimum of makeup, allowing the characterizations of the dueling personalities to come from within. The studio and the director, Victor Fleming, saw things differently. The production was an unhappy experience for Tracy, proving to be his biggest flop and one of the few times he received poor reviews. His only consolation was a love affair that bloomed between him and his leading lady, Ingrid Bergman. The actress had appeared in but a handful of American movies; but, like Hepburn—with her healthy, scrubbed looks and distinctive voice—she had a meteoric rise in Hollywood. Although Bergman was married and a mother, her relationship with Tracy continued beyond their time on the set together. He soon left for Florida to film *The Yearling*; and when that picture shut down, the lovers picked up where they had left off.

I learned over the years that Kate had a rather trustworthy memory of most important moments in her life, but she was genuinely vague concerning those things about which she chose not to know. Of that moment just before she had met Spencer Tracy, she would later write in her memoirs about the details of his performance in *Dr. Jekyll and Mr. Hyde,* how he had been so embarrassed by the theatrical accoutrements demanded for the performance that he used to ride to and from the set in a limousine with the shades drawn. "Ingrid Bergman played the whore," Kate added correctly; "she won an award, I think." About that, Kate thought wrong, though she was clearly trying to bend over backwards to give credit to an actress she greatly admired, even where it was undue. Bergman did not receive the first of her three Oscars until *Gaslight,* a few years later.

Woman of the Year began filming in late August of 1941. As Joe Mankiewicz remembered, "This was the biggest picture on the lot, the one everyone in town was talking about. Of course, anything with Spence was big; and Kate had just come back in a big way. But she knew she was still skating on thin ice. One picture a new career does not make." As if all that were not enough to keep rumor mills grinding, Kate had selected the director for *Woman of the Year* herself; and instead of attempting to duplicate her recent success with George Cukor, she chose to fall back again on George Stevens.

And, briefly, back again into his arms. Although Tracy and Cukor would become intimate friends over the years, Hepburn—

functioning as a quasi-producer on *Woman of the Year*—felt it was essential that Tracy feel "completely at ease" with the director. She said, "I just thought he should have a big, manly man on his team—somebody who could talk baseball."

Within days, however, something extraordinary happened on their MGM soundstage. The very romance depicted in the movie—the unpretentious, plain-talking guy falling for the fancy, hyperactive cosmopolite—played out before the very eyes of the entire cast and crew. At first, producer Mankiewicz wasn't sure if he was imagining things or not; but with each day of the production, he said, more and more people watching the rushes of the film noticed as well. "It's the goddamnedest thing," he asserted years later. "It's there in the finished movie for the whole world to see."

Indeed, apart from their great acting ability, Tracy had never appeared so attractive in the movies before, with a genuine spring in his flat-footed walk. And Hepburn had never appeared so demure, so sexy. She had abandoned many of the mannerisms from her ingenue days and flowered into a striking contemporary woman. "Hell," Mankiewicz explained, "she was gorgeous, and they were in love . . . and it's still pretty goddamned exciting to watch!" The scenes in which Sam Craig first confronts Tess Harding in their editor's office, as she's adjusting her stocking, then when she catches him pursuing her, and later when she agrees to sit in on her first baseball game remain classic moments for just that reason.

Woman of the Year was a romantic comedy, the likes of which had not been seen before. It was modern and sophisticated, with a female character at least as accomplished as the male, strong but also vulnerable. Unlike Rosalind Russell in *His Girl Friday* or even Jean Arthur in *Mr. Smith Goes to Washington*, Hepburn believed it was important to show that Tess Harding was "not trying to be a man. She wasn't even trying to make it in a man's world. She was like me, someone who was making it without thinking about it, working in a man's world, succeeding. And like my mother—who held her own with men without compromising her femininity."

Actually, the film concludes with a great compromise on the issue of feminism, a battle over which Kate never completely forgave herself for capitulating. During the course of the screenplay, Tess and Sam marry, though she continues to be more professional than uxorial, which ultimately sends Sam packing. Upon hearing the vows at her father's second marriage, however, she comes to appreciate her own nuptials with a renewed belief in the sanctity of a relationship built on the principles of give-and-take. Originally, *Woman of the Year* was meant to conclude with Tess at another baseball game, having become an even more ardent fan than her husband. But in 1941—"when men were men and women were still pretty much at home," Kate explained—the executives didn't feel that would satisfy the audience. They didn't want Hepburn to appear to be denigrating the vast majority of non-career women.

So a new finale was fashioned—a nearly farcical, largely improvised scene in which Tess attempts to make breakfast for her new husband and proves she can't even make toast or coffee. It was a gentle form of comeuppance, a means of allowing, as Kate explained, "all the women in the audience to say, 'Even I can do that,' and all the men to say, 'I'm pretty lucky with the wife I've got.' And that Katharine Hepburn, she may be high and mighty, but what she really needs is the love of a good man."

Over the years, many would express their admiration of Hepburn because she had forged her career without compromise. This angered more than amused her, because she believed it was patently false and denied the struggles she had waged. "I had to compromise left and right," she said. "But I was careful to choose my battles. Fight the important ones. The ones I thought I could win. I often lost and was often proved wrong." No question—she compromised plenty. But generally, she stooped only to conquer.

Woman of the Year was a huge hit, coming out shortly after the United States entered World War II, when women in large numbers were, for the first time, working outside the house. The film provided a glimpse of the feminism that the world would be seeing more of over the next half century. More important, it was great fun. The film's basic formula, enhanced by the genuine chemistry of its stars, would provide the template for another eight pictures in which Tracy and Hepburn would appear together over the next twenty-five years, making them the most enduring romantic screen team in history. "Christ," Kate said one day with a belly laugh, "I think we were together longer than Abbott and Costello."

Tracy always got top billing. "That's the way it should have been," Kate explained. "I was just coming back when we started working together. Spence was tops in his field and had never been away. I was just damned grateful he was willing to work with me." At one point, Joe Mankiewicz had discussed the credits with Tracy, asking, "What about women and children first?"

"Hell," Tracy replied. "It's a movie, not a sinking ship."

In my first conversation with Kate—back when I was interviewing her in 1983—I reminded her of her quotation about what Astaire and Rogers each brought to their partnership and asked what she might say in substituting the names Tracy and Hepburn. "Oh, I'm not sure it worked that way," she said. "I think he was so steady and I was so volatile, that we exasperated each other. And we challenged each other, and that was the fun of it. But the truth is, I think we just looked good together." By the end of filming *Woman of the Year,* Hepburn and Tracy were, in the phrase of the day, "keeping company." He never really went home again to his ranch in Encino.

Hepburn surrendered to love as she never had before. At thirty-four years of age, with a string of broken hearts behind her and any number of would-be suitors all around, she was—she told me my first night at Fenwick—"hit over the head with a cast-iron skillet." Hardly a pretty boy, Spencer Tracy had the plain, rugged looks that appealed to Hepburn—"manly" was the word she used time and again, as she did to describe John Ford and George Stevens. Big, redheaded, and completely natural—rather like, as I saw in photographs, Dr. Thomas Norval Hepburn. She believed, without qualification, that Spencer Tracy was simply the best actor in movies. "A baked potato," she often said, referring to his talent—absolutely plain, basic, and essential. His personal life was well known to everybody in Hollywood, and his appeal to former leading ladies certainly contributed to his being attractive to Hepburn.

I sensed that what got to her most was his essential neediness. Tracy exuded a sad loneliness that verged on the tragic. And that brought out the missionary in Hepburn. After living thirty-five years entirely, as she said, "for me, me, me," she realized it was time to start living for somebody else. For the first time, she admitted, it dawned on her that she could love somebody for what she might give more than for what she might get.

She almost consciously decided to devote herself to his wants and needs, often at the expense of sublimating her desires and suppressing her personality. Hepburn—ever striving and often strident, irrepressible to the point of irritating, exhilarating, and sometimes exhausting—assumed the most difficult role of her life. As Tracy's lover and companion, she became supportive in ways that sometimes forced her to be servile, patient to an extreme that often left her patronized, and devoted until she was sometimes reduced to a life in denial. She was periodically subjected to his humiliations, occasionally in front of others. On the set or in a living room, she often sat, literally, at his feet.

They had their most wonderful times together—the best of which, Kate said, were just being quietly alone in each other's company. They lived like married people: eating dinner together, meat and potatoes; reading the Sunday newspaper; taking drives up the coast; painting. Never especially comfortable with his emotions, he could be tender and affectionate when they were by themselves or with their most trusted friends—George Cukor, Garson Kanin and Ruth Gordon, later Bogart and Bacall. They kept separate residences and generally arrived at social events under separate cover. He spoke to his wife regularly.

In an industry where gossip passed for gospel, a brood of columnists had come to wield great power, their word spreading around the world. Louella Parsons and then Hedda Hopper and Sheilah Graham, as well as a string of imitators, were, therefore, feared and fawned over. Hepburn and Tracy generally ignored them. In most cases, such failure to truckle to what Kate called "the rag hags" provoked nasty, sometimes career-crushing, columns. Strangely, Hepburn and Tracy were left alone, with little ever appearing in any of the columns that linked the two outside the studio walls. This tacit hostility proved the easiest way for each side to deal with its obvious contempt for the other's behavior.

I once suggested to Kate that part of the reason the female gossip columnists ignored her relationship with Tracy was that they secretly admired her for it and for the way she sustained herself over the years in a man's world. Later in their careers, Hedda Hopper approached Hepburn at a Hollywood function with her hand held out. "Isn't it time we bury the hatchet and become friends?" the big-hatted reporter asked. "Oh, Hedda," Hepburn replied, "we've gone this long without speaking to each other. Why spoil a perfectly good enmity?"

In the days and decades after *Woman of the Year* ended production, friends of Tracy and Hepburn—and ultimately their fans—spoke with great authority about how they could never marry. His wife would never grant him a divorce, they said; Catholic and guilt-ridden about his son's deafness, he would never seek one. But there was one more factor seldom considered, which Kate insisted was paramount. As she told me that first night in Fenwick, "I never wanted to marry Spencer Tracy."

It has also been suggested that Hepburn was always attracted to men who were, if not married, at least, somehow attached to other women. There's truth to that notion. But I think it was more that the men to whom she was drawn were unmarriageable. Living "like a man," as Kate so often asserted—by herself, paying her own bills, and ultimately, answering to nobody—she liked that arrangement and could afford to live that way.

A leading lady's career seldom extended longer than a decade, which forced many of them into peculiar circumstances. Most stars suddenly found themselves living in a style to which they quickly became accustomed—only to find themselves unable to maintain it for long. That partly explained why practically all of them married repeatedly, at least once for money. (Joan Crawford, Bette Davis, Myrna Loy, Greer Garson, and Jennifer Jones all counted business tycoons among their multiple husbands.) Not Hepburn. Luddy was certainly there to launch her career; and Howard Hughes helped her enter the stratosphere. But she left them so that she would not be further indebted. She wanted less from her men, not more.

With Spencer Tracy, she was able to take that way of living one step farther—appreciating one intense, intimate relationship over a quarter of a century. He and Katharine Hepburn experienced the ups and downs of any married couple; but in never sealing their arrangement legally, they were able to retain an element of unreality in the relationship, a false quality based on neither of them being locked in. In many ways, their time together had the feeling of a "reunion" more than a union, because there was always this escape hatch through which either of them could pass whenever he or she pleased. Tracy periodically slipped out to fight personal demons, resulting in drinking binges and sexual conquests; Hepburn often packed her bags too—for professional conquests, acting roles. It quickly became apparent that even her briefest absences could be enough to set off a cycle of insobriety.

Upon the completion of *Woman of the Year,* for example, they went their separate ways. Against his wishes, Hepburn honored an agreement she had made with the Theatre Guild to appear in a new play by Philip Barry called *Without Love.* While she took it out for a pre-Broadway run, Tracy brooded his way through an MGM production of John Steinbeck's *Tortilla Flat.* When word that he was mixing alcohol with barbiturates reached Hepburn, she felt that she had to suspend the tour in order to spend the summer in California with him. She told the Guild she would return to New York for the play's Broadway opening.

In the summer of 1942, a project intended for Tracy and Hepburn came along. It was the most anomalous of their joint vehicles, but under the circumstances, she considered it a godsend. Donald Ogden Stewart, who had so successfully adapted her two Philip Barry plays for the screen, had just written a screenplay based on a novel by I. A. R. Wylie called *Keeper of the Flame.* It was a melodramatic political thriller, capturing much of the tenor of the times, in which a journalist tracks down the zealously protective widow of a great American hero—Lindbergh-like in some ways—whose Yankee Doodle patriotism turns out to be a front for fascism. It was not difficult for Hepburn to press George Cukor, always eager to prove he could direct drama as well as romantic comedy, into service. She convinced Tracy that this would be a wonderful way to make a worthwhile political statement.

Although the film was meant to emulate Hitchcock—with its whiffs of *Rebecca* and *Suspicion*—the material proved to be far from Cukor's metier. Heavy-handed attempts at psychology and sociology tended to overwhelm the antifascist message of *Keeper of the Flame.* The film succeeded only in allowing Tracy and Hepburn to work together again and to spend time together in a house she rented in Malibu. At night, she would often drive him all the way back into town, to a suite at the Beverly Hills Hotel.

Intense romantic involvements have occurred on motion-picture sets since the days of D. W. Griffith. Most prove to be like shipboard romances, usually ending as the cruise does. By the close of the summer of 1942, the Hepburn-Tracy love affair seemed fated to similar shoals. For months her return to Broadway in *Without Love* distressed her, torn as she was between an old commitment to the theater friends who had resuscitated her career and her new commitment to the one man who, she said, "taught me to love." Tracy made it plain that he wished she would abandon the play.

At that moment, Louise Tracy, who had not seen her husband stray from home this long since his affair with Loretta Young, played her hand. Instead of folding her cards as she almost did nearly a decade earlier, she finessed her way into the public eye with her husband at her side. That fall the University of Southern California announced the creation of the John Tracy Clinic, an organization dedicated to the deaf and their families, largely underwritten by Mr. and Mrs. Spencer Tracy. Louise Tracy's commitment to the cause was never less than genuine. Kate found her timing of the announcement, however, suspect—forcing, as it did, Spencer to play the role of admiring husband and reinforcing his feelings of guilt as a father.

At the same time, Tracy complained that he had never known a woman who kept so many of her old flames ignited—aflicker if not in full blaze—as Hepburn. Leland Hayward periodically checked in with career advice; and after divorcing Margaret Sullavan, he said his losing Kate was the great regret in his life. George Stevens remained friendly with her; and almost until the end of his life, John Ford spoke of retiring to Ireland, taking Kate with him. Howard Hughes told Irene Selznick that he considered his inability to persuade Kate to marry him "the biggest mistake" in his life.

Hughes maintained contact with Hepburn up to the very last years of his life. Until then, he continued to telephone her. At first the calls were ostensibly about *The Philadelphia Story*; but he kept ringing long after there was no business to conduct. A decade later, for example, Kate suddenly found herself looking for temporary lodging in Los Angeles; and during one of their calls, Hughes recommended the former Charles Boyer house, which RKO had bought from the actor a few years earlier as part of the settlement in terminating his contract. It was sitting empty; and, because Hughes owned RKO at that time, technically, he owned the house. He also offered Kate free run of the RKO prop and furniture departments.

Early one evening in 1951, after most people at the studio had gone home, she showed up at the RKO warehouse. She was wandering down a long aisle, looking over some lamps and vases, she said, when she heard a familiar voice call her name. "Howard? Is that you?" she replied, as a hatted figure in khakis and a white shirt approached her, a figure who might easily have passed for a propman—looking ordinary in every way, except for the handkerchief he held close to his mouth in the dusty hall. They hugged and made small talk, then sat for a moment—she on a plain, wooden chair, he (Kate insisted this was true) on a gold-painted throne. "Howard," she laughed, "I see you haven't lost your flair for the dramatic."

Hughes asked if "everything was right" with her; and Hepburn said it was. She made it clear that both her career and her relationship with Tracy were on track. "There was nothing terribly dramatic about the meeting," Kate recalled, "except that it happened at all, and that by then he was clearly becoming this eccentric figure. He was going around the bend, politically speaking, and, I suppose, in other ways as well. Very anti-Communist."

Hepburn said they were happy to see each other; but, she added, "he seemed sad to me. I remember thinking there was something pathetic about the meeting, that he seemed so . . . detached," she said, at last, reaching for the word. "Howard said I should just tell the warehouse supervisor what I wanted and that it would be delivered in the morning." She thanked him, he left, and, said Kate, "That was the last time I saw him face to face." They did continue to talk, with decreasing frequency; and she got reports of his increasing eccentricity through his doctor, Lawrence Chaffin. During one of Hughes's last calls, he asked Kate what time it was. "Four o'clock," she said, drowsily looking at her clock. "Day or night?" he asked.

And why, "for Pete's sake," Tracy kept asking Kate, was Luddy still in the picture? Like Hughes before him, Tracy didn't understand why this ex-husband still had the license to pop in on them in Fenwick and why Kate had never divorced him properly in a United States courtroom. "I didn't realize until then," Kate later admitted, that "Luddy was a kind of a security blanket for me. And Spence made me see that keeping him in my life like that, I was leading him on. I was still being horribly selfish to him. Not letting him get on with his life." In September 1942, Dr. Hepburn appeared in Superior Court in Hartford on behalf of his daughter, as a judge granted a divorce to Katharine and Ludlow Ogden Smith. Within months, Luddy had taken a second wife.

Only when the Theatre Guild applied its heaviest pressure—which included the threat of a lawsuit—did Hepburn agree to honor her vow to take *Without Love* to Broadway. Neither the play nor the critical response was especially good, but she played sixteen sold-out weeks to thunderous ovations. Increasingly, during those four months, Hepburn realized that the adulation of thousands of people did not mean as much to her as the adoration she sought from one man. Because of her growing devotion to Spencer Tracy, she did not set foot on a legitimate stage for the rest of the decade.

At one point, she thought she might retest the waters, by getting Tracy back to the theater. She arranged for him to meet playwright

178

Robert Sherwood and accompanied him to the East Coast as he agreed to appear in a play at the war's end called *The Rugged Path*. But this overwrought and underthought drama about a newspaperman who goes into battle proved to be an unsatisfactory vehicle, despite Tracy's powerful central performance. He never appeared on stage again.

By then, Tracy considered himself a movie actor and nothing more. Benefiting from the number of stars in military service—Gable, Stewart, Fonda, and Tyrone Power, to name a few—he became one of the major attractions of the decade. He took the lead in at least one picture every year into the 1950s and maintained his following with such wartime efforts as *A Guy Named Joe, The Seventh Cross,* and *Thirty Seconds Over Tokyo.* Hepburn's output during the same period was a mere fraction of that, as she put her personal life—supporting the man she loved—ahead of her career, turning down many good roles along the way.

Her only appearance in all of 1943, for example, was a cameo in *Stage Door Canteen,* a fable of sorts about the sacrifices everybody was making for the war effort. It featured dozens of walk-ons, including Tallulah Bankhead, Helen Hayes, Harpo Marx, and Ed Wynn. Hepburn was asked to deliver the morale-building moral of the film, a pep talk meant to inspire the junior hostesses at the canteen, to say nothing of the largely female audiences across the country. Her only film the next year was in *Dragon Seed,* based on Pearl S. Buck's bestselling novel. As Jade, a Chinese farmer's wife, her high cheekbones allowed her to look only slightly more Asiatic than her costars Walter Huston, Hurd Hatfield, Agnes Moorehead, and Aline MacMahon. In 1946 she appeared in a minor contemporary melodrama—directed by Vincente Minnelli and featuring Robert Taylor and Robert Mitchum—called *Undercurrent.* And the next year she portrayed Clara Wieck Schumann opposite Paul Henreid and Robert Walker, as Robert Schumann and Johannes Brahms, in

Song of Love—another of her lesser pictures. It is one of the few times Hepburn appeared as a mother in the movies, tending to a noisy brood of seven. In the film, she did, however, display genuine virtuosity at the piano, the result of months of practice at a keyboard.

Such was the baloney she sandwiched between her pictures with Spencer Tracy that decade. Even those pictures were mixed in quality. In an effort to recapture the magic that had brought them together in the first place, Hepburn got Tracy to appear in a film version of *Without Love*. Don Stewart, who had successfully translated two other Barry works to the screen for Hepburn, punched up the badinage of the script, knowing he had Hollywood's most skilful sparring partners delivering the lines. This rendition was diverting at best, rather silly and a little slow.

The next Tracy and Hepburn picture digressed even farther from the career path they had set for themselves. *The Sea of Grass,* based on a novel by Conrad Richter, was an intense domestic drama set against the plains of the New Mexico Territory. In the film, Hepburn leaves her rough-hewn cattle baron of a husband to have an affair in Denver with his rival, a lawyer played by Melvyn Douglas. "Nobody ever sets out to make a bad picture," Kate later said of the experience. "We really believed in this. Or, at least, we believed we believed in it." The project came, unfortunately, at a time when Tracy was drinking heavily, spending night after night wending his way from one Hollywood watering hole to another—The Trocadero, Ciro's, The Mocambo, The Players—until he'd pass out, somehow awakening in a room at the Beverly Hills Hotel.

Kate felt working together might get him back on the straight and narrow. She was so eager for the opportunity—which would allow her to monitor his behavior at work as well as at home—she overlooked the fact that "the script just wasn't very good."

Knowing a strong director can occasionally mask a weak script with a lot of style and scenery, producer Pan Berman hired the most promising young director on either coast, Elia Kazan—the enfant terrible from the Group Theatre who had recently triumphed in Hollywood with his film version of *A Tree Grows in Brooklyn*. Unfortunately, upon his arrival at MGM, "Gadg" (short for "Gadget," a nickname he acquired in his youth because he had always been handy and useful, a fixer) Kazan learned that the gritty realism he had hoped to bring to this picture was being overruled. The studio had already decided on Walter Plunkett's fancy costumes and process-screen shots on a soundstage instead of playing scenes on location.

Rather than challenge authority—or quit—Kazan chose to settle into luxurious Malibu surroundings with his family. Before he even began shooting, he threw in the artistic towel and passively directed the piece, giving the studio exactly what it wanted and nothing more. He would return to New York ashamed of the job, only to proceed directly to the works for which he would become justly famous, such Broadway milestones as *A Streetcar Named Desire* and *Death of a Salesman*. Several years later, he would return to Hollywood with more artistic integrity, directing such bold films as *Gentleman's Agreement, Pinky, Viva Zapata!*, and *On the Waterfront*. At the time, Hepburn was grateful just to be working with Tracy on a project that went so smoothly. But in retrospect, she said, "I wish Gadg had put up more of a fight. I argued with him plenty as it was, but he never really engaged . . . and for me that's part of the process of moviemaking. If he had, we'd have had a better picture."

Kate was a lifelong liberal who publicly spoke out against the Communist witch-hunts in the late forties and early fifties; and one day, I had to ask how she felt about Elia Kazan's role as one of the most famous show-business personalities to "name names" during that period. "Look, I can't blame anyone for saying things so that he can keep working," she said. "But when somebody says things that keep other people from working, he has crossed a line. Gadg did just that; and I always felt he could have found a way to move on with his career without hurting others. I felt he was a man of enormous talent but very little character. I felt that during *Sea of Grass,* and I was reminded of that experience during the McCarthy period."

The year after *The Sea of Grass,* Tracy and Hepburn reunited onscreen for more standard fare, *State of the Union.* Ironically, the project had not been intended for either of them. The picture, based on the Pulitzer Prize–winning play by Howard Lindsay and Russel Crouse, was made by Liberty Films, a production company owned in part by the movie's director, Frank Capra. In fact, Capra had envisioned reteaming his award-winning leads from his groundbreaking comedy *It Happened One Night.* Clark Gable was meant to play Grant Matthews, a Republican running for President; and Claudette Colbert was meant to play his estranged wife, Mary, who agrees to stand by his side to boost his chances. When she feels she has lost her husband altogether to a scheming newspaper heiress—masterfully played by Angela Lansbury—Mary blows her top at a dinner, haranguing the politicians present for surrendering their values. Nobody is more affected by her words than Grant. Upon realizing that he has forsaken everything he ever cared about, he withdraws from the race.

MGM would not make Gable available, but they eventually invested in Liberty Films and offered Spencer Tracy instead. Colbert was never thrilled with the material, and up until a few days before shooting was to begin, she threw several deal-breaking conditions at them—including her refusal ever to work after five in the afternoon.

At the eleventh hour, Hepburn stepped in. She announced that she was completely familiar with the script and was prepared to play the role at a moment's notice. "I thought it would be wonderful to work with Capra," she said, "and I'd get to work with Spence again." More to the point, she had seen Tracy preparing himself psychologically for the part, and she feared his disappointment if it were scrapped. Sensing his anxiety, Hepburn felt the downtime would send him around the bend. Hepburn called Colbert, whom she liked on- and off-screen, and said, "Look, Claudette, you should know that they're about to replace you in this picture." Colbert said, "Kate, you're welcome to it."

The film plays to this day—with Hepburn's first name misspelled as "Katherine" in the credits—as a hybrid. The style of sentimental and patriotic "Capra-corn" never completely meshed with the more sophisticated Tracy-Hepburn banter. While the film won no prizes, it reminded audiences then that no two movie actors performed better in tandem than Tracy and Hepburn. The public came to consider it an event whenever they partnered; and *State of the Union* reminded the stars that romantic comedy was their long suit.

With that in mind, Hepburn and Tracy sprang to new heights the next year, in their sixth picture together, again under the direction of George Cukor. *Adam's Rib* is the story of a feminist attorney defending a dumb blonde who has shot her philandering husband. She finds herself coming up against her husband, a bright assistant district attorney who has been assigned to prosecute the case. The script—by Garson Kanin and Ruth Gordon—crackled with repartee in both the bedroom and the courtroom and included some feminist arguments that sound progressive fifty years later. Hepburn, in her early forties, and Tracy, almost fifty, continued to "look good together," as Kate said. Because every line they uttered had been perfectly pitched to their key, they seemed to be providing glimpses of their off-camera life. Occasional unscripted improvisational moments—nicknames, swats on the backside, funny looks at each other—did exactly that. In so doing, Tracy and Hepburn became iconic as a twosome—smart, successful, supportive, and still sexy.

While Hepburn continued to boss people around on the set— questioning any detail that offended her—her motives proved less and less selfish. Since 1941, her primary concern was always Tracy's comfort. He seldom argued with directors—simply delivering his lines, then leaving the set. If he had any strong objections, he never even had to voice them. Kate would fight his battles to the bitter end or until he yanked her chain and called her off.

For all her assertiveness, Kate's interests were what she thought was best for the picture. "Now, I have always felt that moviemaking is about the survival of the fittest, but it's never about just one person," she explained one day in her living room in New York. "It's a collaborative medium, but it's not a democracy. And I always considered myself pretty bright with a good sense of what worked with an audience and what didn't. So I would speak my mind. But after I had my say, I knew to shut up. I listened to the good strong directors . . . and I learned from them. I was smart enough to know that if everybody around me looked good, then I looked good."

There was no better illustration of Hepburn's philosophy than on *Adam's Rib,* especially in the development of one of the supporting characters, the dizzy defendant, Doris Attinger. Hepburn, Tracy, and George Cukor were all besotted with Judy Holliday, an actress making a huge splash on Broadway in Garson Kanin's *Born Yesterday.* Holliday, who had kicked around the theater and even made a few film appearances, brought heart and soul to her role in the hit play, making something unique out of what might have been just another dumb-blonde role. Harry Cohn had secured the film rights of the play as a possible showcase for his leading lady, Rita Hayworth. It had not occurred to him to cast Judy Holliday, whom he never considered glamorous enough to be a film star.

The stars, writers, and director of *Adam's Rib* set out to prove him wrong. Not only did they offer her the role of Doris in their movie but they offered to beef it up, enough so that it would be better than any screen test Harry Cohn might make of her, which he refused to make anyway. While filming Holliday's close-ups in *Adam's Rib,* Hepburn remained on the set even when she was off-camera—a courtesy most big stars seldom extended—to provide moral support. Her generosity didn't end there.

Hepburn suggested to Cukor that in shooting Holliday's key scene, he do some big close-ups of her that wouldn't even end up in the picture. For the rest of the scene, he recommended shooting with Hepburn's back to the camera. "Everybody knew what I looked like," Kate explained. "This way he could 'present' Judy, the way he had presented me in *A Bill of Divorcement*."

Then Hepburn went to Howard Stickling, the publicity director at MGM, who leaked to the press some misinformation she had fed him, tidbits hinting that "Kate and Spencer are certainly burned because Judy Holliday was stealing the picture." Once the rumors began to circulate, Harry Cohn asked if he might see some of the *Adam's Rib* footage. Cukor sent him an entire scene shot and edited—complete with the unnecessary "ravishing" shots of Judy Holliday. Cohn promptly cast her in the role she had created on Broadway, assigned George Cukor to direct, and *Born Yesterday* proved to be one of the great successes of 1950. Competing that year against Gloria Swanson for *Sunset Boulevard* and Bette Davis for *All About Eve* (both in "comeback" roles)—to say nothing of Hepburn, who was not even nominated for *Adam's Rib*—Judy Holliday won the Academy Award as Best Actress. The success of *Adam's Rib* was great enough to let Kate breathe easily for a moment, about both Spencer Tracy and her career.

Putting her work in second place during these years had left Hepburn with a lot of time on her hands. She used many of the spare hours to deepen friendships with several older actresses, especially Ethel Barrymore and Constance Collier. Just because she was not performing so much, she realized, was no reason not to keep practicing. Several hours a week she read and rehearsed the great plays with the great ladies of the theater, especially Miss Collier. Hepburn devoted herself to the role of Rosalind in *As You Like It* for a production the Theatre Guild was mounting. They rehearsed for a few weeks in New York, previewed on the road, then opened at the Cort Theatre at the end of January 1950. The reviews ranged from acceptable to wonderful; and everyone granted that Katharine Hepburn was the only movie star of her caliber working on a stage, performing Shakespeare at that. "I just felt I was getting flabby," Kate said of the experience, "and this toned me up."

Predictably, Tracy sank into a drunken depression. He had the willpower to sober up for his appearances in *Malaya* and *Father of the Bride* (with Elizabeth Taylor playing his daughter); and he visited Hepburn in a few of the towns on her tour. But before her departure and during her run, he was drinking harder than ever, often into a stupor.

Whenever Kate spoke to me about Spencer Tracy, I couldn't help thinking he was a textbook alcoholic and she a classic enabler. It pained me to think of her stuck in a role of such powerlessness. One night, after we had both sipped several Scotches by the fireplace in Fenwick, she told me to "give the fire a kick." Colorful sparks sprayed from the saltwater-soaked logs. As I returned to my chair, I asked, without quite facing her, "Did anyone ever think of Alcoholics Anonymous?"

"Of course," she said. "I did." But she wanted me to understand that AA was quite new and mysterious back then. She spoke of it as smoke-filled little rooms with "winos." "Spencer Tracy was the biggest star in the world," she said, "and I don't think he would have been anonymous there for very long. And news of this sort would have killed his career." Kate said she had investigated several private hospitals, where famous people could dry out in seclusion. "But he could control his drinking when he wanted to control his drinking," she explained. "And as long as it didn't interfere with his work, he didn't think he had a problem. And as long as I was there for him, he seemed to be okay." In fact, during that period when Kate was returning to the stage, he told a few friends that he was trying to clean up his act for fear that she would walk out on him for good.

A little past twelve, I stared into the dying fire and stammered out a question I thought Kate was begging to be asked: "Did he ever— strike you?" As I turned toward her, she looked into the few remaining embers.

"Once," she said.

She proceeded to describe a fiendish night at the Beverly Hills Hotel. While Kate was trying to put Tracy to bed, he smacked the back of his hand across her face. She said he was so drunk she believed he neither knew that he'd done it nor that he'd remember. Dignity prevented her from telling him the next day—not hers so much as protecting his. She made her separate peace, privately forgiving him but never forgetting.

"Did you ever think of walking out?" I asked, our eyes now meeting.

"What would have been the point?" she asked. "I mean, I loved him. And I wanted to be with him. If I had left, we both would have been miserable."

Then I remembered Kate's telling me how uncomfortable Tracy had always been at Fenwick. He found the clannish Hepburns—all well-educated, opinionated, and outspoken—so different from his own family. Additionally, he could never appreciate the simple wonders of nature there and the happy solitude it could provide. And in that moment, when Kate voiced her passion for this deeply troubled man, I realized that she was not, in fact, the victim I had supposed. I saw that she possessed the one trait most long-suffering spouses of alcoholics lacked: She ultimately took care of herself. Indeed, returning to the theater had not been strictly a professional decision. Even with Tracy's periods of boozing and brawling, she had the wherewithal to take her leave and perform Shakespeare. She knew too well that "one man in his time plays many parts," and she had learned to go off—whether it was to Fenwick or to Broadway—and play hers.

"What do you think was Spencer's problem?" Kate asked me that night, as I was putting out the fire, leaning the heavy screens up against the hearth. "Why do *you* think he drank?"

"Oh, Kate, I don't know. I mean, I never met Spencer Tracy. All I could give you is some dime-store psychology."

"Well, you always have an opinion on everything else. I don't see why you don't have one on this particular subject."

"Okay," I said. "Here goes." And I plunged into what I felt was a completely embarrassing monologue.

"I have a sense that Spencer Tracy was raised in a rather tough household with a hard-drinking father, a guy who probably wasn't very happy with his lot in life and took it out on his wife and kids. He probably got drunk and loud and knocked them all around a bit. And he probably told Spencer that nothing he did was right, that he was good for nothing, that he was pretty worthless. And so young Spencer hid out as much as he could in his dreams—dreaming of getting out in the world, of being somebody. And every time he tried to express that, his father squashed him like a bug and said, 'Who do you think you are? Don't you know, you're not very bright, you're not very strong, you're not very good-looking. You're worthless.'

"And yet he held on to the dreamy part of his life and made his way into the theater, where he married the first woman who really smiled upon him. And just when things started to break right for him, his baby came into the world deaf. And so, of course, he thinks, 'My father was right. I *am* worthless. And who did I think I was trying to find any kind of life in the theater with a family?' And so, with his genetic predisposition, he drank, and he kept trying to cut himself off from them. He took up with a lot of women, because that made him feel attractive and powerful for a while, and it put a wedge between him and his wife and children. And it all became a vicious cycle, making his worthlessness a self-fulfilling prophecy. And so he drank some more.

"But he kept hanging on to the dream, and lo and behold, he made it and he made it really big. But because he 'knew' he was worthless, he couldn't attach too much importance to all the fame and fortune that fell upon him. What did the world know? And so while he loved getting lost in his roles, he always felt unjustly rewarded for doing such artistic work, something not quite manly. There seemed to be something wrong with the system, something basically wrong with life, rewarding a worthless wretch like him. And so he drank some more.

"And then you came along, and you were the best and most beautiful creature he had ever seen. You got high on life. And he couldn't quite believe that somebody like you could be interested in somebody like him; and he figured he could never keep up with the likes of you. And so he often tried to tear you down, squash your good nature. He made fun of your family and your endless enthusiasm. He tried to cut you down to size. And when he couldn't do that, he started to realize that maybe he wasn't so worthless to have kept somebody like you hanging in there. But periodically, he'd find that too hard to believe, and so he'd drink some more. Or, you would abandon him. You'd go off on location or go off and do a play. And he'd say to himself, 'See, I told you I was worthless.' And so he'd drink some more.

"But in the end, you both hung in there. And that—not all your movies—remains the most important thing in either of your lives. That's what I think."

And then there was silence.

Kate, poker-faced, just rose from the couch. We turned out the lights and walked up the stairs without saying a word, her bad foot clomping behind on the bare wooden steps. When we reached the top, she came into my bedroom to turn down the bed. By then, she looked stunned, even a little wounded. We hugged good night; and, as she headed for the door, she spoke at last.

"Will you be staying up to write?" she asked.

"I don't think so," I said. "It's pretty late."

"See you in the morning, then," she said, closing the door. "But you should write all that down."

VIII

Guess Who Came

to Dinner

After she had worked twenty-five years as an actor—an astronomical twenty of them as a movie star—the next decade and a half proved to be the most intense in Katharine Hepburn's life and career. Spencer Tracy remained the focus of her attention and the locus of her activity, but she did not spend the fifties shackled to him. She continued to meet his demands, usually serving him before he had to request; she anxiously continued to guard against his drinking and clean up after him when she had not been vigilant; and she did admit to falling asleep one night in the hallway outside the Beverly Hills Hotel room in which he had passed out and from which he had thrown her out. That much, she felt, her love demanded she render. But there she drew the line.

During the next decade Katharine Hepburn also traveled farther—geographically and artistically— than she had at any other time in her life, extending herself physically and emotionally. If anything, the strength of her then decade-long union with Tracy only emboldened her to meet new professional challenges. Practically every role she undertook during this period held greater significance for her than its predecessor.

Maybe I've seen *Born Yesterday* too many times—in which bully Harry Brock slaps his dizzy mistress, Billie Dawn, thereby knocking sense into her; but I got a feeling that Hepburn saw the light the night Tracy struck her. Between 1950 and 1962, as most of the female movie stars of Hepburn's age were being put out to pasture, her choices grew increasingly purposeful; and her work in that period remains at the heart of her vast legacy. Ironically, the years in which she was most "married" proved to be the period in which she truly came into her own.

As You Like It closed for the summer of 1950, giving its star some time off before an autumn tour. She returned to Los Angeles and moved, at George Cukor's suggestion, into Irene Selznick's house in Beverly Hills, a beautiful estate complete with swimming pool, tennis court, projection room, and staff. Around that time, Hepburn also thought Cukor might play landlord himself, by allowing Spencer Tracy to move into his vacant guest cottage at the foot of his property, fronting on St. Ives Drive. The little house was completely without pretense, which she knew Tracy would appreciate. Kate cozied it up, though Tracy kept warning her, "Nothing fancy." Because it was to be his place, she obeyed.

While living at Irene's in true luxury, Hepburn received a call from a producer she had never met, a Polish-born "impresario" named Sam Spiegel. He had a few films to his credit; and Hollywood was full of his type—"Big talk. Big dreams. Big belly," said Kate. He asked if she had read a novel by C. S. Forester (author of the Horatio Hornblower series) called *The African Queen.* The book was, by then, fifteen years old; and she had not. Spiegel said that he was working with John Huston in transporting it to the screen and that the female lead was ideal for her.

Spiegel sent the book over, and Hepburn immediately lit up at the prospect of playing Rosie Sayer, the sister of an English missionary in Africa. Rosie gets tangled up with a cockney engineer, a rummy named Charlie Allnut; and together they navigate a dangerous river in the Congo, plotting to blow up a German warship. Stoking Hepburn's interest, Spiegel met with her to discuss potential costars. They ran through the list of every Englishman they could think of— from Ronald Colman and Errol Flynn to David Niven and James

Mason; but each seemed either too dashing or too elegant. Then Spiegel floated Humphrey Bogart's name, suggesting that they simply make Charlie Canadian.

Having reeled in Hepburn, Spiegel used her as bait to hook the other big fish. "That," said Kate about the vanishing breed who knew how to put big movies together, "is producing." (She delighted in the fact that this self-made man—who loved America with the same passion as the generation of flag-waving film moguls a generation earlier—used a pseudonym, S. P. Eagle. "Now isn't that wonderful?" Kate asked with glee.) What intrigued her most about this project was what would have repelled most other movie stars— especially the prima donnas accustomed to studio pampering—the opportunity to work in the wilds of Africa.

At last, director and cowriter John Huston came to call on his star. Kate found him then and forever "one of the most exasperating creatures I have encountered in my entire life." He was "immensely charming," she said, "and he knew it. And while that should have lessened his charm, it didn't." Hepburn thought he could be a ponderous windbag; and every time she brought up the matter of the unfinished script, Huston dodged the issue with a gale of words. But she also found him spellbinding and talented, especially admiring *The Treasure of the Sierra Madre,* in which he had directed his father, Walter, to an Academy Award. "He had this colossal ego," Kate said of John Huston, "and it was completely and totally absorbing, Somehow, it gave me confidence that he would be able to control all the terribly difficult elements that would go into the making of this picture."

Hepburn finished her run as Rosalind in *As You Like It,* and she still hadn't seen a reworked script of *The African Queen.* Then, just weeks before she was to go abroad, her mother died—at the age of seventy-three, on one of the very days she was visiting her in Hartford. Kate suddenly had perfectly good personal and professional excuses to bow out of this "cockamamie" project being filmed at the ends of the earth. "But," she said, "Mother's death, which was sudden, you see, put things in perspective for me. She was a vital woman with a lot in life that she had still wanted to do. And while this movie seemed like a hopeless mess, I wanted to see Africa, and I wanted to work with Bogie . . . and John Huston." She also felt she could find new dimensions of herself in her strong-willed alter ego, Rosie Sayer.

Sailing for England with Constance Collier and her secretary, Phyllis Wilbourn, Hepburn met in London with her producer and director. She was more anxious than ever to see a shooting script, but Huston just kept assuring her not to worry about it. While he and "S. P. Eagle" went ahead to scout locations, Hepburn left for Italy, where Bogart and his wife, Lauren Bacall, were also vacationing. Spencer Tracy turned up as well, a visit they had choreographed in such a way that neither the press nor the public ever caught on that they were there together. It was a glorious holiday, which ended when she called his hotel room one day, only to learn that he had already departed for London on his own. He had clearly foreseen the inevitable, her leaving for Africa, and didn't want to face it.

Hepburn traveled by plane, wood-burning train, and raft to a makeshift village in Biondo, almost fifty miles from Ponthierville in the Belgian Congo. Her hut of palm and bamboo had none of the conveniences of home. Plumbing was crude at best. The star's most pressing desire upon arrival was to work on the script, which, she learned, remained unfinished.

While quickly adjusting to the hardships of life in the jungle, Hepburn gradually accepted that the only way she'd get through this picture was to rely on the instincts of the man at the helm, Mr. Huston—even though at one point he simply disappeared, having gone on safari, with no indication when he would return.

During the next few months, Hepburn felt "something really wonderful was going on while we were making the movie. I had heard that Bogie was a big drunk, and he did drink plenty while we were there. But he was completely and totally professional on the job. Really wonderful, manly, and yet a true gentleman." She also saw that Huston did have in his head the "big picture" of what *The African Queen* would be, thought out to the smallest detail. She recognized that he was enough in control of his cast and crew to allow all the happy accidents that can occur on a movie set to take place. Indeed, much of what would make *The African Queen* so wonderful was its natural, sometimes spontaneous, quality. "We all took John's cue," Kate said, "and realized that we had to work *with* the bugs and snakes and muck and bad weather, not around them all. To have fought against all the elements would have been futile."

"That picture was one great adventure," Kate said; and it also proved to be one of the great challenges of her life. Despite the genuine hardships, Huston was able to capture all her exhilaration on film. That was largely possible because of a now-legendary piece of direction he gave her. On just the second day of shooting—after Hepburn had played the scene in which she had buried her missionary brother—Huston came to her hut, ostensibly for a cup of coffee. "Without stepping on my toes," Kate later explained, "John gently suggested that he had something to say about my part. I had just played this terribly sad scene. All very solemn. But he didn't think old Rosie was a gloomy creature, you see, and that it would be pretty dreary if she went through the picture that way." In essence, Huston was trying to get her to see the difference between being solemn and being serious.

"Have you ever seen those newsreels of Mrs. Roosevelt," he asked, "where she visited the soldiers in the hospitals?" She had. "All very serious," he said. "But Katie, dear—never grim. Because she always wore that lovely smile. Now you've got this sweet down-turned mouth, Katie, and there seems to be something valiant every time you smile." In the most polite tones, he suggested that Hepburn might adopt Eleanor Roosevelt's demeanor by telling herself, "Chin up, old girl. Things'll get better. Have faith. And always the smile. The society smile."

Huston left the hut without further discussion. He was merely tossing a pebble into a lake. For Hepburn it rippled through every scene of the film, defining her character. "You know," Kate said years later, "people often wonder how directors work. And, of course, every one works differently. But that little bit from John was pure inspiration. It was the best goddamned piece of direction I have ever heard—before or since."

Considering all the surrounding hazards, *The African Queen* proceeded without much incident. Hepburn adored working with Bogart and could not imagine anyone else playing the part. "When you're making a picture," Kate explained, "you really have no idea whether it will please anyone or not. You just do the best you can and pray that somebody else will like it as much as you. But on *African Queen,* we all really felt we were making something special. We knew there had never been anything quite like it before. And Bogie and I, well, we just played well together. I think we both liked each other, and we respected each other." (Another bonus from the experience was the fifty-year friendship that evolved between Hepburn and Lauren Bacall. "She's a good girl," Kate often said about her, having admired the way she looked after Bogart and the way she looked after herself. "Great fun," she said, "and she loves to work"—two qualities Hepburn always prized.)

Only toward the end of the location shooting did Hepburn and several members of the crew become extremely sick to their stomachs. The malady was doubly difficult for her because she had scoffed at her director and leading man throughout the shoot for imbibing so much liquor while she had temperately stuck to bottled water. At last, the company doctor determined that the bottled water she had been drinking was nothing more than that—impure water in bottles—while the Bogart-Huston liquid diet had been germ-free—"or at least strong enough to kill any bug that might have gotten inside them." By the time they had completed their filming in Africa, Hepburn had lost twenty pounds. The company moved on to six weeks of shooting at a studio in London, where she was met by Spencer Tracy and put under a doctor's care.

The African Queen was released just before year's end and became a huge hit among critics and fans. Facing stiff competition that year, Bogart would receive his only Academy Award. Hepburn would receive her fifth Oscar nomination but lose to Vivien Leigh for *A Streetcar Named Desire*. Fifty years later, the American Film Institute would conduct a survey among filmmakers, critics, and historians, asking them to select the greatest screen legends of the century. Bogart and Hepburn—who never worked together again—were the number-one choices.

Back in California that fall, Hepburn leased a secluded house above the Beverly Hills Hotel (where she often came down to play tennis, sometimes with "Big Bill" Tilden; other times she played with Chaplin on his nearby court). By then, Tracy had settled into George Cukor's guest cottage. The two stars happily reunited, in life and on the screen, this time in another comedy by Garson Kanin and Ruth Gordon, again directed by Cukor.

Pat and Mike was Hepburn's favorite of the nine films they made together. This story of a plodding sports promoter who takes on a prodigious female athlete was the most feminist in its attitudes, one of the few films that believably allows the female of the species to demonstrate her physical superiority. In so doing, it allowed Hepburn to show off her athletic prowess—her running, swimming, golfing, basketball, and tennis skills. At forty-five, Hepburn had the body of a woman twenty years younger. "Not much meat on her," Mike says of Pat, "but what's there is cherce."

Tracy, hoary and paunchy, was at times looking at least ten years older than his age, then fifty-two.

The plot of *Pat and Mike* veers into implausability from the start, with Pat's losing her concentration every time her dull fiancé appears at one of her competitions. But that silliness had the positive effect of making light of what were strong feminist images for the Eisenhower-era audience, which liked to view women as happy homemakers. For further box-office appeal, George Cukor resorted to a lot of stunt casting, including such well-known athletes of the day as Babe Didrikson Zaharias, Gussie Moran, and Don Budge. The picture became one of the team's most critically acclaimed and popular. Tracy hoped it might mark Hepburn's return to Hollywood for a good while.

But she had her eye on the road again. While she had been in London, she had met with some producers to discuss a production of George Bernard Shaw's *The Millionairess*—a role the playwright had hoped a decade earlier that Hepburn might perform. Epifania— a rich, spoiled heiress, the capitalistic incarnation of the Shavian Life Force—suddenly appealed to Hepburn. As she would literally throw over one silly suitor (Cyril Ritchard) for another, a brainy Egyptian doctor (Robert Helpmann), the role demanded that she perform all sorts of strenuous physical business while spouting pages of dialogue in practically every scene of the play. "I always found her too bossy and without much humor," Kate said, by way of explaining why she had long resisted the part. "Now, I never really minded the bossy part, but I didn't like her being so serious. Once I found a way to make her more fun, I thought this could be a splendid role for me. And I think every actress should get to play Shaw, and so few realize that. I think old GBS liked me because I was agile—I was quick on my feet and quick with words, and you really need to be both if you're going to play any of his women. I'm sorry I came around to his work too late to have played Ann in *Man and Superman,* because it's a great part and I think I could have done a good job with her. Mother, of course, knew every word of Shaw backward and forward, and he was so much a part of our growing up. That's probably why I rediscovered him so late in life"—alas, after Kit Hepburn had died.

Hepburn's performance would have done her mother proud. Critics in London (and later in New York, when the Theatre Guild brought the production to Broadway) agreed that *The Millionairess* was second-rate Shaw and that Hepburn often worked too hard playing to the second balcony. But nobody denied that it was an entertaining, often thrilling, tour de force. Audiences raved.

Spencer Tracy brooded. Not only was he in one of the few sloughs in his career—slogging through several forgettable pictures—but, once again, he felt abandoned. George Cukor told me that "whenever Kate was gone, he was like a sulky little boy." During Hepburn's run in *The Millionairess* and his filming *The Plymouth Adventure,* a lugubrious look at the Pilgrims coming over on *The Mayflower,* he indulged in an affair with his leading lady, Gene Tierney, the haunting star of *Laura* and one of the most stunning faces ever to appear onscreen.

Kate never mentioned the Gene Tierney affair to me, though others did. It obviously coincided with this new era in Hepburn's career, the start of their second decade together, when she seemed to be making up for lost time and lost parts. Hepburn was still prepared to sacrifice almost anything for Spencer Tracy; but she was not willing to throw in the towel on her career. She worked tirelessly, for example, with Preston Sturges —"truly brilliant man, unfortunately a terrible drinker"—trying to transcribe *The Millionairess* into a film. "I think he wrote one of the funniest scripts I have ever read," Kate said, "a real gem." But even after agreeing to work for nothing and to pay Sturges out of her own pocket to direct, she couldn't find anybody to underwrite the project. "Here was a man who had directed a half dozen of the cleverest comedies ever made, and in his mid-fifties, nobody would hire him," Kate said. "And let's face it," she added, "this was another rough patch in my career. People liked me enough when I had a picture out there, but studios were courting a new generation of stars"—Elizabeth Taylor, Doris Day, Marilyn Monroe, and Audrey Hepburn (who was not a relation), to name a few. At the same time, Joan Crawford was scrambling for parts in a few anemic melodramas; and after *All About Eve* in 1950, Bette Davis found herself in but nine pictures for the rest of the decade, her former output for a typical year or two in her heyday. *The Millionairess* would not become a film until 1960, when Sophia Loren would play the lead opposite Peter Sellers, in a bastardization that bore virtually no resemblance to anything Shaw ever wrote.

Tracy revived his career by going to Arizona for what would become an Oscar-nominated performance in a provocative film called *Bad Day at Black Rock*. Around that same time, Hepburn realized that there was a way to bring balance to her life by remaining true to Tracy and being choosy about her work, selecting only important roles. In the summer of 1954, she went abroad again, this time to etch one of her most unforgettable performances.

David Lean, a former film editor who had graduated to directing *Brief Encounter, Great Expectations,* and *Oliver Twist,* was in Venice making a contemporary drama, largely his own adaptation of Arthur Laurents's play *The Time of the Cuckoo.* Retitled *Summertime* (*Summer Madness* in Great Britain), it tells the story of Jane Hudson, a middle-aged spinster from the Midwest, who has packed all her romantic hopes up for a holiday in Venice. There she falls in love with a shopkeeper, only to learn that he is married and has several children. He leads her past her inhibitions, enough to spend a few days of passion together on the nearby isle of Burano. In time, she realizes their relationship is finite, that she must return home; but she is a changed woman.

Much of the film is David Lean's valentine to Venice, stunning shots of canals and bridges and the glories of the Piazza di San Marco. But the city never outshines its star. Weaving through the most gorgeous movie set in the world, Lean also photographed Katharine Hepburn—lonely at first, later in love—in ways nobody had before. Almost fifty, there were times she looked her age—still beautiful, but not glamorized—with lines on her face, her hair unfashionably pulled back, with scarcely a touch of make-up. Because Lean was a perfectionist about the composition of every frame of his pictures, Hepburn had never felt more challenged by a director, often having only a moment, in which a cloud was about to blow over or the sun would be ducking between buildings, in which to reach some acting crescendo.

Lean's direction made Hepburn feel safe enough to plumb previously unexplored depths. Her performance as Jane Hudson is the most neurasthenic but naturalistic she ever gave. Before a setting sun, when she speaks of love with her inamorato—suavely played by Rossano Brazzi—her voice displays a vulnerability and raw sexuality never heard before. In our conversations, Hepburn always seemed slightly uncomfortable talking about this picture, self-conscious; she got embarrassed whenever I noted that her performance stood apart from the rest of her work. Upon my suggesting that of all her roles, this one might have been the most self-revealing, Kate quickly diverted the conversation, crediting her director for her characterization. "I've never worked with anybody in my entire career who understood film, really understood it, the feel of it, better than David," Kate said. "I honestly think film editors, whose senses are so alive to the impact of the images, make the best directors."

Or Kate would retell the most famous chestnut about the making of *Summertime,* the story of the scene in which Jane Hudson, taking a home movie, falls backwards into a canal. The Venetian waterways were, of course, famously polluted; and Hepburn took every precaution before shooting the scene, putting lotion all over her body and even antiseptic unguents on a small cut on one of her fingers. As soon as Lean got his shot, she immediately bathed and gargled with disinfectant. But it never occurred to her to wash out her eyes; and the next morning the whites had turned crimson. A staph infection plagued her for the rest of her life, causing her to tear. "But it's a cute moment," Kate said, "—fun," as though that made it all worthwhile. Hepburn's performance earned her sixth Academy Award nomination, but that year's Oscar went to Anna Magnani, in *The Rose Tattoo,* who was a few years Kate's junior. The other nominees that year—Susan Hayward, Jennifer Jones, and Eleanor Parker— were all ten to fifteen years younger.

During Hepburn's absence, Tracy's behavior reverted to its most self-destructive. In preparing to work on a picture that would later be called *Tribute to a Bad Man,* he had a brief but not-so-private affair with his intended costar, Grace Kelly. Instead of running back to him, Hepburn kept pursuing her career. She spent the summer of 1955 in Australia with her friend Robert Helpmann and the Old Vic Company performing *Measure for Measure, The Taming of the Shrew,* and *The Merchant of Venice*—earning serious plaudits. Shortly after shooting began on *Tribute to a Bad Man,* Tracy went missing in action. While he was still off on a drunken tear, the studio replaced him with James Cagney.

After her Australian tour—which theatergoers there remembered with enormous fondness a half century later—Hepburn felt ready to come home. "I suppose I had to prove something—to myself," Kate later reflected. "I felt I had reached out as an actress and felt more fulfilled. And so I wanted to reach out to Spence. I knew that he had to help himself, but I also knew that I could help him too—once I had fortified myself." Having been more apart than together in the last few years, Hepburn privately vowed from then on to share their lives as much as the vagaries of show business would allow. Having climbed her own personal summit, she went on location with Tracy to the French Alps, where he filmed *The Mountain* with Robert Wagner. When the film was being completed on the Paramount backlot, Hepburn again felt it was safe to accept what became another of her trademark roles, in a Paramount picture shooting on a neighboring stage.

Not unlike her part in *Summertime,* Lizzie Curry in N. Richard Nash's hit play *The Rainmaker* is a spinster. She lives with her father and two brothers on a drought-plagued farm in the Southwest. Enter Starbuck, a conman who promises to make rain for the vast sum of $100. Although Lizzie resists Starbuck's charms at first, and discourages her father from buying into the scheme, she gradually succumbs to him, becoming a more fulfilled woman for it.

Starbuck was played by Burt Lancaster, then the hottest actor in town. He had recently taken Hollywood by storm in *Come Back, Little Sheba, From Here to Eternity, The Rose Tattoo,* and *Trapeze.* His own independent production company had produced the Best Picture of 1955, *Marty.* Kate found him "a most peculiar man, full of unexpected rushes of energy" and felt she never connected with him. But that blind acceptance fit right into her role. She received another Oscar nomination, clearly finding a place in the hearts of Academy members, critics, and the public in playing love-starved spinsters.

"Did you have a maiden aunt in mind when you took on these roles?" I asked Kate one day during a walk in Fenwick.

"Well, of course, there was my Aunt Edith," she said, "but I wasn't playing her. With Lizzie Curry and Jane Hudson and Rosie Sayer— I was playing me. It was never difficult for me to play those women . . . because I'm the maiden aunt."

In the midst of this third flowering in her career, Hepburn got snookered into what she would always consider the worst film on her resume. Spencer Tracy discreetly accompanied her to London, where Bobby Helpmann had induced her into costarring with him in a film called *The Iron Petticoat*. It was a knockoff of "Ninotchka," with Hepburn playing a coldhearted captain in the Russian Air Force who spars with an American pilot about communism, only to warm up to the comforts of capitalism. Her leading man was to be Bob Hope!

Hepburn knew that going in; but with a script by Ben Hecht that was witty enough, she felt safe. She did not know that Bob Hope was, as she later recounted, "the biggest egomaniac with whom I have worked in my entire life." Nor did she know that he would immediately turn the picture "into his cheap vaudeville act with me as his stooge." Hope brought in his own team of writers to punch up his lines, and he shamelessly ad-libbed. "I had been sold a false bill of goods," Kate explained. "I was told that this was not going to be a typical Bob Hope movie, that he wanted to appear in a contemporary comedy. That proved not to be the case." Kate claimed never to have seen the finished product.

She atoned for her sin by accompanying Tracy to Cuba, where he was to film *The Old Man and the Sea* for director Fred Zinnemann. Before the production team was summoned home to Hollywood, under the helm of a different director, John Sturges, Hepburn and Tracy were able to squeeze in some pleasant vacation time together. Although she never cared much for restaurants, gambling, or clubs, she allowed herself to go out on the town with Tracy and sample Havana's nightlife. By day, they both painted a lot, with Kate taking up watercolors. For all the sincerity of Tracy's performance in the film, it proved to be a sluggish exercise, taking almost as long to watch as to read the book.

So upon its completion, it came as something of a relief when Twentieth Century–Fox asked Tracy and Hepburn to reteam. The vehicle they had in mind was a tepid reworking by Henry and Phoebe Ephron of a play called *The Desk Set,* to be directed by one of Fox's contract directors. It meant the stars could work together again for the first time in five years in their most public-pleasing genre—romantic comedy.

Desk Set was the story of Bunny Watson, the know-it-all head of the reference department of a large television network who comes up against Richard Sumner, the inventor of a huge electronic brain, which is about to render Bunny and her colleagues obsolete. In the end, humanity prevails, and Bunny winds up in Sumner's arms. It was a hybrid of the early Tracy-Hepburn films and the later Hepburn-as-spinster films—appearing, as she does once again, with her hair pulled back and pinned up tight. As such, *Desk Set* is little more than an amiable one hundred minutes of romantic comedy, with a moral that addressed a new fear of its time, that of machines taking the jobs of people. Hepburn was grateful for the opportunity to work with Tracy in an eighth film.

Most actors worry that each job will be their last. Spencer Tracy's deteriorating health offered good reason for him to believe as much. In his mid-fifties, he increasingly spoke of retirement, repeatedly saying, "I really don't need this anymore." Intent upon looking after him, Hepburn knew such idleness would surely hasten his deterioration. She believed more than ever that work—the harder the better—was the essence of life. She kept an ear open for new projects for him; and she could not resist an invitation for herself. The Shakespeare Festival Theatre in Stratford, Connecticut, asked her to appear in *The Merchant of Venice* and *Much Ado About Nothing* that summer. The great Yiddish actor Morris Carnovsky played Shylock to her Portia, and Alfred Drake played Benedick to her Beatrice. Even more than her deservedly good reviews, Katharine Hepburn continued to be the only Hollywood headliner of her day willing to risk her reputation by tackling Shakespeare.

Although Stratford was a short drive from Fenwick, Hepburn chose to live that summer in a red fishing shanty right on the Housatonic River. She remembered it as "the happiest summer of my life"—waking up at dawn to see the local fishermen, swimming in the river and biking through the country, performing Shakespeare to packed houses every night. During our weekend jaunts through Connecticut, we'd periodically drive by the site of the old shack and she would stare longingly at other little houses built on other rivers throughout the state. I knew she was remembering that summer of 1957. I realized that while she enjoyed the perquisites of fame and having more money than she ever needed, her supreme ambition was to be an actress, a player who took her work seriously and was appreciated.

That winter, Hepburn and the Stratford company took *Much Ado About Nothing* on the road. Although she always had a chauffeur, she liked taking the wheel, driving herself and Phyllis Wilbourn—who, upon the death of Constance Collier, had joined her "family." During a rehearsal of the play one afternoon, Kate was standing in the wings while Alfred Drake was running some lines. Phyllis, she was startled to notice, was standing there herself, murmuring all the lines to herself. "Oh bliss!" remembered Kate of the moment.

In the summer of 1960 Hepburn would rejoin the Stratford company. She appeared as Viola in *Twelfth Night,* opposite Robert Ryan, another Hollywood player testing his mettle, whom she greatly admired. She fulfilled another commitment she had made to herself—and to Constance Collier—by starring in *Antony and Cleopatra,* playing what they both considered the greatest of the Shakespearean heroines.

Life back in Hollywood proved every bit as dramatic as it was onstage, as Hepburn kept returning to Tracy—a man who had, of late, been raging like Lear and drinking like Falstaff. She used her influence with John Ford—then nursing his dream of ending up in Ireland with Kate—in getting him to cast Tracy in *The Last Hurrah,* a film based on a novel drawn from the career of Mayor James

Curley, the legendary political boss from Boston. During the production and afterward, Hepburn assumed her role as loyal spouse, smoothing all the rough waters on the set, turning Tracy's dressing room into a homey apartment, taking long weekend walks with him along the beach.

The next year, while Tracy was preparing for the Clarence Darrow–like character in *Inherit the Wind,* Hepburn assumed the most iconoclastic role of her career—the bizarre Violet Venable in *Suddenly, Last Summer.* It came nearly a decade after *The African Queen,* with Sam Spiegel's reapproaching the star, this time with the rights to Tennessee Williams's controversial play, what had been one act of a double-bill called *Garden District.* Gore Vidal was adapting this nightmarish story of a rich young man named Sebastian Venable, whose strange and sudden death has traumatized his beautiful young cousin, a witness to his grotesque demise. The imperious mother of the deceased goes to great lengths to protect her family name, to the extent of offering a million dollars to a hospital to perform a lobotomy on the babbling niece, to keep her from remembering any sordid details of cousin Sebastian's final moments. Resorting instead to truth serum, a neurosurgeon uncovers the fact that Sebastian has used his cousin to lure young men, as he had formerly used his beautiful mother; and on this occasion, the scheme backfired, inciting a pack of boys to kill him. The play had been one of the most controversial in years, no simple pouring of tea and sympathy but a dark brew of the barely speakable—homosexual procurement, even cannibalism, with plenty of Oedipal undertones stirred in.

"I felt Tennessee Williams was the greatest living playwright at the time," Kate said, "—brilliant and full of poetry. And I knew it would be a challenge to perform many of his speeches. But I thought he was a truly tragic figure, and this play showed that. I remember reading it and thinking this man keeps going farther and farther 'out there,' and one day he won't be able to come back." She found the part of Mrs. Venable "fascinating, showy, and tricky." She agreed to appear in Spiegel's production but asked for changes that would tone down the material, to keep it from being "cheap and sensational." All smiles, Spiegel even dropped George Cukor's name as a possible director.

He chose Joe Mankiewicz instead; and he surrounded Hepburn with two of the most high-strung stars of the day—Elizabeth Taylor to play the niece and Montgomery Clift to play the brilliant doctor. "The entire production was a nightmare," Kate said, "—from day one." Clift had recently been in a car accident that had slightly disfigured his beautiful looks; he was on pain medication and was what Kate called "a psychological basket case." Taylor seemed to be ailing through much of the shoot herself and made a point of being the last to arrive on the set every day. "There's nothing more frustrating than wanting to work and not being able to," Kate observed in talking about Miss Taylor. "It's the rudeness I minded, keeping people waiting when they're all ready to go. Not just the other actors, but the crew . . . and the people paying the bills." Unlike herself, Hepburn felt that Taylor "preferred being a movie star to being an actress. But don't be fooled," she added, "because I think she is a brilliant actress, truly brilliant. Especially with the Williams stuff. Look at her performance as Maggie the Cat [in *Cat on a Hot Tin Roof*]."

For most of what she remembered as "a completely miserable experience," she blamed the director. "Joe Mank had nothing to offer me in the way of direction, and he spent most of his time with Monty and Elizabeth, and not in a way that I felt was productive. He was absolutely cruel to Monty—tormenting him when he was clearly having a hard time. And rather than try to help him, he just kept beating him down. He was even worse with Elizabeth. I thought he sensationalized her part, had her posing unnecessarily. And it was simply vulgar. Some directors love to work with actors, to play with them. I don't think Joe really liked actors. He felt quite superior to them, and I think got great pleasure out of demeaning them. Some actors need to be treated that way."

Hepburn did not. On the last day of filming, after the last take of her last scene, she turned to her director and asked, "So that's it? I'm finished?"

"You're finished," Mankiewicz said. "And you're marvelous. It's just great."

"But you're sure you're finished with me? You don't need any close-ups or reshoots?"

"I'm sure," he said. "Your work is finished here."

"You're absolutely sure?"

Mankiewicz again assured her there was nothing more for her to do on the picture. With that, Hepburn turned to the director and said, "Well, then, goodbye." Then, she said, in front of the cast and crew, she spat in his face and walked off the set. Mankiewicz later confirmed the story, except he said she spat at his feet. Irene Selznick, a stickler for accuracy, also told me that it was at his feet . . . and that Kate then marched to Sam Spiegel's office and bade him a similar farewell.

In truth, there were probably a few more reasons that *Suddenly, Last Summer* had been such a miserable experience for Hepburn. For one, she never felt completely comfortable with the raw substance of the play. And though she never mentioned it to me, I thought more than once that it could not have been easy for her to be appearing in a motion picture in which for the first time she was not, strictly speaking, the female lead. There she was playing an exotic mother-figure alongside an erotic beauty, then considered not only the most glamorous woman but also the hottest commodity in Hollywood. The Academy would nominate Hepburn for the eighth time as Best Actress, alongside Taylor. The picture became a great success, a trailblazer in breaking taboos and bringing a new frankness to the screen.

The entire experience was enough to put Hepburn off making any more movies. She rededicated herself over the next few years to Tracy, who continued to age rapidly. While succumbing to binges less often, he continued to drink steadily. He gained weight; he developed ulcers and skin cancers; his energy waned. Like him, Kate smoked cigarettes and shared his diet of red meat and ice-cream sundaes. But she remained fit by playing tennis regularly at the Beverly Hills Hotel and swimming in George Cukor's pool. She maintained a separate residence—a favorite among her many rented houses, this one a former home of John Barrymore, the Aviary, up on Tower Grove Drive in Beverly Hills. As often as possible, she dragged Tracy out for walks around the Franklin Canyon Reservoir or on the beach at Malibu, where they liked to fly kites.

Hepburn still believed work was the best tonic for each of them and was grateful every time an opportunity presented itself to Tracy—even if it meant shooting on location, which had become difficult for him. Despite the additional strains on her, she accompanied him to Hawaii in 1960 and sat with him on the set of *The Devil at 4 O'Clock*. The next year she accompanied him to Germany, where he filmed *Judgment at Nuremberg* for producer-director Stanley Kramer. She had pressed hard for him to accept the role as the presiding judge not only because she knew it was too good for him to pass up but also, as she explained, "I couldn't bear the thought of watching somebody else in that part, especially delivering that long verdict in the picture"—practically a fifteen-minute speech. "Who else," Kate asked, "could have done it?"

By 1962 a seemingly irresistible offer came to Hepburn and Tracy. A television producer in New York had a small budget with which to film a production of Eugene O'Neill's *Long Day's Journey Into Night*. The playwright's autobiographical tragedy depicted the

Tyrone family during the course of a day and night in 1912—two sons and their father, a former Irish-American matinee idol, and their mother, a faded beauty who has become addicted to morphine. Kate thought the O'Neill play was "the greatest this country has ever produced" and that the aging mother, Mary, was "the most challenging female role in American drama." The raging father, James, Sr., was no less formidable—so daunting that Tracy did not seriously consider it for a moment. "I think he would have been brilliant," Kate insisted; and she suggested at first that she thought he didn't feel "up to the physical challenge." Later she implied that material as profound as that made Tracy so self-conscious that he doubted his ability to master it. Even though he knew the film was to be shot back east, he felt Hepburn must not let this opportunity pass her by. He sent her off with his blessing.

Sidney Lumet, a young director who had already demonstrated a flair for adapting heavy drama from the stage to the screen, surrounded Hepburn with three superb actors. Jason Robards, Jr., and Dean Stockwell played the emotionally afflicted sons, and Ralph Richardson the beguiling but paralyzing father. The thrill for Hepburn came in rehearsing with the talented company for three weeks, before moving onto their sets at a studio in Manhattan and a dowager Victorian house on City Island in the Bronx. Because of the subtle transitions of emotion throughout the play, it was filmed largely in sequence, an unusual practice.

Except for Spencer Tracy, Hepburn never spoke of an actor more glowingly than she did of Sir Ralph Richardson. "He was mad as a hatter—until he got inside somebody else's character," she observed. "What was so thrilling about this performance," she noticed in their scenes together, "was that his character never lost his charm, not even in his most horrible moments."

Kate believed her work in *Long Day's Journey Into Night* was the best she ever did on screen. It was one of the few performances I ever heard her brag about—for both taking it on and pulling it off. Once, when a mutual friend of ours was raving about the performance Constance Cummings gave in the same role in a television production of the play, Kate listened politely for a few minutes of his gushing, then said, "All right, that's quite enough."

At the end of shooting, there was a small wrap party—supper and a few musicians—which Hepburn attended. Kate was talking to Richardson's wife, actress Meriel Forbes, known as Mu, when he came over and asked his costar to dance. "Oh, Ralph," she said, begging off (pronouncing his name in the Irish fashion, "Rafe"), "I haven't danced in years." But Mu encouraged her to step out onto the floor with him. For a number or two they tripped the light fantastic until, at last, the music stopped—at which point Richardson held her by the shoulders and stared into her eyes. "I say," he said with a look of astonishment on his face, as though seeing her for the first time, "you're a very attractive woman!"

"Mad as a hatter!" Kate howled, after telling the story. "But brilliant. Maybe the best of those boys"—meaning Olivier, Gielgud, and Richardson.

Hepburn received her ninth Academy Award nomination for her portrayal of Mary Tyrone but lost to Anne Bancroft in *The Miracle Worker*, a performance she had admired immensely on Broadway. Then she disappeared from the stage and screen for the next five years—far and away the longest time she had been out of the public eye since embarking on her career in 1928.

"I never talk about that period," Kate had said to me during my first visit to Turtle Bay, referring to 1962–1967. Over the years she did—but only to reveal that it was an extremely quiet time in her life, sad but satisfying. Her father, who had married his nurse just months after the death of his wife, died in 1962 at the age of eighty-two after a few years of pain and a general diminution of his faculties. Although a generation younger, Spencer Tracy was beginning to decline into a similar health pattern. Keeping a tank of oxygen close at hand became more necessary than precautionary, and his kidneys were slowly failing; he was hospitalized for a pulmonary edema and a prostatectomy; he was chronically fatigued. After one medical emergency at a house she rented at Trancas Beach, Hepburn accompanied Tracy in an ambulance to the hospital, called Louise Tracy, then disappeared before the press arrived. Even then, Tracy chose not to recuperate at home with his wife but rather in his cottage on the Cukor property. Kate moved in to nurse him back to health.

In 1963 Stanley Kramer induced Tracy into a few weeks of work, playing the dramatic foil to dozens of comedians in *It's a Mad, Mad, Mad, Mad World.* Aside from that, he and Hepburn contented themselves with quiet pursuits: reading ("Spence always loved his dime novels, his mysteries, but he began reading some big, serious novels too. Even poetry. Yeats."); listening to music ("He liked jazz but was listening to classical music. Beethoven symphonies. Schumann."); and they both painted a lot. "We were just quite happy being quiet together. Truth be told," Kate revealed after I had been coming to Fenwick for about five years, "not much to say about those years. We just loved each other. Nothing more to say."

One early afternoon in late July 1984, Kate and I were in the backyard at Fenwick, weeding one of the flowerbeds, when Phyllis came running out of the house. She had just taken a call from "Mr. Jackson" and said he would be calling back in five minutes. "I must go in to take that call," Kate said. "You keep weeding."

A few minutes later she returned, stood over me, and said, "Guess who's coming to dinner."

I didn't put two and two together, until she said, "Michael."

Kate had met Michael Jackson in the summer of 1979, when she filmed *On Golden Pond* on Squam Lake in New Hampshire. Jane

Fonda—who, Kate said, "wanted to do the film with her father to work out her life's problems with him"—had invited the pop star to the New England location, then all but disappeared when he arrived. Feeling sorry for him—having come all that way only to be abandoned in the woods—Kate befriended him.

"He fascinated me," she said. "He's an absolutely extraordinary creature. He's worked his entire life, entertaining professionally since he was three, and he's never lived a single moment, I mean not a moment, in the real world. He doesn't know how to do anything but write his songs and thrill an audience. He's this strange artistic creature, living in a bubble, barely touched by anything in the outside world." Kate had been quite stern with Michael one morning in New Hampshire, when she discovered that he had not made his bed, then was stupefied to learn that he didn't know how. "He had never made a bed in his life!" she exlaimed. "He's E. T.!"

Over the next few years, Kate and Michael cultivated a friendship. She invited him to dinner when he was in New York City; and he reciprocated with tickets to his concerts. She showed up at one of his events at Madison Square Garden (with Phyllis in tow); and a lot of pictures of the two stars together were snapped that night. Frankly, it was a good photo opportunity for each of them. Kate didn't really care much for the music, but she thought he was a masterful showman—"a great dancer," she said, "with a cute little backside."

Alas, Katharine Hepburn and Michael Jackson didn't have a lot to talk about. So, I didn't even have to invite myself to dinner the following week. Kate said, "I don't think I can do this alone." She wouldn't have to. With Michael Jackson at the peak of his fame, tickets for his upcoming "Victory Tour" performances at Madison Square Garden being scalped for $700 apiece, and "Michael Mania" in the air, she would have no difficulty rustling up guests for a private dinner. (Kate called Irene Selznick that week, ostensibly to get a doctor's name but really to drop that of her upcoming dinner guest. Uninvited, Irene did ask me a little longingly who was to be at the dinner, and she insisted I remember every detail.) Kate invited her niece Katharine Houghton, who had become friendly with Michael as well, and Cynthia McFadden. We were all told to keep the event under wraps.

As the night approached, it occurred to Kate that perhaps Michael had something personal to discuss with her. And so she told Cynthia and me that we were invited for drinks . . . and if she signaled us to leave when dinner was being served then—as she said—we "would have to blow." Fair enough.

We were all in our places in the living room at 244 East Forty-ninth Street a few minutes before six that evening—Kate in her chair, the others seated around the room, while I tended the fire. (Yes, even on hot summer nights a fire was necessary, to compensate for the air-conditioning, which Kate cranked up.) Nobody was more excited than Norah, who had been anxious for days. Because there might be as many as six of us for dinner, it had been decided that we would eat downstairs in the dining room—a rare occurrence. As she carried up the tray of whiskey and glasses, she was visibly nervous. "Norah, you must calm down," Kate said. "We've had dinner guests before."

"But Miss Hepburn," she protested, "this is Michael Jackson. He's the greatest staaa—I mean, the second greatest star in the world!"

Moments later the doorbell rang, and Norah ran down to answer the door. "Now, don't wet yourself!" Kate called out. Norah was hardly listening. In a moment our visitor had ascended the staircase.

He was wearing sunglasses and a satiny blue uniform trimmed in gold braid. Onstage, it would probably look dazzling. Up close it looked flimsy and gaudy, like something Professor Harold Hill might have sold to some boys in Iowa along with some tin trombones. Kate held out her hand to him, apologized for not standing because of her bad foot; and he leaned over to kiss her on the cheek. They were happy to see each other. Kate introduced us all, and Michael found a place on the couch, at Kate's immediate right.

I found it difficult to take my eyes off him—not because he was a star, but because he looked so unusual. His body was even slighter than pictures suggested; his skin was taut and a beautiful tawny shade; his nose, with its tiny bridge, bore little resemblance to any other I had ever seen. At twenty-five, he had the demeanor of an extremely polite ten-year-old. He spoke in a gentle voice, full of sweetness and wonder.

"Is it too bright in here?" Kate asked her guest. He said no.

"Well, then, Michael, you really must take off your sunglasses, so that I can see your eyes. If you don't, then I'll have no idea where you're looking." He reluctantly obeyed. "I think you wear your sunglasses far too much," she continued. "It can't be very good for your eyes, and in the getups you wear, it's hardly as if you go anywhere unrecognized. So let us see your eyes. They're the window to your soul."

After a moment of silence, I asked if I could fix Michael something to drink. Kate interjected that Michael didn't drink alcohol and asked what he wanted—"Juice, soda, fizzy water, plain water, tea, 'funny' tea?" He wanted nothing. "Are you sure?" Kate asked, then ran through the entire menu again. "Nothing, thank you," he said sweetly, then sank back into silence. Having had her glass of grapefruit juice, Kate handed me her glass to be filled with Scotch and soda, tossing me a look that suggested this was going to be a bumpy night.

For the next few minutes, everybody took a turn at trying to get the ball rolling, but the best our guest could muster were monosyllabic answers to perfunctory questions. Thinking we might have appeared to him like the Inquisition, Cynthia and Kathy and I peeled off into our own private conversation. But we could all overhear that it was rough sledding for Kate, left alone to chat with him. We were drawn back into their conversation when Michael raised Charlie Chaplin's name. Kate said she knew him a bit and had played tennis with him but that Michael should really talk to Phyllis. Constance Collier had been a great friend of Chaplin, she explained, and Phyllis had spent a lot of time with him. "Yes, that's true," Phyllis said. "He was very amusing."

And that was it. Conversation ground to a complete halt. "Thank you very much, Miss Phyllis, for enlightening us with those fascinating comments," said Kate.

I asked Michael if he liked movies, and he sparked to that subject. Oh yes, he assured me. He spent most of his afternoons and nights watching videos of old movies. Katharine Hepburn, he said, was his favorite movie star. "Mine too," I said. "And which of Kate's pictures are your favorites?" He turned to me with the sweetest smile; and, with what looked like heavily made-up eyes glowing right into mine, he said, "I'm not sure."

I told him my favorite was *The Philadelphia Story*. He said he had not heard of that one. "What about *Holiday* or *Bringing Up Baby?*"— vintage comedies that I thought would appeal to a video junkie. He didn't recognize those titles either. Trying the other end of the spectrum, I asked if he had seen *Long Day's Journey* or *The Lion in Winter*. No, he didn't know those. *The African Queen*?

"Is that the one in Africa?" he asked. Never saw it.

"*On Golden Pond*," I said assuredly—after all, it's how they met. Never saw it. Aha, I finally realized; he liked this older, white liberal woman because of *Guess Who's Coming to Dinner*. Nope, never saw that one either. "Well, Michael, there's got to be some movie of Katharine Hepburn's that you've seen!"

"That one with Spencer Tracy," he chimed in. "*Adam's Rib?*" No. Thinking sports, I say, "*Pat and Mike?*" No. "*Woman of the Year?*" "*Desk Set?*"

"No, the one where Spencer Tracy plays a fisherman, and he saves the little boy. . . ."

"*Captains Courageous*?!" Kate asked incredulously.

"Yes," Michael said. "He was very strict, but he was sweet to the little boy." Kate, with a look of madness I hadn't seen since the last act of *Long Day's Journey,* simply held up her empty glass.

Cynthia came to the rescue by inquiring about Michael's famous menagerie, asking him what animals he had. At last, he felt at home. With great enthusiasm, he spoke of his ranch with his llama and monkey and his boa constrictor, Muscles. "Now, Michael," Kate said, "I have always liked animals, but honestly, what do you do with a boa constrictor?" Excitedly he described his huge terrarium, behind a curtain, in which Muscles lived, and how every few days, he and special guests would sit down in front of the great glass window, open the curtain, and watch as a small rodent was placed in the snake house. This was an evening's entertainment, watching the snake capture, constrict, and consume the animal. We all sat there speechless. Kate held up her glass and, in a choked voice, called out, "Too weak."

There was some commotion downstairs, which was explained when Norah came scurrying up with a tray of hors d'oeuvres—none of which Michael ate—and a note for Miss Hepburn, which she read on the spot. "Unbelievable," said Kate. The missive had come from Stephen Sondheim's house (formerly Max Perkins's) next door. "The nerve!"

"I didn't think you and Mr. Sondheim spoke to each other," I said, knowing the only real communication between the neighbors came on the occasional nights when he played piano too loudly and too late—"entertaining gentlemen callers," Kate said—and she had to go outside in her nightclothes and pound on his rear windows.

"We don't," she said. "This is from his dinner guest, Mr. Stoppard."

The playwright Tom Stoppard had dashed off a note saying that he had young sons at home in England and that he had heard that Michael Jackson was having dinner next door and that if he didn't do everything he could to obtain an autograph for them, he would never forgive himself. "Out of the question," Kate barked. As we had all been sworn to secrecy, I asked Kate how Sondheim had even caught wind of the dinner. "Norah," she said, without having to think about it. "She and Louis [Sondheim's housekeeper] know everything about everyone on the block." Then it occurred to her that perhaps she was being harsh.

"Of course, it's not really my decision. Michael, how do you feel about signing autographs?" Kate explained that Stoppard was a great playwright.

"I like to do things for the children," he said. "I'll sign something for them."

Kate deputized Kathy and me to go to Sondheim's and notify Stoppard that he would be granted a brief audience with Michael Jackson. We were graciously received by Sondheim, who seemed tickled by the whole turn of events, even as his dinner guest left with us to go to Kate's. Stoppard was effusively grateful to his hostess and her special guest, who signed some pieces of paper. It wasn't until Stoppard left that I noticed that Michael was wearing his sunglasses again. All the hubbub genuinely amused Kate, her perturbation notwithstanding.

Dinner was served. We all descended to the dining room, where we sat at the big round table—which normally served as Hepburn's secretary's desk and was usually covered with correspondence and an IBM Selectric typewriter. Because Michael did not eat meat, Norah had prepared a vegetarian meal, starting with bowls of cold beet soup. A plate of toasted Portuguese bread got passed around, as did a small tub of whipped butter. When the butter reached Michael, he dipped in his soup spoon, then dropped a big white dollop into his soup, which he started to eat. Kate saw what was happening and apologized, saying it was her fault that he had mistaken the butter for sour cream. She called for Norah to get Michael a fresh bowl of soup. No, Michael insisted, he would eat this one. Kate said absolutely not, that it would taste terrible with all that butter. But Michael persisted—finishing the entire bowl, glob of butter and all. The rest of the dinner—which was a lot of beautifully prepared vegetables, potatoes, and a macaroni-and-cheese casserole—ensued with neither incident nor much conversation. Kate was astonished when Michael, who ate little more than vegetables all his life, did not know the "white broccoli" on his plate was something called cauliflower.

Before the dishes were cleared, Kate suggested we all move upstairs again. It was a little after eight. As we paraded up the narrow staircase, with Kate and Michael bringing up the rear, I heard him ask if he could speak to her privately. Cynthia, Kathy, and I returned to the rear living room, while Kate and Michael entered the front living room and stood by the windows overlooking Forty-ninth Street, their heads bowed down in serious conversation. Every now and then we could hear Kate say, in a low but firm voice, "Absolutely not. I'm terribly sorry, Michael, but absolutely not." Within minutes, they had rejoined us, but Michael did not sit down. He said his goodbyes, and we all followed him to the front door, where a driver-bodyguard stood waiting. He ushered Michael from the door into a waiting vehicle, a television repair truck with no rear windows. They zoomed off into the night.

Kate closed the door and looked at all of us assembled and cried, "Whiskey! Norah, get the whiskey!"

Upstairs we poured our nightcaps, and Cynthia asked what had happened in the front living room. Kate explained that Michael had wanted a photograph of the two of them. Kate had said she would send him a picture of herself. No, Michael said, he wanted one of the two of them—and he had a photographer with him, who had been sitting all night in the television repair truck. "Absolutely not," Kate had told him. This was meant to be a private dinner among friends, not a stop on his publicity junket. She thought Michael understood, until he had asked, "Do you know Greta Garbo?"

Kate said that she did know Garbo, but they had not seen each other in years. "Oh," he asked, "do you think you could introduce me to her?"

"Absolutely not, Michael . . ."

It was nine o'clock. Kate downed her drink and said, "I'm exhausted. I can't recall a more peculiar night in my life, and I'm going to bed." Which she did.

I said, "I'm hungry. I'm going somewhere to eat some meat." We all said our goodnights. I was staying that trip with a friend on the Upper West Side; and on my way to his apartment, I went to the nearest pay phone, where I called another writer-friend, whom I knew ate late. I asked if we could meet for a hamburger somewhere. He suggested a place within walking distance of each of us. On my way, I saw the strangest thing—

During my walk of five or six blocks, I saw four different limousines cruising the avenues of New York, each with a back window open, enough to allow a glimpse of a young, light-skinned African-American wearing sunglasses, and a hand crooked out the window, wearing a sequined glove.

Sworn to secrecy, having vowed never to reveal the details of my dinner during Hepburn's lifetime, I said little during my second dinner that night. That didn't matter. I could hardly shut my friend up. He was bursting with tales from his girlfriend, a journalist, who had covered Michael Jackson's concert the preceding night at Giants Stadium in New Jersey . . . and she actually went backstage and saw him!

I called Kate the following afternoon, and, without any prompting, she said, "If you show me the pages you wrote, I'll show you mine." They were pretty similar, except she had forgotten the butter in the soup.

In fact, Kate had been writing fragments of her life for years—usually in the morning, in bed, over her pot of coffee—scribblings on a long yellow tablet that got typed by a secretary and filed away. In 1987 she published a short, lavishly illustrated book, *The Making of* The African Queen *or How I Went to Africa with Bogart, Bacall and Huston and Almost Lost My Mind*. It became a bestseller, received glowing reviews, and encouraged her to keep writing. It also became a satisfying way to fill an hour or two of each day.

Although she seldom indulged in nostalgia with most of her friends, Kate liked me to pepper her with questions about the past, as though I were interviewing her. A week or two after we had talked about a certain film or person, I would discover she had composed a vignette on the subject—usually written in short staccato phrases, much like the way she spoke—very often with dashes in lieu of standard punctuation. Publishers—especially Knopf, which had done so well with her first book—were eager for a second volume from her. But she was reluctant. She didn't fancy herself as a writer; and to her, it seemed more than ever like throwing in the towel on her acting career, which was still going strong.

An agent without much experience had worked her way into Hepburn's life and arranged for several publishers to court her at East Forty-ninth Street. When I asked Kate why she chose to do business with somebody so new to the game, she simply said, "I've always been attracted to mutts. And if I don't help her, I don't know how she'll pay her rent." I did my best to trumpet the merits of my new publishers, Putnam's; and Phyllis Grann was thrilled to have a private audience with Hepburn. In the end, Bob Gottlieb, who lived across the private garden in Turtle Bay, eased her into signing a multimillion-dollar contract with Knopf, though he left the company to edit *The New Yorker* weeks later.

In the autumn of 1990, I prepared to take up residence in New Haven so that I could work my way through the Lindbergh archives. Kate and I were both delighted by Yale's proximity to Old Saybrook, not forty-five minutes up the coast. She suggested that I live at Fenwick and commute; but I said I could spend the travel time more constructively on campus each day, and that I would rather save Fenwick for the weekends, when the Manuscripts and Archives division of the library was closed.

Then Kate had another brainstorm. The weekend before I intended to start work, her driver took us to New Haven, where we dropped in unannounced on a cousin of hers, Edie Hooker, who lived in a stately house on the choicest street in the city. "Edie lives alone in this big, beautiful house," Kate explained on the way down. "And she has a guest apartment as well. It's perfect for you." It sounded as though it was, but I asked, "Shouldn't we tell Edie Hooker we're coming to visit her?" Kate told me not to worry and to leave all the talking to her. "You just stand there," she instructed me, "and try not to look like a homicidal maniac."

We pulled into Edie Hooker's driveway, and Kate stood there yelling, "Hey! Hey! Edie, come out here." Out trotted a handsome elderly woman, who was surprised and delighted to see her famous cousin. "Now, Edie," she explained, "this is Scott Berg, and he's about to start writing an important book, and he has to live in New Haven a while, and you're alone down here; and I thought—"

Edie interrupted her to say that, in fact, she had a guest apartment, but that she had recently rented it out to a very nice young couple. "Well, I don't suppose we can get rid of them then," Kate mused.

Hepburn suggested we tour the house. "Now look, Edie, this place is just too big for you to be rattling around alone—" Poor Edie tried to explain that she was very happy living alone and that her tenants were close by in an emergency. At last, she had no alternative but to offer me a room. I thanked her for her kindness but said that I would like to look for a place a little closer to the library, and that if I couldn't find anything, I would be most grateful to accept her generous "offer." Fortunately, the next day, I found exactly what I was looking for, a small apartment within a huge house on the same street as Edie Hooker, and an easier walk to the campus.

Most Fridays for the next two years, I'd leave the library a little early and catch a commuter train—"The Shore Line East"—to Old Saybrook, where Kate and her driver would meet me at the station. Sometimes she'd even stand at the platform waiting for me to disembark. We'd make a stop or two in town—"Do you want an ice cream cone at James's?"—before crossing the causeway to Fenwick. Then we'd sometimes take a swim and meet up by the fire at six for drinks and dinner. (Although I stopped entering the water from the end of September until May, Kate continued to take her sunrise swims in the dead of winter, trotting across even snow-covered sand.)

The clocks at Fenwick seemed for the first time that year to be winding down. Phyllis, by then in her late eighties, had slowed considerably, physically and mentally. Not long after sunset, I would usually set up the dinner tables before the living room fire and help serve her and Kate. Eight-thirty became a late night.

"Would you like to read something?" Kate would ask on her way upstairs practically every weekend of my first year in New Haven. Then she'd produce the latest batch of writing she was working over. I was instructed to make notations—"Be tough, but not too tough"—in pencil. I usually worked the pages over until eleven then left my marked-up copy outside her bedroom door. I rewrote none of her sentences. For the most part, I simply posed questions, urging her to fill in more details. "More milk, Bossy," was a comment I jotted in many a margin. By the time we met again in her bedroom for breakfast in the morning, she had done most of her rewrites and we'd discuss those comments she had not understood. Within a year, there were enough finished pieces to fill a book—*Me*, which Knopf prepared to publish in the fall of 1991.

Almost every Saturday for the two years I lived in Connecticut, we would drive to Kate's sister Peg Perry, who lived upstate. We'd leave late in the morning, sometimes drop in on her brother Bob outside Hartford, leaving time to arrive at Peg's cow farm for lunch. Phyllis would sit in the front seat of the car and invariably fall fast asleep within minutes. "She's amazing," Kate would say, incapable of understanding how anybody could sleep in the middle of a day. "She has absolutely nothing going on in that head of hers."

The youngest of Kate's siblings, Peg was both the toughest and the tenderest—and perhaps the prettiest of the Hepburns as well. She wasn't glamorous but had a natural strength of character reflected in her strong face, the weathered look of a woman who had worked outdoors much of her life, as she had. She graduated from Bennington College, married, and raised three sons and a daughter. One of her sons had long been missing in action in Southeast Asia. She is, if you can imagine, the most opinionated of all the Hepburns. And the minute you try to slot her into one category or another she'll surprise you with an exception to her own rules. She thinks the world has become overly permissive—from parents mollycoddling their children to teachers losing authority; she believes in the right to bear arms. She can't stand bleeding-heart liberals or dyed-in-the-wool conservatives. She truly believes in justice for all.

Our lunches at Peg's rectangular dining room table usually included a friend or two of Peg's as well as a son or grandchild who might drop in. The meal was always a very hot macaroni and cheese pulled right out of the oven, usually some cold meat, some freshly baked bread, salad, and cold milk. Kate was always served first and had usually cleaned her plate by the time the last of us was getting started. Then we'd move on to dessert and hot coffee, and even hotter discourse from Peg, who would rail about the public library getting upset with her for shoveling the snow from the walk because the man hired to do the job didn't do a good enough job or about the town elders who wouldn't provide a tax incentive for somebody's business, thus driving dozens of jobs to another town. Like Kate, Peg always saw the humor in the situation. Her bark is worse than her bite. "But you don't want to cross her," Kate told me after one heated discussion, "because there's always the possibility she'll shoot you!"

After lunch we'd drive back to Fenwick, often stopping along the way at a general store or cheese shop or museum. One day Kate, Phyllis, and I drove through New Britain and made our way to the Museum of American Art, a lovely small collection, with some Marsden Hartleys, which Hepburn especially liked. Upon entering the small museum, we all signed the guestbook, even Kate. On our way out, I noticed that the page with our signatures had already been ripped out of the book by some souvenir collector. When I got into the car, I reported this fact. "Oh," Kate said to me, "I had no idea you were so famous!"

Phyllis began to sputter. "Oh, no, why you're the famous one. They wanted your signature."

"Yes, dear. Thank you."

Every now and then we'd go to Fairfield, where the legendary agent Audrey Wood—who had nurtured the careers of playwrights from Tennessee Williams to Lanford Wilson—was in a nursing home, in a coma. She and Kate had not been great friends, but Kate always respected her. "This is a terrible irony," Kate would say, "because this woman believed in euthanasia. I heard her talk about it many times. She was desperate not to be allowed to linger. But all that was before she had made all the proper arrangements for herself. And so she had a stroke and went into this coma." For years Kate made a point of popping in to visit, unannounced—just to see that she was being cared for. She would check to see that the floors and bathroom were clean, that Audrey's hair was washed and combed, and that her fingernails were clipped. Satisfied, she would depart with as little fuss as she had entered.

I don't remember a single day with Kate that she wasn't reading. She was always in the middle of a big book—historical nonfiction and biographies her favorites; and there was always a pile of new novels within easy reach from her bed in New York and Fenwick. She became intrigued enough with Derek Humphry's *Final Exit,* a detailed account of how to take one's own life, to have two copies, one on each bedstand. "You're too young for this," she said upon giving me a copy, "but everybody should read it." She loved to talk about books and pass her favorite current selections along to me. I could always tell how intensely she had liked each book by how much chocolate I found smeared on its pages.

Sundays we usually ate an early lunch. Kate went through a succession of drivers in the years I knew her, all remarkably kind and slightly eccentric men (three of whom died young) who doubled as cooks at Fenwick on the weekends. We all pitched in around the house; and it irritated her if a visitor ever asked, "What can I do to help?" Nothing was always her reply. If you didn't have the initiative and know-how simply to muck in, she would rather have you out of her way.

When it came time to make lunch, I had become the official grape-slicer for the chicken salad—"Vertically! Vertically! They don't taste the same cut across," she continued to admonish. Phyllis made the toast, which had to be buttered before placed under the broiler; and Kate liked to make fried eggs for everybody, punching a hole out of a piece of bread with the top of a glass, then placing the bread in a frying pan and cracking the egg into the center. Dick would wander in and out, usually in some long underwear, preparing a roast, some confection, and a huge boiling pot full of anything else lying around the kitchen. Neither Kate nor Dick ever trespassed to the other's side of the kitchen—except at night, when she'd check to see that he'd turned off all the burners on the stove. "One day he's going to blow this house up," she'd say on the one out of four times she'd find a flame still burning. The rest of us were always encouraged to hunt and gather from his sector—a turkey drumstick or a slice of cake as an appetizer to the meal being prepared on Kate's side of the kitchen.

The unspoken rivalry between Dick and Kate stretched as far back as childhood and increased as her fame grew. Any hope of restoring balance in their relationship was lost forever when, in the early forties, Dick wrote a play about a multimillionaire courting an actress. While it was clearly written as farce, it was plainly based on Howard Hughes and Kate. She resented the intrusion; and the entire family stood behind her. Dick claimed that it contained some of his best writing and that he intended to get the play produced. Only after all the Hepburns came down on him did he back off. In so doing, he had established a foundation of resentment toward his sister, one sound enough to make her feel responsible for his livelihood. That he was never too proud to accept her charity only furthered his resentment.

One weekend Dick gave me one of his later plays to read, a work that periodically caught the eye of a producer. It was a witty account of an eccentric New England family that made me see he could have had a playwriting career, had he actively pursued it. "The theater is tough," Kate said, accepting only a small measure of responsibility for standing in his way; "but that play about Howard and me was cheap exploitation and would not have made his career. It would have been a stunt. If Dick really wanted the career thing badly enough, he should have written another play just as good, and another one after that." He never did.

While privacy among the Hepburns was, of course, held in high regard, one afternoon I came into my room and found Kate rifling through my overnight bag. I had clearly caught her red-handed. All she could do was smile sheepishly—for a moment. "Did you find anything interesting?" I asked. "No," she said, stuffing my clothes and some papers back into the bag. "Not a goddamned thing!" Except for a box of chocolates—from which she took a piece of almond bark, which she ate as she walked out the door.

There were lots of rules at Fenwick, but they were changed as often as they were broken. One day we were preparing a big fruit salad; and while peeling apples, I dropped a piece on the floor. I picked it up to throw in the garbage, and Kate yelled, "What are you doing? It's perfectly fine." Without even washing it, she threw it into the bowl. "Oh yes," Phyllis added. "My father used to say a man eats a peck of dirt before he dies." A few weeks later, I lost my grip on a carrot and—against my better judgment—I tossed it into the bowl. "Oh my God!" Kate shrieked. "Do you think we're animals around here?" She fished it out of the bowl and chucked it into the garbage along with several leaves of lettuce she felt I had also contaminated. "What about the peck of dirt a man eats before he dies?" I asked. "Oh," said Kate, "that's one of those utterly ridiculous English expressions." Every week there was a new policy regarding bed linens, as I prepared to change mine every Sunday morning. Sometimes she'd insist I leave the sheets on until my next visit, other times she'd declare, "We change all the sheets in this house every few days." (She often expressed strong sentiments against anything but white sheets, but, periodically, light blue would appear on my bed.) In any case, Kate almost always took part in making the bed; and I never saw anybody derive as much pleasure from a good hospital corner as she did.

Sunday after lunch brought the most dreaded moment in the week. That was when we packed the car for the drive back to the city—the hour in which all passengers and their baggage, as well as all perishable foodstuff and all living cut flowers, were packed into the white sedan. Even with her worsening foot, Kate would tear from room to room, gathering a shirt and pair of shoes from one bedroom, bouquets of huge lilies and tall stems of Queen Anne's lace from the living room, jars of Peg's stewed peaches and leftover zucchini soup, wheels of cheese, tins of cookies, loaves of bread, and coolers of meats and fruits and vegetables from the kitchen. Meantime, food was being prepared for the drive down—deviled eggs (heavy on the cayenne) and little sandwiches of ham and chicken with the crusts cut off.

Once everything was gathered in the front hall, Kate oversaw the actual packing with military authority and surgical precision— "Coolers. Large suitcase. Small vase. Small suitcase . . ." After a good half hour of jostling and rearranging, the trunk was closed. Then came the last two commands, the same every week. "My leather bags," would come the cry—which meant grabbing two pouches that looked as though the Pony Express had once carried them, filled with her latest writings, address books, wallet, and current mail. And then, just as we were ready to take off, "Where's Phyllis?" Miss Wilbourn, who had taken to wandering, physically and mentally, would be herded into the front seat, where she was given a huge vase of flowers to hold all the way to New York. Kate and I would pile into the back, the leather pouches and food for the ride between us. Sometimes there'd be an additional passenger, which, of course, complicated the procedure by twenty percent. All hands still on deck—Dick, his lady friend, Virginia, any other Hepburn siblings or nephews—continued to come out front for the 1—2—1-2-3 salute, though over the next few years, the tradition would fade away for lack of enthusiasm.

We usually stopped at a vegetable stand, then took the turnpike to New Haven, where I was delivered to my front door on St. Ronan Street. I'd go to bed early on Sunday nights—thoroughly refreshed by the weekend, too exhausted not to get a good night's sleep, and too stuffed to want to eat for several days.

Kate and I would speak on the phone once or twice during the week, to confirm our weekend plans. Every few weeks, however, she would say, "We're in a rut. We're like an old married couple. You better spend the weekend in the city." She said there was nothing in the world better than having somebody else's apartment in New York when the owner wasn't around.

During the late eighties, the friendship between Kate and Cynthia McFadden intensified. As Cynthia enjoyed a meteoric rise in her career—becoming enough of a star reporter on *Court TV* to be invited to join the powerful team at *ABC News*—she often lived upstairs on Forty-ninth Street. She and Kate also traveled a great deal together—to Los Angeles or Canada, when Kate was working on a television movie, to Boca Grande, Florida, for vacations. So it was with mixed emotions for Kate, when Cynthia fell in love and agreed to marry a man absolutely besotten with her, Michael Davies, the elegant publisher of *The Hartford Courant*.

Cynthia told Kate that she dreamed one night of being married at Fenwick, and Kate made the dream come true. I can think of no greater sign of Kate's love for her young friend and protégée than opening her private sanctuary to Cynthia and her family and friends. All the "Forty-ninth Street Irregulars" gathered for the event as well—Phyllis and Norah, of course, and also Tony Harvey, an old friend from Philadelphia named David Eichler, and me, along with Kate's siblings and Kathy Houghton. There was a merry party the night before the wedding at the couple's sprawling new house in Lyme, Connecticut, just across the river.

Midday, September 9, 1989, we all gathered in the little church at Fenwick. A longtime friend and photographer of Kate, John Bryson, was there to take pictures. After the short, sweet ceremony, almost everybody walked over to the Hepburn house. Kate, in a cream-colored jacket worn over a white turtleneck shirt and white pants and white sneakers, rode. We enjoyed a beautiful late-summer garden party under a marquee at the rear of the house. Kate's foot ached that day, but she circulated among all the guests before finding a chair. Even then, she hardly sat, as she made a point of standing for each person who approached to say hello or goodbye. When it came time to cut the five-tiered creamy cake, the bride called Kate over to share in the first piece—which she pushed into Kate's face. Everybody laughed, mostly Kate.

Kate was obviously happy seeing Cynthia so happy, but she was already starting to miss her company. In truth, they would continue to see almost as much of each other as before she married, but Kate knew that she could no longer be the central person in Cynthia's life. Kate also felt that there was a great imbalance in the relationship, that the groom loved the bride more than she loved him. Kate wondered why it had been necessary to marry him.

By five that afternoon, all the guests and the help had left. Kate and I were alone, under the tent, killing a bottle of club soda after the day's champagne. She said she thought it was unfair for Cynthia to marry Michael, that Cynthia was more concerned just then with her career than with pleasing a husband and that that was no way to enter a marriage. The more she talked, the more I felt she was talking about her own marriage to Luddy. And the more she talked, the angrier she got. At last we just sat there, watching the sun pass over the Long Island Sound, in silence—until Kate said, "Pig."

"Let's go in," I said, putting my arm over her shoulder. She reached up and squeezed my hand tightly.

Kate's driver took me to Hartford, where I caught a plane to New York, in order to make a connection late that night to London, where I was going to promote my Goldwyn book. I had a few minutes at JFK, during which I called Irene Selznick. As soon as she heard my voice, she said, "Revolting."

"I'm sorry," I said, trying to catch up with her mind.

"The cake in the face. I know all about it. Absolutely revolting. Do you think she's lost her mind?" Irene pressed me for every detail of the wedding, though she seemed to know most of them already. I flipped through the guest list in my mind to ascertain who had filled her in. To this day, I don't know the identity of her mole. (I suspect Norah.) But I did know that after almost sixty years of friendship, everything Kate did of late irritated her. And Irene never dealt well with pain.

Although I always found her extremely democratic in her thinking, Irene had been raised a princess. She liked—expected, even—everything in her life to be special, exclusive. (She titled her discreet memoirs, in which she kept her most revealing stories between the lines, *A Private View*; and she prided herself on a life full of people and experiences few could match.) For her, it wasn't fame or wealth that conferred prestige so much as uniqueness. Accordingly, it pained her to see Kate become increasingly public.

One day Kate got into an argument with a traffic warden on Forty-ninth Street over her momentarily double-parked car. When the altercation made the newspapers, complete with pictures, Irene was mortified. Not long after that, Irene was sick in bed, and Kate decided to bring some of Norah's soup to her apartment at the Hotel Pierre. Irene was moved by the gesture; but, she reported to me, "She got into the elevator here looking like Raggedy Ann, and the elevator operator wouldn't take her up. She had no idea who this 'bag lady' was. And Kate had to go to the manager to get permission to come up. Kate! I'm talking about Kate! Katharine Hepburn!"

Irene was devastated. It was hard enough for her to feel she had lost her friend to a gang of younger people she didn't know, or that Kate forged valiantly on with her career, despite her own physical maladies. Irene had come to feel excluded from Kate's life, and she was unwilling to try to be included any longer. She decided Kate was becoming a commoner. More than once that year, Irene talked about her "noble" friend—and suddenly burst into tears.

There was one more thing. During her last visit to East Forty-ninth Street, Irene discovered a young woman she did not know who had been staying there. At one moment her eagle-eyes witnessed an exchange between the two of them that suggested a level of intimacy she had never allowed herself to believe. "Now everything makes sense," Irene said to me. "Dorothy Arzner, Nancy Hamilton—all those women. Laura Harding. Now it all makes sense. A double-gater. I never believed that relationship with Spence was about sex."

"Irene, I think you might be getting carried away," I said. "I sure get the feeling that Spencer Tracy was a pretty sexual animal, and they wouldn't have lasted that long if sex wasn't involved."

"In the beginning," she said. "But you can't drink as much as Spence did and maintain a relationship built on sex."

"But like most great relationships," I suggested, "shouldn't it become about something more?"

Irene granted that was the case with Hepburn and Tracy; but she was disturbed by her new understanding of Kate's sexual nature. "Irene," I said, "you don't know what goes on with all these women. I mean, Kate herself says, 'Nobody really knows what goes on between two people when they're alone.'"

"That's my point," Irene replied. "You're too young to have known all those other women, those single women. I knew them. I knew who they were."

I said that I felt that Kate was simply more comfortable with single people of either sexual persuasion, that she felt she could get closer to individuals with no other attachments, and that while I had told her of a relationship in my life that began about the time she and I met, she almost never wanted to hear about it. "I don't like to think of you living anywhere," Kate had said to me shortly after giving me the key to her house. "I like to think that this is your home."

Again, sexuality was not really the issue between Kate and Irene. It was the exclusion that troubled Mrs. Selznick—that there had been a dimension of Kate's life that had never been revealed to her, one that Kate could now be sharing with people she had never even heard of. This realization became a turning point in their lives, the moment at which Irene, feeling hurt, began to lose interest in her friend of some sixty years.

In 1990 Irene seemed to be suffering physically, but so far as I knew, no doctor could put his finger on a specific problem. Her body ached ("Of course it aches," Kate would say, "she never moves in or out of that goddamned apartment!"); and her appetite was diminishing. In some ways she was happier than I had seen in more than ten years, largely because, for the first time since I had known her, she was feeling good about the lives of both her sons at the same time. Jeffrey had married a beautiful woman named Barbara who "loves him and looks after him better than he deserves"; and not only had Danny married into the Sulzberger family but, Irene observed, "They think he's Cary Grant." Her will, which she emended regularly as long as I knew her, was in order.

So it came as a shock to me that summer when I received one of the most unforgettable phone calls of my life—one in which, after a few minutes of pleasantries, Irene said, "I'm calling to say goodbye."

"Goodbye? Where are you going?"

"I said, 'I'm calling to say goodbye' . . . goodbye . . . the big trip." It dawned on me what she was saying, but I couldn't believe it.

"Is everything all right?" I asked. Irene said, "Don't I sound all right?" I replied that she sounded better than she had in ages. "That's right," she said, "That's why I'm calling to say goodbye."

Irene explained that for the first time in years, she was happy with her life. "Everything's in order," she said. And because she was relatively free of pain, she didn't want to endure "the real thing" when it came along. "Well, maybe it won't come along," I suggested, and she could go on in her present state for many more years. "I don't want to go on for many more years," she replied.

"But don't you want to see your children's lives play out, and your grandson. You adore him. And what about your friends? I've just started this book, and I want to be able to share it with you."

"Darling," she said, "I do care about your book. So we'll keep talking to each other every few days . . . and you'll come to see me every few months. And I'll ask about your book, and you'll tell me, and I know how this whole chapter of your life will end. I'm tired of watching things when I know how they'll end."

I suggested that she was probably going through a kind of depression, and maybe a little time and perhaps some medication would change her attitude. "Do I sound depressed?" she asked. "I can't remember the last time I felt this good."

"So why are you calling then? What can I do?" I asked. She told me that I could just carry on being her friend as though this call had never happened. She explained that she was calling five or six people, whom she named. Kate was not among them. She said we had become "special friends"; and she didn't want me to pick up the paper one morning and suddenly read her obituary.

"Well, you're smart enough to know that this is a cry for help, then," I said. "And I'm going to call somebody—a mutual friend, a doctor, your boys, Kate."

"No!" she shouted into the phone. "If you discuss this call with anybody, I will never speak to you again."

We talked for another two hours, and I reluctantly agreed to her terms. But I begged her to discuss the matter with her sons. If she didn't, I argued, she was putting an unfair burden on her friends. She agreed.

"So is this really goodbye then?" I asked before hanging up. "No," she said, "—probably late September, but certainly by the first week of October."

I was stunned. I thought, perhaps, a doctor had given her a death sentence of some kind. A recurrence of her cancer, maybe? But Irene had said that was not the case; or, I tried to recall, had she merely issued a non-denial denial? So I played by the rules and said nothing to anybody. Our conversations with each other continued without further reference to the phone call, though I did send her missives with small comments that revealed that I had listened to everything she had told me over the years. She replied with grateful notes.

On October 11, 1990, during a break at the Yale library, I picked up my phone messages from Los Angeles, which included an urgent call from John Goldwyn, Samuel Goldwyn's grandson and Irene Selznick's godson. He told me the news that Irene had been found dead that morning, wasn't it shocking?

Over the next few weeks, I learned of a few others who had received Irene's farewell phone calls. She had discussed the matter with her children, I learned, though they were obviously unable to thwart her plans. She had not called Kate, who probably would have been more supportive of her exit plan than she imagined. Then I learned that Irene died under circumstances even more mysterious than I had imagined.

There was apparently no evidence that Irene had committed suicide. I was told she had stayed up late that night, fussing with papers and making a few calls. She was found dead in her bed in the morning, with her hands folded over her chest, holding her eyeglasses, and wearing a beatific look. I have since pursued the story of exactly how Irene Selznick died, and the best answer seems to be that she, as only she could do, simply willed it.

The memorial service was arranged for November ninth at the Ethel Barrymore Theater. Kate had no intention of attending. I called her the week before and the night before and argued that I thought she would feel better if she went, that Irene had played an important role in her life. "What's the point?" Kate asked. "She's dead. She won't know the difference."

"What about Danny and Jeffrey?" I asked. "It would mean a lot to them." There was no arguing about that.

I swung by the next day and her driver took us to the Ethel Barrymore before the doors inside had even opened. Kate barged in and I followed, and several ushers called out that she couldn't enter yet, as they were still setting up. Hearing the commotion, Danny, who was producing the event, came up the aisle, told the ushers it was all right, and embraced Kate. Her eyes welled up seeing him. He asked us where we wanted to sit, and we selected center orchestra seats. Minutes later the few hundred others were admitted. All the speakers that afternoon were concise, eloquent, funny, and on the mark, just as Irene would have insisted. She came across as a no-nonsense woman whom everybody found challenging.

After quickly escaping to Kate's waiting car, she said, "Don't ever have one of those for me." I said I was sure some tribute was inevitable. "Well, luckily I won't have to be there for it," she added, "and neither should you." I suggested that Irene's service had provided some comfort for everybody there. "Not me," she said. "She's dead, and nothing's going to bring her back. Better if everybody had stayed home and thought about her for a moment, then gone on with their lives. And that's all they should do when I die. And if anybody wants to do more than that, they can rent one of my movies."

A few dozen of us, Kate included, went back to Irene's apartment. The rooms were filled with several recognizable faces from an earlier era of show business. They all focused on the foyer when Katharine Hepburn entered. While she spoke to Danny Selznick, I fixed two plates of food. After a few minutes, Kate was making motions to leave, when a short, old man made a beeline toward her, calling out, "Will you speak to me?" I could see she didn't recognize him, and I was able to whisper "Elia Kazan" before he was standing in front of her.

"Gadg," she said to a man she had not spoken to in more than forty years, "that can't be you." He beamed and leaned over to kiss her on the cheek. While they exchanged greetings, I could see another elderly man watching the reunion. Emboldened, he walked over as well, and said, "And will you speak to *me*?"

"Of course, I will," she said, having no idea who was then pecking at her other cheek. As he spoke to Kazan for a moment, I whispered, "Joe Mankiewicz."

"Good God," she said.

For the next two minutes everybody was all smiles. Then Kate said she had to leave. I accompanied her to the street. She said she was going home but that I should go back to the party and come over when it was done. She climbed into the backseat of the waiting car, and before the driver pulled away from the curb at the Pierre's Sixty-first Street entrance, she rolled down her window and said, "Do I look as awful as they do?"

"God no, Kate. At least they knew who *you* were."

I returned to the tenth floor. After a few minutes, I slipped away from the living room and retreated to the den, where Irene and I had always sat. A guard was posted there, watching over the artwork and personal effects. I went to the little refrigerator and pulled out the bottle of "Cary's aquavit" and poured myself a shot. Then I sat in the chair in front of the Mary Cassatt picture of the little girl and cried.

IX

Always Mademoiselle

"No, I couldn't in all truth say I was surprised by the offer," Kate remembered of that afternoon at the end of 1966. "But, honestly, can you imagine me as a fireman's wife?"

Stanley Kramer, who had become Hollywood's most socially conscious filmmaker and who had directed Spencer Tracy three times already, visited the Cukor guesthouse with a new idea for a movie he was hatching with the screenwriter of *It's a Mad, Mad, Mad, Mad World*, William Rose. A handsome—and alcoholic—American expatriate living on the Channel Island of Jersey, Rose was plotting the story of a wealthy British couple whose daughter brings home the man she intends to marry, "perfect in every way"—except for his being of another race. Sidney Poitier, then the most successful man of color ever to have appeared in motion pictures, had already expressed interest in playing the fiancé, a cultivated professional man, the kind of role model that had not appeared in a mainstream film. With that piece in place, Kramer set about casting the costars.

A devoted friend and fan of Spencer Tracy, Kramer had suddenly thought this film might provide a glorious last hurrah for the ailing actor. By transplanting the story from its English locale to American soil, Tracy could easily play a retired, middle-class Irish-American, a former cop or fireman. Having broached the idea to Tracy without being brushed off, Kramer continued to spin his gears. If, indeed, this was likely to be Spencer Tracy's last appearance in motion pictures—in a love story at that—he asked himself what would be more moving than casting him opposite his romantic partner of twenty-five years.

By the time Kramer had arrived at the cottage, the story had shifted even further. "Once I heard Stanley describe the setup, and he was suggesting that the fireman be in a more elevated position," Kate recalled, "I knew that he was thinking of me to play the wife." The three kicked around several possibilities that day. Tracy, who had for decades played the "conscience" in so many dramas—the all-American voice of truth and justice—would be wasted playing a priest in this romantic story; and he had already portrayed a judge for Kramer. They discussed his being a newspaper publisher, a man who had long been a liberal voice of reason, a man who stood for social justice—who suddenly balked when the ultimate test of his liberalism landed on his own doorstep. He would find himself coming up against his wife, who would be speaking from the heart, a sensible woman who would be the voice of romance.

Kate had mixed feelings about the project. She thought it sounded like a wonderful film—"with something important to say"; and she was eager to do it. For the first time, however, she worried that Tracy was not physically able to complete the job. Even in the world of studio doctors who routinely signed off on major health risks so that movies could get made, Spencer Tracy had become uninsurable. Knowing that, Kramer made two unusual promises to the actor. He said he would arrange the entire shooting schedule around Tracy, so that he would only have to shoot a few hours a day—and in the morning at that, when he was at his best. Furthermore, he said if Hepburn and Tracy would not make this movie, neither would he.

Columbia Studios agreed to finance the picture only if Hepburn would put her quarter-million-dollar salary in escrow along with the director's half million until the completion of principal photography. That would provide enough insurance to reshoot with another actor, should that eventuality arise. Kramer put his money where his mouth was, an act of faith and friendship that Hepburn never forgot. "All of Stanley's movies came straight from the heart," she said. "There are damn few like him."

He retreated to Jersey with writer Rose, who knocked out the script of *Guess Who's Coming to Dinner* in a matter of weeks. In some ways, the material might have been better suited as a play. A handful of characters—the young lovers, their respective sets of parents, and a priest and maid for some comic relief—converge upon a single set, the San Francisco home of Matt and Christina Drayton, where they deliver speeches that argue all sides of the issue of the impending interracial marriage. But knowing they had Tracy and Hepburn—with at least one of them in a valedictory role—gave Rose and Kramer not only the voices to work with but also years of cinematic history.

Unlike Garbo and Gilbert, Myrna Loy and William Powell, Jimmy Stewart and Margaret Sullavan—even Abbott and Costello—Tracy and Hepburn had matured as a couple. Over a generation, the public had watched them encounter a number of different situations together, always a little ahead of their times. Paradoxically, this unmarried twosome had become the symbol of the all-American couple, exemplars of family values and, even more, of human values. Kate told me years later that while working on his script, "Willy Rose said he'd often ask himself, 'Now what would Spencer Tracy and Katharine Hepburn say here?' Not the real Spence and the real me. But the images everybody knew. Queer, isn't it?"

As a result, the entire film gave audiences the feeling that they were eavesdropping, listening in on relatives who had long been part of their collective consciences. The conceit was further enhanced by the actress who debuted in the film as their daughter, Katharine Houghton. The daughter of Kate's sister Marion, and a stunning, literary graduate of Sarah Lawrence College, Kathy burst onto the screen displaying a lot of her aunt's zealous personality. Naturally, she looked enough like her to give rise to the rumor that she was, in truth, Tracy and Hepburn's love child and that Kate's sister had simply been their cover. "Now that's one I haven't heard," Kate said of the canard when I mentioned it to her. "Too bad so many people are alive who remember when Marion was pregnant."

Everybody's anxiety over Tracy's health only fostered greater efficiency on the set of *Guess Who's Coming to Dinner.* But it was a nervous-making shoot for Hepburn, who had to perform double duty—always looking after him and performing a considerably challenging role herself. While the two actors had always stuck around for each other in the past, feeding lines for the other's close-ups, most shots of Hepburn alone were delivered to the script supervisor, thus allowing Tracy to go home early each day, as promised. "I shouldn't say most movie sets, but certainly on a lot of movie sets, you develop a sense of family," Kate recalled; and, she added, she couldn't remember that feeling ever being so "strong" as it was on the set of this picture.

Tracy and Hepburn had long approached their work differently. He had a phenomenal memory, could read a script, absorb the lines, look over a scene the night before it was shot, and was usually word perfect on his first take. She liked to study a script, learning not only all her lines before production but most everybody else's as well. She considered every possible reading she could give—and was known to pass along advice to other actors as to how they might deliver their lines as well. In the past, when she had suggested they rehearse together, Tracy generally dismissed the notion by saying, "I'm saving it for the set."

On *Guess Who's Coming to Dinner,* however, Tracy asked Hepburn to run lines with him every night. He felt he owed as much to his director, for putting his salary on the line. He felt he owed Kate even more, for having put her career on ice for five years. He seemed eager to make this picture especially good, if only to help get her career back on track. So it was disconcerting for the actors to discover that, for the first time, he was having trouble remembering his lines.

The climax of the film was Spencer Tracy's delivery of its message, a kind of verdict. After starting out as the leading opponent to his daughter's marriage and listening to each character articulate his or her position, he takes exception to a comment made by the mother of Sidney Poitier's character, played by Beah Richards. She avers that he has become an old man who has forgotten what it is to love. That spurs him to render his ultimate opinion that "in the final analysis it doesn't matter what we think. The only thing that matters is what they feel, and how much they feel for each other. And if it's half of what we felt," he says looking toward Hepburn, her eyes brimming with tears, ". . . that's everything." It was a flawless performance; and there was not a dry eye on the set. Everybody knew that Spencer Tracy was a great actor; but that day, they felt he wasn't acting. On May 26, 1967, Tracy shot his final scene and went home. Kate thanked the cast and crew for all their cooperation.

Hepburn had been residing full-time in the Cukor guest cottage on St. Ives, though she continued to rent the Barrymore aviary a few minutes away on Tower Grove Drive. Phyllis spent her nights there. Kate generally sat up late with Tracy in the bedroom on St. Ives until he dozed off; then she repaired to the maid's room off the kitchen. A buzzer sat on his bedstand and she carried the bell, attached to a long wire, wherever she went in the house. Day and night, she monitored his movements, as always, anticipating his needs. Before retiring, she'd put a big kettle of water on the stove, which she kept simmering all night, so that he could instantly prepare a cup of tea if he couldn't sleep.

At three o'clock in the morning of June 10, 1967, Kate heard Tracy come out of the bedroom and into the kitchen. She was getting out of bed to join him when she heard a teacup smash against the floor and then a thud. By the time she reached him, Spencer Tracy was dead of a heart attack. While he had been slowly dying over the last few years, she found immediate comfort in the fact that the death itself had come so swiftly.

Hepburn immediately summoned Phyllis, George Cukor, the couple who lived on the grounds, and Howard Strickling, the MGM publicity chief, who had decades of experience dealing with the press at the death scenes of Hollywood stars. She was packing up her personal belongings and removing them from the premises when she suddenly came to her senses. "This was my house too," she realized, "and I had lived with this man for most of my adult life." She returned to the house and called Louise Tracy, their children, and Tracy's brother.

"It seemed the least awkward thing to do," Kate explained to me. "To have done otherwise would have required a series of lies and would have served nobody." Over the next few hours, she did her best to stay out of the way, to let the Tracy family have their final moments of bereavement—thus depriving herself of that same moment of closure. "It was all like a bad dream," Kate recalled more than twenty years later, "a real nightmare." It reached its most surreal when the morticians asked how the body should be dressed. Kate had pulled out an old jacket and some trousers, but Louise Tracy took umbrage at not being able to select the clothes herself. In that moment, Kate snapped. "Oh Louise," she said, "—what difference does it make?" By six o'clock, a doctor had examined the deceased and the undertaking firm of Cunningham & Walsh had taken him away. The press would arrive midday—when they were told that Mr. Tracy's friends Miss Hepburn and Mr. Cukor had come down to the cottage at eleven that morning.

For three evenings the mortuary received mourners. Kate showed up each night after hours. One night she placed an oil painting she had done of some flowers into the casket. The next night she learned that the casket had been sealed at the family's request. She presumed her painting remained with him.

Upon Tracy's death, Hepburn behaved rather as she had during his lifetime, remaining unseen in public with the man she loved. Early on the morning of the funeral, Kate and Phyllis drove to the mortuary and helped place Spencer Tracy's coffin into the hearse. Then from a respectable distance they followed the parade of black cars to the Immaculate Heart of Mary Church in Hollywood. When they got close enough to see that a crowd had formed, they turned around and headed for home. "Goodbye, friend," said Kate.

After the funeral, a handful of Tracy's closest friends—those intimate enough to have been part of his actual domestic life—stopped by the house on St. Ives. Hepburn greeted Garson Kanin and Ruth Gordon, writer Chester Erskine and his wife, Sally, director Jean Negulesco and his wife, Dusty. Hepburn seemed to be in complete control of her emotions. "I wasn't really putting up a brave front," she later said. "I was just in a complete daze." It wasn't until the Negulescos left, and Jean made a comment about how angry he was that Spencer had left them, that Kate collapsed into his arms and sobbed.

One night, some weeks later, Kate told me, she telephoned Mrs. Tracy. Thinking she might be of some help with the children, she said, "You know, Louise, you and I can be friends. You knew Spencer at the beginning. I knew him at the end. Or, we can just go on pretending—"

"Oh yes," Louise said. "But you see, I thought you were only a rumor."

Kate never got over this story. "A rumor!" she said to me. "Can you imagine? Thirty years her husband isn't there, and she thinks I'm a rumor." For a minute or two Kate tried to imagine what could possibly have been in Louise Tracy's mind—what hoops of denial she must have jumped through to believe that. I suggested to Kate that Louise Tracy knew the score all along and simply said what she had to get her goat. "But why would she want to do that?" Kate asked in a state of agitation. "Exactly," I said.

Guess Who's Coming to Dinner opened the following year and became the most successful picture at the box office that either Tracy or Hepburn had ever appeared in, together or apart. It was nominated for ten Academy Awards—including Best Picture, Best Director, Best Actor, and Best Actress. William Rose won an Oscar for his screenplay. The late Spencer Tracy was up against Warren Beatty for *Bonnie and Clyde*, Dustin Hoffman in *The Graduate*, Paul Newman in *Cool Hand Luke*, and Rod Steiger for *In the Heat of the Night*; the latter won. Hepburn's competition was not quite as stiff: Anne Bancroft for *The Graduate*, Faye Dunaway for *Bonnie and Clyde*, Dame Edith Evans for *The Whisperers*, and Audrey Hepburn for *Wait Until Dark*. With this, her tenth nomination, Hepburn won her second Oscar—thirty-four years after her first. "I felt that was the Hollywood community's way of honoring Spence," Kate said years later, with undue modesty. There's no denying that sentiment played heavily into the voting that year. But if the Academy was honoring a life and not that particular performance, this was probably more the Academy's way of applauding Hepburn's return to the public arena. By the time her Oscar was presented—as before, in absentia—she had already completed work on another movie and was in the middle of filming yet another.

F. Scott Fitzgerald once commented that in American lives there were no second acts. Had he enjoyed a normal life span, he would have been able to see the curtain go up on the fourth act of the life of one of his favorite actresses, Katharine Hepburn—then sixty years of age.

Kate recuperated from her loss on Martha's Vineyard as the guest of the Kanins. Long swims, long drives, and long talks contributed to her recovery. But, as always with Hepburn, it was work, not recreation, that brought her back to life.

That summer the arrival of a screenplay called *The Lion in Winter* spurred her into action. James Goldman had adapted his own successful play, the story of the marriage of Henry II of England and his imprisoned wife, Eleanor of Aquitaine, who is sprung for the Christmas holidays in 1183. During the course of the play, they argue the question of succession, a decision that will affect nations on both sides of the Channel. Peter O'Toole, who had played Henry II in *Becket,* would wear the same crown once more.

"What was fascinating about the play," Kate said, "was its modernness. This wasn't about pomp and circumstance but about a family, a wife trying to protect her dignity and a mother protecting her children." She grew even more excited about the project after seeing a film made by the director O'Toole was favoring— *Dutchman,* which presented a harsh look at urban life, with a woman stabbing a black man on a New York subway train. It hardly seemed an appropriate screen test for a film about twelfth-century European royalty, but Kate found director Anthony Harvey's work "absolutely riveting. It grabbed you by the throat. Exactly the approach that our material needed. Not that glossy old MGM stuff, but cold people living in cold castles." Furthermore, Harvey—an Englishman then in his mid-thirties—had been a film editor (for Stanley Kubrick, no less, on *Lolita* and *Dr. Strangelove*); and Hepburn had long been partial toward the profession. Similar to what she had said about David Lean, Kate reminded me that "nobody has the same love affair with film that cutters do. It's a tactile medium for them." She felt an instant rapport with the director, and they became great friends for the rest of Kate's life. Nobody championed him more than she; and in her final years, nobody cared for her more than he.

The company—which included a young Anthony Hopkins as her son Richard (soon to be "the Lion-Hearted") and an even younger Timothy Dalton as King Philip of France—rehearsed for two weeks in the Haymarket Theatre in London. Then they all moved to Dublin to shoot interior scenes and to Fontvieille, a small village in the south of France, where they filmed in an old abbey.

Hepburn admired everyone in the cast. O'Toole was wild and rambunctious, "sometimes utterly impossible, a real Irishman," Kate said, "—too much charm and too much liquor. But I was used to that. And what an actor! Great voice. Great performance. Great fun." His great vigor, she suggested, helped restore her vitality. Years later, she would take pride in the deserved success of Hopkins. And when Dalton was hired to play James Bond, she bragged that she "knew him when."

The film was another triumph for Hepburn, with the public and within the industry. Again, her film was nominated in all the major categories—Best Picture, Director, Actor, Actress, and Screenplay. Again the screenwriter won . . . and so did Hepburn. This third victory was unprecedented. (So was the fact that there was a tie that year—with Hepburn sharing Best Actress honors with twenty-six-year-old Barbra Streisand, who had debuted in *Funny Girl*. After saying, "Hello, gorgeous" to her gleaming trophy, Streisand said what an honor it was to be in the same company as Hepburn, whose award was accepted by Tony Harvey.)

By then, Hepburn had left one locale in southern France for another, this time to appear in a production of *The Madwoman of Chaillot*. When she had signed on to appear in this film version of the Jean Giraudoux play, John Huston was meant to direct. By the time shooting began, however, Bryan Forbes had replaced him. "John was no fool," Kate said of his abandoning this allegory, in which a quixotic noblewoman, the Countess Aurelia, takes on the greedy capitalists of the world. She holds a mock trial and lures all the villains into a bottomless pit by telling them of an oil reserve beneath her house. "The big problem," Kate said, "is that material like this plays better on a stage than on screen, which requires something more literal. I mean, you have to photograph something. And I think it's difficult for a movie audience to accept an entire film that is so abstract and stylized."

Ely Landau, the producer of *Long Day's Journey Into Night*, produced this picture as well, hiring a charm bracelet of international stars—including Charles Boyer, Claude Dauphin, Oscar Homolka, Yul Brynner, Donald Pleasence, and Danny Kaye; the Countess Aurelia's conspirators were played by Edith Evans, Margaret Leighton, and Giulietta Masina. "I think the real problem with the picture," Kate said, "is that none of us ever really figured out how to play our parts, how to speak that dialogue, which was terribly artificial. The old girls, we all started impersonating Edith Evans, who really was terribly amusing . . . but I don't think she knew what she was doing any more than we did. It was really quite hopeless." It was ultimately difficult for an audience—to say nothing of the star herself—to accept Katharine Hepburn as somebody who had truly lost her mind. She ultimately came across as more eccentric than mad.

Undaunted, Hepburn found that work begat more work, and her resurgence inspired her to new challenges. In 1969 she agreed to return to the stage after close to a decade's absence . . . in a genre she had never attempted. Alan J. Lerner had been at work for a year on a musical based loosely on the life of Gabrielle "Coco" Chanel, the legendary clothes designer; and he wanted Hepburn—also a woman of style, stature, and staying power—to assume the title role. "Now, I'm sure I saw Ethel Merman in something, and I adored *My Fair Lady*," Kate recalled, (though it turned out to be the Cukor-directed film version of the Lerner and Loewe classic that she recollected), "but I honestly don't remember ever sitting through a Broadway musical. I certainly never thought I could sing my way through one."

Hepburn herself admitted that after a lifetime in the theater she never learned to vocalize properly; and the only tunes she felt comfortable carrying were hymns. "But I can be loud," she said, "and I figured if Rex Harrison could star in a musical, so could I." She worked up a few songs with musical arranger and vocal coach Roger

Edens, which she tried out one night at Irene Selznick's before the guests of a small dinner party, which included Alan Lerner and Frederick Brisson, the play's producer and husband of Rosalind Russell. After bellowing a captivating rendition of "Miss Otis Regrets," everybody seemed convinced that she had enough equipment to carry a musical. What she lacked in euphony she made up for in guts. Ultimately she found both the challenge and Alan J. Lerner—a man of extraordinary wit and intelligence—irresistible.

Coco proved to be the most arduous production of Hepburn's career, a constant uphill battle. She continued her voice lessons six days a week. "I'm not sure I ever really learned to sing," Kate admitted, "but I acted well enough to give the impression that I was singing!" The lyrics of *Coco* were among the cleverest Lerner ever wrote, but neither they nor the star were helped much by the music of André Previn, mostly forgettable tunes, some of which sounded like remnants from *Gigi.*

Then the show's director, Michael Benthall, who had guided Hepburn in *The Millionairess,* began to stumble. When he proved unable to tackle all the elements of the musical—which included not only a complicated revolving set but also several characters out of Coco's past appearing on large screens in filmed segments—he was sidelined. The choreographer, the young Michael Bennett, stepped in and assumed directorial duties as well. Bold and brash and full of his own ideas, he clashed constantly with Lerner and the star—both of whom, he felt, had somehow turned the show from the life of Chanel into that of Katharine Hepburn— an independent female artist, who gets through life by remaining "always mademoiselle."

In fact, that was the title of the big finale; and several of its sentiments came straight from Hepburn's mouth. One night while she was getting extremely frustrated with the entire production, Kate threw her hands up at dinner and said to Lerner, "Who the devil cares what a woman wears!" He said, "Kate, that's a good lyric," and used it. In the same number he also adopted one of Hepburn's firmest beliefs about character, that actions define a person, that—as Lerner lyricized it—"One is as one does."

With the exception of George Rose, who played Coco's friend and manager Louis Greff, Hepburn felt the cast was "pretty mediocre." "With all the actors in New York," she said, "it always amazes me how difficult it is to find a few with real talent."

During one number, Bennett staged a routine in which a dancer had to stand in front of Hepburn and perform a series of fan kicks, first swinging his right leg over her head, then the left. "I'm sure Michael kept hoping that man would miss one night and kick me right in the face," Kate said. Everybody lived in constant fear that the set wouldn't revolve properly, and on more than one occasion it didn't. The audiences on those nights got perhaps the best show of all, as Hepburn would step center stage and regale the crowd with show-business anecdotes until the machinery was functioning again.

Once the show opened, the week before Christmas 1969, none of the problems seemed to matter. For eight months fans came steadily to see this sumptuous showcase for Katharine Hepburn, with its Cecil Beaton sets and costumes. While some critics quibbled over her warbling or quarreled over the writing, everybody succumbed to the power and energy the trim, Chanel-tailored sexagenarian exuded on the stage of the Mark Hellinger Theatre eight times a week. It remained a strained production, for which Hepburn shouldered much of the responsibility. "How couldn't it be tense?" Kate asked. "I was nervous about every performance . . . wondering what the hell I was doing out there." She left *Coco* in August 1970, and was replaced by Danielle Darrieux, who performed admirably. But the production closed shortly thereafter. (Hepburn recorded the cast album and resurrected the show on the road before soldout standing ovations.)

Through the 1970s, Katharine Hepburn remained in perpetual motion, tackling one project after another. Work remained the best antidote against grief. In fact, she refused far more offers than she accepted, agreeing only to those that provided the opportunity to work with unique talent or special material. Never having performed Greek tragedy, she went to Spain at the end of 1970 to appear in a film version of Euripides' *Trojan Women*. Michael Cacoyannis, who had directed *Zorba the Greek*, had also enticed Vanessa Redgrave to costar. Kate considered her the most accomplished actress of her generation— "a thrill to look at and to listen to." (Years later, in fact, there was talk of turning Hepburn's memoir about the making of *The African Queen* into a film, which didn't excite her until she learned that Redgrave might play her. "I don't know who else could possibly do it," she said.)

Kate worked next on two projects that she ultimately abandoned. She was meant to star in a film version of Graham Greene's *Travels with My Aunt*, which George Cukor was directing. After receiving no satisfaction from several different versions of the script, Hepburn took to rewriting it herself. Shortly before shooting was to begin, the studio announced its displeasure with her version and that they were going back to earlier drafts of the script. "When I said I had no interest in any of the earlier drafts," Kate recalled, "they said, 'Thank you very much.'" She was replaced by Maggie Smith in what proved to be an unsatisfying production, released in 1972.

And, at the height of their friendship, Kate worked for years with Irene Selznick on a project called *Martha*, based on a series of books by Margery Sharp about a young artist. Irene intended to produce the film, with Kate directing. The project was subsequently aborted—"not because I didn't think I could direct . . . and not because I didn't think Irene could produce a movie. I think it's simply because I was afraid we'd kill each other."

Then producer Ely Landau approached her for the third time, on this occasion touting something called the American Film Theater.

He was producing cinematic versions of important dramas, which would play on television and have theatrical film distribution. The play in question was Edward Albee's *A Delicate Balance,* a family drama about a seemingly complacent older couple in suburban Connecticut whose lives are suddenly thrown off-kilter by the unexpected arrival of their best friends; this visit becomes a strange incursion, compelling the characters to examine the debts and deceptions in their lives. "I'll be honest with you," Kate divulged, "I knew that Albee was considered 'the great white hope' of the American theater, but I had absolutely no idea what that play was about."

Surrounded by an elite corps of actors—which included Paul Scofield and Joseph Cotten—and directed by Tony Richardson, a highly intelligent and fussy British expatriate, Hepburn came to appreciate the point of the play. "I think it's about self-protection," she said, "—how our homes become our domains, and how we want to protect that from outsiders. And we even come to see that this marriage is really made up of two people trying to protect themselves, from each other. He's a stuffed shirt, and she's a bossy old thing, and that's the only way they can save themselves. At least that's what I think. But I must tell you, for the first time in my life, I had no idea what I was saying. Maybe that tells you how *good* the dialogue in that play is." Several people had told her the play was funny; but Kate confessed, "I never really saw a grain of humor in it."

Then producer David Susskind, who had been attempting for years to mount a television production of *The Glass Menagerie,* asked Kate to play the mother. She was loath to accept the offer. Having starred in motion pictures for forty years, she had a knee-jerk reaction against a work made directly for television. She also had Laurette Taylor's performance as Amanda Wingfield ingrained in her memory. Agreeing to the project meant she would get to work with

Anthony Harvey again, which pleased her enormously; but what ultimately convinced her to take the part was the opportunity for her niece Kathy Houghton to play her daughter once again, this time the crippled Laura. Hepburn signed on, only to learn that Kathy Houghton was not interested in playing the role. "She would have been perfect," Kate said. "It's a great part for her." But Kathy had other acting plans at the time, as well as writing aspirations. Kate never really appreciated that it might be difficult for her niece to perform in her shadow.

While Hepburn was not ideally cast as the Southern mother, who endlessly recalls her days as an alluring belle, she brought all the requisite power to the role, which she delivered with grace and intelligence. Tony Harvey directed a strong supporting cast—Sam Waterston, Michael Moriarty, and Joanna Miles. The program became one of the great television events in 1973, commanding huge ratings. Its success opened Hepburn's mind to the possibilities of future work in the medium.

Then Hepburn's friend George Cukor, in his mid-seventies, was offered an elegant script by James Costigan—for television. *Love Among the Ruins* was an Edwardian story of an elderly actress who turns to a former beau to defend her against a younger man suing for breach of promise. Cukor thought it would be ideal for Hepburn and Laurence Olivier. Hepburn agreed and made a crucial suggestion to the director. "Look," she said, "we both know Larry; and he will do this project only if you go to him first. Then suggest several other actresses, until he mentions my name. Then you can say, 'Larry, if I knew you were doing this play, I'm sure I could get Kate.'" Olivier bought Cukor's act.

Hepburn enjoyed working with Olivier—though she was still recuperating from a hip-replacement operation at the time. She thought he was "a first-rate actor." But she felt compelled to add that she thought he was "a second-rate person." More than finding him a posturing egomaniac, she based her judgment largely on his treatment of his former wife, Vivien Leigh, a talented though troubled woman, with whom Kate had been friendly. "Larry always wanted to be a big movie star," Kate said, "and while he was considered the greatest actor on the stage, he was never in the first rank as a star in the movies. Then Vivien comes along and gets Scarlett O'Hara. Wins the Academy Award. Biggest picture ever made. Suddenly Larry says, 'Oh darling, we really must get you out of Hollywood now. Let's go off and do Shakespeare together.' Now Vivien could do anything, but he was clearly trying to keep her in her place, which was billed beneath him. Then a few years pass and Vivien returns to make *Streetcar*. And she's brilliant. Wins the Academy Award. Most talked-about movie of the year. And suddenly Larry says, 'Oh darling, we really must get you out of Hollywood now. Let's go off and do Shakespeare together.' Small man. Giant actor. Very small man." *Love Among the Ruins* was a great success, collecting rave notices, big ratings, and Emmy Awards for the director and his two stars.

Hepburn next teamed with John Wayne. She had not worked with him before, and she hadn't played opposite an actor who seemed so different from her since she and Humphrey Bogart navigated the Congo River. In many ways, this picture, *Rooster Cogburn,* was a carbon copy of *The African Queen*—a Bible-toting minister's daughter ends up on a journey with an aging marshal, who is after a gang of bad guys. The title hero was, in fact, the same character Wayne had played in *True Grit.*

There wasn't much more to this movie than the two legends firing stereotypical dialogue at each other. But both stars had a good time making it. Coming from two different political camps, these rugged old-timers simply avoided controversial subjects and chose to enjoy each other's company. Said Kate, "I can honestly say I never met a man who worked harder or played harder than Duke. He was a total straight-shooter, decent, and fun. Just a natural. We were up in the Cascades, and some days we got on our horses and rode all day. Great fun. Big man. Small backside." The stunt casting alone was reason enough for some people to see the film, though not many.

In 1976 Hepburn agreed to a three-month run of a play called *A Matter of Gravity* by her friend Enid Bagnold. This was a lighter version of her hit play *The Chalk Garden,* a look at several generations in a big English country house. In London, Edith Evans had played the dotty matriarch in the decaying home. Bagnold was only too happy to alter the part to suit the grande dame of the American theater. In retrospect, one of the play's greatest distinctions was its appearance of Christopher Reeve as her grandson in one of his first roles. Kate took a shine to the handsome young actor. So the day I heard that Reeve had been paralyzed in a near-fatal accident, I called Kate to give her the news. "Part of me thinks you'll say, 'He'd be better off dead.'"

"Mmmm," Kate said, passively agreeing. Then she added, "But I don't think so. He's strong. Strong body, strong spirit. He's got a family he loves. He's got guts . . . and unlike a lot of actors . . . he's got a brain."

Before taking *A Matter of Gravity* on a successful nationwide tour, Hepburn appeared in an odd, forgotten little movie called *Olly Olly Oxen Free,* in which she played the owner of a junkyard who helps two children repair a hot-air balloon. "All I really remember about it," Kate said, only five years after making it, "is that I got to ride in the balloon. And one night we filmed a scene in which I brought the balloon down right in the middle of a performance at the Hollywood Bowl. I'd say that was probably worth the price of admission for all of us."

After the *Matter of Gravity* tour, Hepburn worked again with George Cukor, then seventy-nine, remaking Emlyn Williams's *The*

Corn is Green. Bette Davis had appeared in the acclaimed 1940s film version, and Kate was pleased when the television production won more kudos for everybody involved.

So, in the fifteen years since Spencer Tracy's death, Katharine Hepburn had been almost as active as she had during any previous period of her life. She cheerfully graced magazine covers and granted interviews, including one with Dick Cavett, the host of a popular late-night television program. In 1974 she startled a worldwide television audience—and a thousand people sitting in the Dorothy Chandler Pavilion—when Academy Awards host David Niven unexpectedly announced the next presenter by saying, "To me, this is a star—Katharine Hepburn."

She strode out in a black pantsuit and clogs, as the stunned crowd rose as one. Hepburn quieted the audience and thanked them for their moving welcome. "I'm also very happy that I didn't hear anyone call out, 'It's about time,'" she said. Then she added, "I'm living proof that a person can wait forty-one years to be unselfish." She was there to present the Irving Thalberg Award to her old friend Lawrence Weingarten, who had produced *Adam's Rib.* After they walked offstage, Hepburn left the winner to face the press alone, as she disappeared into a waiting limousine, leaving as suddenly as she had arrived. Hepburn sightings in Los Angeles and New York—playing tennis with Alex Olmedo at the Beverly Hills Hotel, shoveling snow on East Forty-ninth Street, theatergoing on and off Broadway—became less uncommon but no less thrilling.

By the 1980s most of the male movie stars of Hepburn's generation had died, and the few remaining female stars of her vintage had fallen from sight. A tremor—mostly her head, sometimes her hands—had become increasingly pronounced; her voice quavered; and skin cancers periodically erupted on her face—"too much time in the sun. No good for redheads." But her strength and energy had not noticeably diminished.

She and her friend Noel Willman, who had directed her in a few plays, drove down to Wilmington, Delaware, one day to catch a performance of a play called *On Golden Pond,* by Ernest Thompson. Hepburn found it a "true" depiction of an elderly married couple, coping with the difficulties of old age. Although she found the actors at least a generation too young for the parts they were playing, she thought it would make a good movie.

So did Jane Fonda. She was intrigued by the relationship between the incommunicative and undemonstrative father and his daughter, who had long sought his approval. It mirrored her relationship with her legendary father, Henry. Not until Jane's production company put the film together and the director, Mark Rydell, introduced them, did the two mythic older stars meet.

"It was strange," Kate said of being cast in the film. "It seemed as though I was the mother Jane had fantasized having . . . and if her father and I could make everything all right in the movie, somehow things would be all right in her life. There was certainly a whole layer of drama going on in the scenes between her and Hank, and I think she came by to watch every scene he and I had together. There was a feeling of longing about her."

By the end of the shoot—during which Hepburn's character, Ethel Thayer, tries to instill some Yankee virtues into her unforgiving daughter and unyielding husband—Hepburn was full of admiration for Jane Fonda. "We all had a good time making the picture," Kate said. "It was fun." And it allowed Kate to show how spunky she still was—diving fully clothed into Squam Lake, singing and dancing an old campfire song, perfusing her failing husband with love and wisdom. She walked away from the production thinking how hard it must have been for Jane, being the daughter of this famous figure who was so remote. "Hank Fonda was the hardest nut I ever tried to crack," Kate said. "But I didn't know any more about him after we had made the picture than I did at the beginning. Cold. Cold. Cold."

At the start of production, Hepburn had given Fonda one of Spencer Tracy's favorite hats; and at the end, the actor had reciprocated by presenting her with a painting he had done of three hats, Tracy's in the middle. Kate was touched by the gift—until she realized he had made a print of the picture and given dozens of them away, to publicists and friends of friends. "Strange man," she said. "Angry at something. And sad."

Hepburn had her hand in the script—more, I suspect, than she let on. She turned suddenly modest one evening talking about the speech in which Ethel tells her husband that he's her "knight in shining armor," and that he's got to "go, go, go." When I suggested that it sounded like "pure Hepburn," she immediately spoke of all the hard work the writer had done, defining those characters. Ernest Thompson won an Academy Award for Best Screenplay that year. So did Henry Fonda, his first, which his daughter accepted while he watched on television from his bed, only a few months before he died. Breaking her own precedent, Katharine Hepburn won as well—for the fourth time.

By then, Hepburn was already appearing in a new work by Ernest Thompson, a play called *The West Side Waltz*. It was another gerontological study, a woman refusing to bow out of life gracefully. She had hoped somebody might buy the screen rights for her, to costar with either Elizabeth Taylor or Doris Day; but nobody did. Instead, she committed herself to a film originally titled *The Ultimate Solution of Grace Quigley*. Kate said the writer had literally thrown the script over her fence and she had fallen in love with it—a black comedy about an old woman who hires a hit man (played by Nick Nolte) to bump off her dying friends. Few beyond Hepburn saw the humor.

Over the next few years, Kate continued to lose friends and acquaintances as well as longtime "rivals" from the thirties (most of whom she barely knew, if at all)—Bette Davis, Joan Crawford,

Myrna Loy, Jean Arthur, Mae West, Irene Dunne, Barbara Stanwyck. Later Garbo, Dietrich, Greer Garson, Sylvia Sidney, and Claudette Colbert died. Kate's first great friend from the theater, Laura Harding, lived an increasingly sedentary life on her estate in New Jersey, which irritated Kate as much as it bored her.

In what proved to be his final months, Kate restruck a warm relationship with Luddy, then a widower and suffering from inoperable cancer. For a while he accepted his first wife's open invitation to Fenwick; but when the trips became too difficult, she visited him at his own bedside. "I tried to do everything for Luddy that I possibly could, knowing I could never repay him for all the support he had given me," Kate told me two decades after his death. "Unimaginable—my life, had it not been for Luddy. He was heaven-sent."

More than ever, Hepburn cultivated her newer friendships. Cynthia McFadden divorced her husband and, after joining the *ABC News* team, always made time for Kate; Tony Harvey moved from the city to the Hamptons, but visited regularly at Turtle Bay and Fenwick and even got her to call on him on Long Island. David Eichler often made the trip north from Philadelphia for dinner and the night. She always got a charge out of seeing Martina Navratilova, one of whose tennis racquets she proudly displayed in the living room; and she always seemed buoyed by gossip columnist Liz Smith, despite her being engaged in what Kate called "a moronic profession."

Kate also found herself making time for people she normally would never have tolerated. She would invite Corliss Lamont, a highly intelligent but rather ponderous old author and philosopher, to dine anytime he called, even though he would sit there for fifteen minutes at a time without uttering a word. Kate had gone two decades without speaking to Garson Kanin because of his chatty book *Tracy and Hepburn*; but even he won his way back into her good graces, simply because he was available. "Oh," she said wearily the day after their reunion, "I'm too old to be carrying grudges." But her dance card was no longer filled every night. As often as not, Kate and Phyllis ate dinner alone, in increasing silence.

Into her eighties, Hepburn remained professionally active. She continued to make movies for television, which gradually deteriorated in quality, though not necessarily in popularity. She participated in documentary films—sometimes as the subject, just as often to contribute anecdotes about others, be it Spencer Tracy or George Stevens.

She tinkered for years on a screenplay titled *Me and Phyllis,* scenes of their lives together. It climaxed in the car crash in which Kate almost lost her foot and Phyllis her life. One night in the living room on Forty-ninth Street, Kate performed the entire script for me. She captured the dialogue between the two of them in funny detail; and she brought me close to tears a few times in revealing her gratitude for having had somebody so dear as Phyllis in her life. Beyond that, it was a strange piece of work that was meant to be a quasi-documentary, with Hepburn reenacting scenes from her own life. She asked me what I thought of it and how she might improve it. For a moment, I felt like William Holden stumbling into Norma Desmond's parlor in *Sunset Boulevard.* "Now, remember," she said, before I could speak, "don't spoil an old woman's delusions."

"Well, it certainly played great tonight," I said, "but do you think it would be as funny on the screen? I mean, wouldn't it be strange?"

"Well, you laughed, and I'll be playing me again."

"Yeah," I said, "but you were performing the whole thing as a kind of reading. It'll be different if you're staging it for film, which literalizes everything. Besides," I said, "who could possibly play Phyllis?"

"Quite right," Phyllis interjected. "Nobody could possibly play me."

Kate asked for casting suggestions; and I proposed Mona Washbourne and Mildred Natwick, both of whom had some of Phyllis's fey quality. "It's a shame Nigel Bruce is gone," Kate said.

"Nigel Bruce?" queried Phyllis indignantly. "To play me? That's ridiculous."

"You don't have to worry, dearie. He's dead."

In fact, several producers showed an interest in Kate's script, though I think a few of them were just interested in spending time with her and shopping her name around town. Joseph E. Levine—a producer with a long and spotty track record—actively pursued the project and claimed for months to have the financing in place. Talks progressed far enough that Kate was once willing to have lunch with him in public. She told me it would be the first time she had eaten in a restaurant in at least twenty years. As that made it an occasion in itself, she selected The Four Seasons. She ate caviar and drank champagne and thoroughly enjoyed herself; but the deal soon fell apart.

No matter. Hepburn finished her second autobiographical book, *Me,* the compilation of pieces she had been pulling together over the years. Sonny Mehta and everyone else at Knopf backed the book in a tremendous way. When the American Booksellers Association held its large annual tradeshow in New York late in the spring of 1991, just months before publication, Kate opened her house to the owners of the major bookstores and chains for a cocktail party.

For the first time I saw her panic about the book. While dozens of people milled around the house, some spilling out into the garden on the warm spring evening, Kate pulled me upstairs and said, "Why am I doing this?" I assured her that this party was great public relations, that meeting her was one of the biggest thrills for everybody in that room. "No," she said in frustration. "Why am I publishing this book? I mean, I've gone this long. Why bother—"

"Maybe because the public has given you a lot over the years. And you should think of this as giving them something back. A small piece of you for those who care."

Kate returned to the party all smiles; and when the books were produced, she autographed copies for everybody who had a hand in its publication. She even agreed to selective publicity. While the book never got penetratingly personal, it illustrated a life of hard work, adventures, and fun.

On my next visit to Fenwick, I found a copy of the book just sitting on my bed, autographed with the author's love and thanks. Flipping through the finished work, I also found my name listed with a dozen others in the acknowledgments—calling me her "chief critic." I went downstairs and said, "I assume this copy of your book is for me."

"Mmm," she said, not wishing to make much of it. "Is it all right?"

"Yeah, it's great. Thank you for your kind words. But honestly, Kate. I'm not a *critic*."

"What are you talking about? Of course, you are. You're always correcting and criticizing, and having the last word."

"That's not true," I protested. "I may make the occasional suggestion—"

"It's *quite* true. You're doing it right now. My God, you're completely hopeless!"

One day later that week, when we were back in New York and *Me* was number one on the bestseller lists, I asked Kate what her most satisfying role had been. "I'd have to say," she replied, pausing, then looking up at the wooden goose hanging from the ceiling as it had years earlier back in the Cukor guest cottage, "—those years I wasn't working."

I knew she meant those five years just before Spencer Tracy's death. And then she surprised me by remembering exactly the first

266

time that topic had come up. "But," she added with a smile, now that we had covered a lot of ground in the years since then, "I never talk about that time."

"Who's Donovan?" Kate asked over the phone one day in the summer of 1990.

"Donovan?" I asked back. "Why do you want to know about Donovan?"

"Who *is* he?"

"Well, he's a singer, kind of a folk-rock singer from the sixties. Why do you want to know about Donovan?"

"Because I'm going to do his program."

"His program? What kind of program?"

"His television program."

"Kate, this guy was a hippie singer and songwriter from the sixties. I don't think he has a television program. What sort of show do you think he has?"

"It's one of those talk shows. Like Cavett. Only it's during the day, and he's apparently very popular with all the housewives."

"Got it. Kate—his name is Dona*hue*. Phil Donahue. Yes, he's got a very popular show. It'll be great for your book. But you had me worried for a minute. I thought you were going on some show wearing a headband and love beads."

It didn't take much to promote Kate's book; and she did what she was asked. Cynthia McFadden made her promise not to appear on *Sally Jessy Raphael* or any of the other down-market shows. There was no need to worry. Nobody knew how to sell Katharine Hepburn better than Katharine Hepburn. In fact, she often talked about herself in the third person—as "the creature." She said "the creature" had become an institution, much like the Flatiron Building or the Statue of Liberty, a bastion that had withstood the tests of time. *Me* became a phenomenal success, cresting the bestseller list for over a year.

After the rush of the book, however, as the sales, interviews, and publicity died down, there was little on Hepburn's plate. For the first time in a long time—at age eighty-five—she didn't know what she even *might* do next. Scripts still arrived regularly, but most of them were terrible—patronizing screenplays about "cute little old ladies— what a goddamned bore," she said. She received umpteen renditions of *The Aspern Papers,* one of which, she hooted with incredulity, was pornographic.

Her primary occupation became her mail. A secretary sorted through most of it, then presented her with those letters that required a response. A few warranted handwritten replies—usually written with a black Flair pen on KATHARINE HOUGHTON HEPBURN notepaper. Others received dictated responses later in the day. The important missives were alphabetized and filed in fat accordion folders and stored away.

Most of the mail came from rapturous fans. Little peeved Kate more than an extravagant letter from an admirer who rhapsodized about her talent and beauty and influence on his or her life, then addressed the envelope to "Katherine Hepburn." "God," Kate would splutter, "you'd think the first thing they'd learn is how to spell my name." It pleased her that people enjoyed her work, but she found the letters from those who wrote of spending countless hours watching her movies, night after night, deeply disturbing. "If they're really inspired by what I've done with my life," she asked, "—why don't they do something with theirs? Not just watch old movies."

More disturbing were the occasional crank letters, sometimes hate mail, usually about her position on abortion. Occasionally there were threats. Whenever she received such a letter—or read about an abortion clinic being bombed by some religious fanatic—Kate would declare, "So much for 'God is Love!'" The hate mail was separated from the rest; but Kate held on to it, tucking it away in a closet off the living room.

For Kate, the most distressing aspect of the 1990s was Phyllis's behavior. Her age had long been a mystery, but everybody presumed she was at least a few years older than Kate. As such, she was something of a medical miracle, still going through the motions of her rigorous job every day, seven days a week. In truth, Kate had really looked after Phyllis more than the other way around for years. Everything about her had slowed; she often needed to lie down; she was frequently confused. "Phyllis needs a Phyllis," Kate said; and she hired people to look after her, mostly to see that she didn't wander into harm's way. One Sunday afternoon I came upon Phyllis in the foyer at Fenwick, just standing there in a daze with one arm in the sleeve of her coat. I asked her if everything was all right. "Oh, fine. Just fine," she insisted. "I just can't remember whether we're coming or going."

Kate was becoming lonely. Although Cynthia McFadden saw Hepburn as much as possible, her fast-paced career, new romances, and a baby consumed more and more of her time. Tony Harvey in the Hamptons and David Eichler in Philadelphia found themselves in Manhattan with less frequency, while Kate's pianist friend Laura Fratti suffered from ill health and didn't get around much. And I finished my research on Lindbergh and had to go home to Los Angeles to write. For the next few years, I had little reason to travel to the East Coast except to visit Kate.

At first I tried to steal away every month or two. Gradually, my visits decreased to four times a year, then two. I tried to stay in touch by telephone, but Kate always acted slightly hostile toward the instrument or those at the other end. Whenever I called, she would ask where I was, then say, "Well, you're of no use to me there." Then she'd usually add, "You should come back soon . . . before I'm dead."

Our visits remained pleasant, but they were changing. With less stimulation, her life had become stagnant. She moved more slowly; her energy ebbed. Gone were the conversations until midnight, or ten, or even eight. Sometimes she'd want dinner as early as five o'clock; and she'd clamber up the stairs to bed—literally using her hands and feet—by six, before the sun had set.

The only thing that kept her downstairs a little longer was to have a drink or two after dinner. In the late eighties she had changed brands of Scotch, from her King William IV to Famous Grouse. She had been introduced to it by her wealthy relatives in Boca Grande, Florida. "Now, Kate," I said, in mock irritation, "I've been telling you about this Scotch for years, that all the right people in England drink it. And you ignored me. Now because some Houghtons drink it, it's okay." She recalled my having discoursed on the subject of Famous Grouse more than once. "You've caught me, and now you know the truth," she said. "I'm a hopeless snob."

I learned from Norah and the other caretakers around both houses that these days Kate was usually having two drinks before dinner and one or two postprandially. They never seemed to affect her physically, but they fogged her mind. She was forgetting things. This new condition worried Norah enough for her to take it upon herself to water down the whiskey. During my visits, she told me she was pouring half the Scotch out of the Famous Grouse bottles and diluting the rest with water. "It's funny," Kate said to me one night at dinner. "I've completely lost all sense of taste. I take a drink, and it has no flavor."

Unconsciously, Kate was using the liquor as an anodyne—not only to kill the mildly depressing bouts of loneliness but also her physical pain, which I had long suspected was worse than she ever let on. Emotional situations—a sad scene in a movie, a touching story, a death—could bring her to tears; but only once did I see her cry because something physically hurt. It was a late afternoon in 1992, when she was trying to step onto the bench in the living room to water some plants. She thought she was alone in the room, and I could see she was in agony. At last, she swung her bad foot up and it clearly ached. She let out a small cry, and I ran in to help her. There were tears in her eyes, and she said she had tripped.

Another time in the summer of 1992, we drove to a park near Fenwick to take a walk. It had just started to sprinkle when Kate came upon a great bunch of Queen Anne's lace. There was one absolutely magnificent blossom she insisted on having. She pulled and pulled on the huge flower but it would not uproot. Then she tried to snap the stalk, but it would only bend, not break. She asked me for the car key, which she used as a saw on the fibrous stem. For several minutes she stood hunched over the flower, hacking away, as the drizzle turned to rain. Mother Nature was clearly going to win this round; so I said, "Kate, let's go. It's really starting to come down." As she gave up on the plant, I noticed how wet her eyes were, and not from the rain. We drove back to Fenwick in silence.

That disturbed me far less than another drive some months later, in the spring of 1993. Kate's chauffeur of the last few years, a man of great equanimity, had suddenly died, and a new man was at the wheel. On a Saturday morning we made the trip from Fenwick to Peg's house for lunch, a trip she had made several thousand times. Approaching Hartford, US 91 offered exits to the east and west, and the driver called out for directions. "East," Kate said firmly.

"Aren't we going to Peg's?" I asked.

"Of course we're going to Peg's," she said. "Where do you think we're going?"

"Well, Peg lives to the west of Hartford."

"East. East," she called out to the driver, then said to me, "You never had any sense of direction. She lives to the east."

"Kate," I said, reaching for a map, "unless Peg has moved, she lives to the west of Hartford." I spread Connecticut out on my lap and said, "Here's where we are, and here to the left is Peg."

Kate looked thrown but tried to shrug it off. "All this time," she said, "I always thought that was to the east."

Close to six months passed before I was again able to leave Los Angeles and visit Kate. By then, she was spending most of her time in Fenwick, using the trips to New York City for meetings with doctors, lawyers, and accountants—appointments that seemed merely a way of differentiating the weeks. In the early fall, I found a free weekend. Because I didn't want her to anticipate my visit for too long with the possibility of my canceling at the last minute, I didn't call her until Thursday afternoon. I said that I would arrive at Fenwick in time for dinner the next night. We had a nice long talk, and we joked that she would have to wait at least until five-thirty before eating dinner.

Early the next morning I left for New Haven, where I picked up a car and drove on to Old Saybrook. The timing was perfect. I crossed the causeway to Fenwick a little after five and pulled into the driveway. A concerned woman looked out at me from the kitchen. This was Hong Luong, the new housekeeper at Fenwick, a strong but kind soul and an able cook. "I hope you're expecting me?" I said, reading on her face that she was not.

"Don't worry," she said. "There's plenty of food."

But I was worried. As I walked into the living room—which was darker than usual, and dead quiet—Kate and Phyllis were sitting in their places with television tables set before them, waiting to be served. "Remember me?" I asked.

"What are you do—" she started to say, then stopped to amend her greeting. For the first time, I saw Kate embarrassed, even a little ashamed, as she said, "You are entering a house of the very old."

I poured a glass of Famous Grouse—a double, neat. And it tasted of nothing.

X

Travels with "My Aunt"

Actors occupy a peculiar place in the social phylum—people who literally stand out from the rest of the species, wanting to be looked at as much as the rest of us want to look at them. They bring stories to life, tapping into our emotions, often becoming the vessels that allow us to experience a moment of realization, sometimes self-recognition. Many become reference points common to people around the world, elements in universally shared experiences. We tend to look upon the practitioners of the acting profession as special. We pamper and praise them; some people practically worship them.

Then there are movie stars, a breed unto themselves. The stakes are so high for those rare few who, decade after decade, captivate us, that we shower rewards upon them. Some are compensated with millions of dollars for a few days of work; their opinions on all subjects are held in higher regard. We create special rules for them, private entrances and exits for them to pass through.

The lives of the biggest movie stars—the "superstars"—are generally as "unreal" offstage as the characters they portray. There is a near-constant frenzy around them—the whirl of managers and agents and publicists and assistants tending to the constant demands for the star's time: interviews; photograph sessions; public appearances. The ringing telephone becomes an addiction, often sending a star into withdrawal when it stops.

For those who became famous under the old studio system, the lack of reality to their lives was even greater. Because the contract stars of the thirties, forties, and fifties had worked constantly, everything off the set was less important than what they did before the cameras. The studio heads paying the bills protected their own interests and took care of everything in their stars' lives. On the set, doubles were always available for the dangerous or unpleasant duties, whether it was performing a stunt or standing under the hot lights. Off-camera, everything was tended to. Not just clothing and grooming and personal chores but even indecent, occasionally illegal, activities were cleaned up, swept under the carpet, fixed.

Many stars begin to believe their own encomiastic press releases. After a year or a decade, and, in a few cases, a lifetime of fabulous salaries and fringe benefits, there naturally comes a sense of great expectations. With most movie stars, there also comes a sense of entitlement.

Perhaps the most attractive aspect of Katharine Hepburn's personality was that she held no such feelings. She made plenty of demands; indeed, she knew how to get what she wanted long before she was a star. In part, that's how she got to be a star. But she always remained grounded. In twenty years I never found a trail of bodies she trampled over in order to reach her goal. For all her impatience, there was always a sense of humility and humanity, even a sense of gratitude for her good fortune. She was never above making a bed, cooking a meal, chopping wood, or working her garden. Indeed, she found pleasure in those activities. Almost every time I saw her in the kitchen in Fenwick, she was wiping a sponge across the countertop, cleaning up after somebody.

In short, she never lost her work ethic. She believed the point of making money was to allow you to live comfortably enough to work some more, until you simply could work no longer.

"Retire?" she had exclaimed one night at dinner, when Irene Selznick had found a gentle way of broaching the topic. "What's the point? Actors shouldn't walk away from the audience as long as the audiences aren't walking away from them. As long as people are buying what I'm selling," she added, "I'm still selling." Kate never understood how people got stuck in jobs they didn't enjoy.

Stars who bemoaned the hardships of their profession—the impositions, the loss of privacy—rankled her, as though she were embarrassed to be one of them. "These actors who complain in interviews about twelve-hour days!" she said with incomprehension. "You sit there for eleven of them. It's not as if we're carrying sacks of feed all day!"

"What does he expect?" she said upon reading about Sean Penn punching out a photographer. "You can't go around saying, 'I'm special. I make my living asking you to look at me, to pay to see me,' and then get upset at somebody for taking a picture. If you don't want to be a public figure, don't pick a public profession and don't appear in public. Because in public you're fair game." She also didn't understand stars who sued newspapers over printing lies about them. "I never cared what anybody wrote about me," Hepburn said, "as long as it wasn't the truth."

While she sought the limelight all her life, Hepburn believed actors received too much attention and respect. "Let's face it," she said once, "we're prostitutes. I've spent my life selling myself—my face, my body, the way I walk and talk. Actors say, 'You can look at me, but you must pay me for it.'" I said that may be true, but actors also offer a unique service—the best of them please by inspiring, by becoming the agents for our emotional catharses. "It's no small thing to move people," I said, "and perhaps to get people to think differently, maybe even behave differently." I pointed out to Hepburn that she had used her celebrity over the years for numerous causes—whether it was marching in parades for women's equality or campaigning for Roosevelt, speaking out against McCarthyism, or supporting Planned Parenthood. "Not much, really," Kate said. "I could've done more. A lot more. . . . It really doesn't take all that much to show up for a dinner with the President or to accept an award from an organization so it can receive some publicity. Oh, the hardship! Oh, the inconvenience! Oh, honestly!"

Los Angeles is, in many ways, a one-industry town. There is, obviously, a thriving financial sector; real estate, aerospace, and the music business have all played a large part in the economy and ethos of the city. But motion pictures dominate, pervading all walks of the city's life. Photographs of movie stars decorate the walls of liquor stores, restaurants, even car washes—with best wishes from the likes of Burt Reynolds, Zsa Zsa Gabor, and Rock Hudson. Although most people in Los Angeles have never met a movie star, everybody there seems to "know" them all—through a common trainer or hair stylist or florist or dry cleaner or checker at the supermarket.

For close to seventy years, Katharine Hepburn sightings remained the most coveted of show-business personalities—even more than those of Garbo, who could be counted on to take her daily constitutional on the streets of New York. One rarely heard a firsthand Katharine Hepburn story. Although some of my friends knew of my relationship with her—mostly because her name appeared on the dedication page and in the acknowledgments of *Goldwyn*—few ever invaded *her* privacy by even asking me about her.

Although I had "known" Warren Beatty through several friends and my older brother, Jeff, the head of International Creative Management, a major talent agency, I had never met him until early 1993. Then I began receiving calls from his wife's agent. He said Annette Bening had long been fascinated with Anne Morrow Lindbergh, and she was hoping I might be able to meet her sometime to talk about what I had gleaned from the Lindberghs' private archives. An insistent third call from the agent expressed the fact that Warren Beatty was eager to meet me as well and that somebody would be calling very soon to arrange a dinner. Five months passed in which I heard nothing.

In mid-July the agent called again to set our date. I said this no longer seemed like such a good idea, that after half a year there seemed something slightly forced in the situation. No, the agent explained, Warren Beatty was extremely interested in our meeting. I had not heard from anybody, he explained, because Warren had, in fact, been occupied producing, rewriting, and starring in a film called *Love Affair*. It was a remake of the 1957 movie *An Affair to Remember*, which starred Cary Grant and Deborah Kerr, which was a remake of *Love Affair*, made in 1939 with Charles Boyer and Irene Dunne, all based on a story by Mildred Cram. He and Annette, I was told, very much wanted to get together as soon as possible.

On Wednesday, July twenty-first, Kevin McCormick, a film producer who had recently become an executive at Twentieth Century Fox, and I drove from our house in the hills above the Sunset Strip to Mulholland Drive, where we were buzzed through the Beattys' gate at exactly seven-thirty. In the living room, we found Warren playing with his eighteen-month-old daughter, entertaining two other guests, the agent and a female executive from another studio. Annette darted in, to say hello, and then went to put her daughter to bed. For several minutes, our host chatted with all of us; then we repaired to the dining room for dinner, where Annette joined us. Few movie stars look as good in person as they do on screen, where they benefit from makeup and lights. The Beattys, however, did. He was taller than I had expected, and his face was starting to show some attractive character lines I hadn't seen on film. She glowed.

The house was comfortable and unostentatious—though the dining-room ceiling could be retracted, letting guests feel as if they were outdoors. We ate "indoors" that night, a tasty but extremely dietetic meal of chicken and vegetables and a fruit dessert. A bottle of wine sat on the table, but neither of the hosts indulged, imbibing only water. Conversation quickly turned to my work on Lindbergh. Annette and the three other guests just sat and ate, as Warren peppered me with questions about the famous aviator. He was surprised (and pleased) to learn that the story included so much politics, starting with Lindbergh's grandfather (who had been elected to the Swedish Riksdag and had been forced to leave his homeland because of a political and sexual scandal), including Lindbergh's father (who had been a controversial five-term Congressman), right up to Lindbergh himself, known for his role in the little-understood America First movement. I tried to include everybody at the table in the discussion, often lassoing Kevin in for his astute political commentary. But Warren was not much interested. That night I was the only person on whom he fixed his attention.

A little after ten, the conversation changed, but the conversants did not. While the other guests grew restless, our host shifted the dialogue to *Goldwyn*. "Is it true I was the last person Sam Goldwyn talked to before he died?" Beatty asked me. Not quite, I explained. But Warren Beatty had, in fact, been the last name recorded on Goldwyn's telephone sheet before suffering the stroke that ended his career. Then, just as the other guests were getting up from the table—bored to tears, I feared—the conversation took another sudden shift.

"I guess you know Katharine Hepburn pretty well," he said. "Because I see you dedicated your book to her." While Annette started shepherding the others toward the door, Warren lingered behind with me, quickly measuring the depth of my friendship with Kate. "Do you think she'd like to work again?" he asked. Not right away, I said, as she had recently finished a rather uninspiring television movie. "Well," he followed up, "do you think she's able to work again?" I said she was definitely capable, but her interest was waning along with her health. She had skin cancers on her face, she was not sleeping soundly, and was suffering from dizzy spells. Her shaking often became more pronounced, I said; and she had taken to working off cue cards. "Oh, that doesn't matter," Warren said. "Jack uses them too"—meaning his friend Mr. Nicholson.

"Because there's a great part in our movie," he continued.

"The old aunt?" I asked, slightly incredulously. "Is that really a great part?"

While the old aunt in *Love Affair* was but a supporting role, the character did serve as a kind of fulcrum, appearing in one extended scene in the middle of a sentimental story about a longtime bachelor about to marry. This man-about-town meets a singer, also about to marry, on a cruise; and their sudden love for each other becomes apparent during a brief layover at a European port, where they meet the man's elderly aunt, who is charmed by the young woman and wishes them Godspeed. (The ageless beauty Cathleen Nesbitt played the part in the Cary Grant version, the character actress Maria Ouspenskaya played opposite Boyer.) In this new version, the port-of-call had become Tahiti, the exteriors of which had already been shot. Beatty told me that Hepburn would have to travel no farther than the Warner Brothers lot in Burbank, where her character's house was being built on a sound stage. Her dressing room would be constructed literally steps from the set.

"Even if she wanted to work again," I told Warren, "you've got to remember that Hepburn has never played anything but the female lead. With the exception of her scene in *Stage Door Canteen*, she has always been the star. No supporting roles. No cameos. No commercials. And the only reason she did *Stage Door Canteen* was as part of the war effort." This picture, I thought, isn't exactly in the national interest.

As he and I made our way out to the driveway, where the other guests were driving off and Kevin was talking with Annette, Warren explained that the film was virtually finished except for this one long scene—which required an actress of stature. Moreover, he said, he wanted an actress in her eighties who looked as though she was in her eighties—not an octogenarian who had been tucked and pulled nor a sexagenarian caked in makeup. Not only that, he said at last, "I've always been in love with Katharine Hepburn."

Ever since he had been a young man, he said, she had bowled him over—with her brains, her beauty, and her attitude. "She's very sexy," he said.

"That's what Howard Hughes thought," I replied, knowing that Beatty had talked of producing a film about Hughes for more than a decade. "Yeah, what about that?" Warren said, as I was getting into the car, which Kevin had started up. "Did she ever talk to you about Hughes?" After I told him that she had, I could see he was prepared to pump me all night. I figured the only way we could leave was if I threw him a bone. So I said, "Kate often told me, 'What you must always remember about Howard is that he was deaf. And from an early age that affected him.'" As the car began to move, Warren followed along for a few paces, continuing the conversation—mostly about how chancy a sentimental love story was these days.

"Well," said Kevin as we reached the end of the driveway, "—now I see what that dinner was all about." I said he was being ridiculous, that the purpose of the evening was to learn about Lindbergh, and now that Warren had heard all I was willing to impart, that would be the last I would ever hear from him. We arrived home at eleven.

At 11:05, the phone rang. Kevin said, "Warren."

"This is Warren Beatty, the movie star," said the exuberant voice at the other end of the line. "It was really great meeting you guys," he said. Then he chatted aimlessly about Lindbergh for a few minutes before asking, "So do you think Hepburn might be interested in doing this part?" I reiterated that it seemed unlikely, but

I volunteered to inquire discreetly. "This much I can tell you," I added. "Don't approach her right away. She likes to feel she's coming in to save the day. She loves to save the day." In the meantime, I advised him to tailor the scene in ways that might especially appeal to her. I further advised that he think of other actresses who could play the part, so that he wouldn't be stuck in the probable eventuality that she wouldn't do it. Obviously, Beatty had already compiled such a list.

I pushed Frances Dee, Hepburn's costar in *Little Women,* saying that I had seen her in recent years and that she was an extremely attractive older woman with all her wits. "I know," Beatty said, "but I think the part needs a bigger name, a real star." I mentioned Luise Rainer, who had won back-to-back Oscars in the 1930s—for *The Great Ziegfeld* and *The Good Earth*—and who was also in her eighties. Furthermore, I argued, she had been off the screen for decades, so the studio could probably get some publicity mileage out of the casting. "No," Beatty whined, "she just doesn't seem right." I argued that the part sounded more appropriate for her than for Hepburn. "I could see Luise Rainer languishing in her final days in Tahiti," I said, "but not Kate. No balmy breezes for her. Greenland, maybe. Or the Yukon. But not Tahiti." That seemed like a frivolous technicality to Beatty, who added, "I just don't see Luise Rainer as my aunt."

"I've always found Hepburn really sexy," he told me again. In that moment, what I had long known became perfectly clear. I realized that even for movie stars, Katharine Hepburn was the actress they all wanted to meet and the one with whom they all dreamed of working. Once again I said I would sound Hepburn out but that he should also think about Wendy Hiller, Loretta Young, Jessica Tandy. "The old lady lives in Tahiti," I suggested before hanging up; "how about Dorothy Lamour coming out in a sarong?"

I called Kate the next morning—waiting until seven-thirty Los Angeles time, knowing that one could no longer call her "at any

282

time." In fact, she often didn't awaken until eight, sometimes nine, and then she lingered in bed reading, writing, and sorting through her mail. I told her about my evening with Warren Beatty and his interest in getting her in his movie. "Tell him you spoke with me," she directed, "and that I have absolutely no interest in the film. Is that the one where the girl gets hit by the car on her way to the Empire State Building?" she asked. I complimented her on her memory. She seemed to have been approached to appear in this version of the film already, and she wrote the story off as "pretty silly stuff."

"My God," she added. "Have I become Maria Ouspenskaya?"

Strangely, our conversation on the subject did not end there. "Is he interesting?" she asked, indicating Warren Beatty. "I'm not sure," I said. "He's certainly engaging. He gives the big rush. And he has a kind of courtliness. I think you'd like him."

"Why does he want to remake that movie?" she asked.

"Cary Grant, I think."

"Cary Grant?"

I told her a story I had heard years earlier about Cary Grant walking into a big Hollywood party in the sixties, where he saw all the gorgeous women in the room swarming around the young Warren Beatty. Grant was said to have commented to a friend, "See that guy. That used to be me."

"Now," I told Kate, "I think Mr. Beatty wants to be Cary Grant. No man aged more gracefully on the screen than your friend Cary, and when he was fifty-three he made *An Affair to Remember*."

"How old is Warren Beatty?" she asked.

"Fifty-six."

"Is he any fun?" she asked. "I'm not sure." I said. "He takes himself extremely seriously, but I think that's so people around him will take him seriously. But I have a hunch he's kind of goofy underneath it all."

"Hmmm," Kate said. "Well, *that* could be fun."

I reported most of the conversation to Warren and suggested that he leave her alone as long as possible, that in closing the door she had left a slight crack. It was a clear signal that Hepburn was ready neither to end her career nor to commit to anything new. I told him that I would be visiting her in New York in early September and I could take her pulse in person.

At that dinner in New York, I raised the subject of the Warren Beatty movie. Again she was noncommital. With such a small role, she asked, what was the point? I said that it might be fun to do such a part—one that would make a great impression and wouldn't require much time or effort. Besides, I argued, it would be nice circumstances under which to visit her friends in Los Angeles, something she hadn't done in years. "They're all dead," she said.

"Well, I'm not," I protested.

"If you keep talking about this movie," she said, "you will be."

Most people, even in Hollywood, don't know exactly what a producer does. In fact, producers come in all varieties and perform any number of functions. Some seize an idea or get their hands on a piece of unpublished material and shepherd it to a studio, where they develop it as a motion picture; others simply raise the money for the venture. Studios often stir other producers into the stew because of their ability to lure big stars and prominent directors. Still other producers get assigned to a film because of their ability to "make the trains run on time," seeing that the dozens of artists and technicians and drivers and caterers all perform their tasks according to the budget. Such extensive division of labor accounts for the large number of producers one finds in the credits of motion pictures today.

In the golden age of Hollywood, each film generally had one producer, and perhaps an associate who monitored the mechanics of the physical production. In more modern times, there are very few producers who conceive a film project and oversee its journey from inception to exhibition. The conglomeratization of the studios is, in part, the reason for the increase in number of producers—as bean-counting corporate heads want to insure their ever-increasing investments by hiring high-paid specialists to perform each production task. Another reason is that there's little room for the big personalities that existed in the old studio system—men like Goldwyn and Selznick and Thalberg, whose passion practically willed their movies into existence.

Not long after remaking *Love Affair* popped into my life, I asked a venerated member of the Hollywood community what he thought of Warren Beatty. "As an actor," he said, "he had one of the greatest ten years an actor could have. And since then, his career has pretty much slipped, and so has his acting. As a director, he's had a couple of good pictures. But as a producer, he's one of the best I've ever seen in this town. He can get anybody to do anything. That's producing."

Into the fall of 1993, I watched Warren Beatty produce. He made contact with Hepburn herself and her no-nonsense financial adviser named Erik Hanson. Upon learning that Kate liked cut flowers, Beatty began sending arrangements—one after another. I too began to receive his calls. At first they came once a week, to devise a game plan; then once a day, soon five times a day, analyzing every word she had said to him and strategizing every word he might say back. The calls were always flattering and full of excitement, manipulation so overt that it was comical. Kate was amused as well and called one morning to say, "Please tell your friend Mr. Beatty to stop sending me flowers. It looks like a funeral parlor around here."

She clearly enjoyed the seduction; but as December arrived, the courtship had to end. The film's remaining scenes had to be shot—with or without Katharine Hepburn. Feelers had been put out to Frances Dee, who was standing by in case her old friend Kate declined.

Meantime, Hepburn's health was failing. Her energy was not what it had been even the year before, and her short-term memory came and went. She found it difficult to concentrate. She asked what I thought of the script, as she could make little sense of it. When I told her I had not seen it, she asked me to call Warren Beatty and request a copy.

I did, suggesting that Hepburn herself realized that this might very well be her swan song and that she wanted it to be special. Toward that end, I said he should consider interpolating a few lines that would be "personal"—not just in style but also in substance. I was thinking of dialogue that might comment upon the character's life and philosophy but which was obviously drawn from Hepburn's as well, rather the way Spencer Tracy had spoken his heart in *Guess Who's Coming to Dinner.*

Beatty messengered a script over—not the entire script actually, just the fifteen pages that featured old "Aunt Ginny." They didn't seem like much to me. In the first of my calls from Warren the next day, I asked, "Who wrote this?" The simple question elicited a most complicated answer—of the sort one found in most of his interviews, rambling and evasive: "Oh, it's really hard to say. A lot of people have had their say, and of course it goes back to the original movie and Mildred Cram and . . ." The best I've gathered since is that Robert Towne wrote the script with Beatty rewriting, or vice versa.

Hepburn also called that day and asked what I thought of the script. I said I thought it was pretty mediocre, flat and charmless. "I thought I was the only one," she said. "That puts an end to that." But, I added, there was still plenty of time to fix it, because it was a potentially wonderful scene. "What's the point?" Hepburn asked. "Why bother?" The fact that she even asked, that none of her refusals to do this movie had sounded definitive, made me think she really wanted to take the job. If they could have shot the scene in New York, I don't think she would have hesitated for a moment. But this would mean uprooting herself and moving to California for several weeks; and I think that, for the first time, she was factoring her age and health into the equation. Beatty promised to find her a comfortable house, one that could easily accommodate Norah and anyone else with whom she wanted to travel. Of course, she could select the personnel tending to her hair and makeup and costumes.

Kate seemed to be wondering if she would be alone during this venture. Laura Harding had been there for her in the old days, but she was estate-bound in New Jersey; Phyllis had become too feeble to make the trip; and Cynthia McFadden, who had become Kate's favorite companion on both business trips and vacations, could no longer simply take time off from work. When Kate asked again what the point was in doing the film, I felt she was asking whether or not I would be around.

"I think you should do it," I said. "You always said, 'Actors act.' So I think you should act. Do you need this movie for your career? I don't think so. But I think it could be fun, we can have some adventures in L.A., and you'll be starting your seventh decade in movies. Now that's pretty great—a career that goes from John Barrymore to Warren Beatty."

"Jesus!" she said. "I might have to say 'yes' just to stop him from sending any more flowers."

"I believe that's part of his campaign, Kate, to show the kind of attention he'll lavish upon you."

"We've run out of room here," she said. "So it shows me that he's a goddamned fool for wasting so much money."

I updated Warren Beatty, explaining that Kate would probably flip-flop another dozen times in the next two weeks and that left to her own volition, she would prefer to stay at home. "She is eighty-five," I reminded him. All that said, I told Beatty that I would be willing to fly east to reassure Hepburn of the soundness of this venture and that I would accompany her to Los Angeles. I also said that if he wanted to act on his own, that would be fine with me as well. In any case, I added, "you really should let up on the flowers."

Christmas Day, a Saturday, Beatty called to say if my offer still held, we should leave on Monday, the three p.m. flight. Hepburn still had not committed to the role, but her deal had been negotiated, her backup team was on alert, and accommodations were being arranged. We just had to lure the lion out of her lair. Because we would be arriving in New York long after Hepburn's bedtime, I asked him to book a hotel room for me on Monday night and to make a dinner date with Hepburn for Tuesday. Meantime, I would call Kate and arrange to be with her Tuesday afternoon to discuss the trip. I would stay for dinner, and spend the night upstairs—because Wednesday morning she would rise with absolutely no intention of leaving for California.

Monday morning, Beatty called to say a car would pick me up at two o'clock, return to his house to fetch him, then we'd go to the airport. "Isn't that cutting it a little close?" I asked. He said he didn't think so, but I could have the car come whenever I wanted. He asked if I would bring a copy of Hepburn's *Me,* which he had not read; and for comfort's sake, I asked for an extra fifteen minutes. That quarter of an hour proved worthless, because when I arrived at Beatty's house on Mulholland, he was still running around gathering things for the trip and fielding phone calls. We met in the kitchen at 2:15, where he insisted we eat some roast-beef hash the cook was preparing. At 2:25 I suggested we move along if we were to catch our three o'clock flight. "Okay," he said, downing the last of the hash.

At five minutes before the hour, we arrived at the American Airlines terminal, where a special representative met us curbside. We must have walked through security, but I don't remember it, as we were escorted right onto the plane. The first-class stewardess had our names and greeted me and Mr. Mike Gambril—the name of Beatty's character in the movie. The first-class section was empty except for

288

us; and Warren used the flight to whip through Hepburn's book, periodically asking for amplification on one chapter or another.

We were whisked through JFK and taken to the Carlyle Hotel, where I was shown to an enormous suite—a big bedroom, two baths, and a huge living room—easily costing $1,000 a night. It was only nine o'clock California time when Warren rang and asked me to accompany him to P. J. Clarke's for a bite.

The restaurant was quiet at that hour, except for a rowdy group of young Italians sitting a few tables away. They periodically pointed to my dinner companion and chanted, "Deek Tracy! Deek Tracy!" Our chatty waitress kept lingering at our table; and when she brought our salads, she seized the moment to ask Beatty if he remembered her. She said they had "dated" some ten years prior. He said he did remember her, which put a big smile on her face; and when she left, he told me that even though she had put on some weight, he did recognize her. As we were leaving the restaurant, one of the Italian men asked "Deek Tracy" for his autograph, which Beatty happily provided. "Where does Hepburn go out to eat?" Warren asked as we headed out.

"She doesn't," I said.

"No—I mean, when she goes out, what restaurants does she go to?" I explained that she hardly went to restaurants at all, maybe three in the last twenty years, and only once in the last decade that I was aware of. "Why?" he asked in disbelief. "First of all, she knows she'll get better food at home. And she also knows that people will be watching her every time she lifts the fork. And then there's those guys," I added, pointing back to the jovial Italians. Warren laughed, put his arm on my shoulder, and said, "That's the reason I *do* go out to restaurants."

It was after one when we returned to the hotel, but it was still early on Warren's wristwatch. Although it was already evident that alcohol was not part of his diet, he asked if I'd join him for a drink in the hotel bar. "What do you drink?" he asked; and I told him a single-malt Scotch or Famous Grouse. "What does Miss Hepburn drink?" he asked. The same, I said. He ordered two Famous Grouses. "How do we like it?" he asked me. Neat, I said. "Neat!" he called out to the bartender, delighting in making his request. For the next hour we sat at the bar—"Another!" he called out with glee—and he was warm, funny, self-deprecating, inquisitive, and positively reverent every time he spoke of Hepburn, to whom he hoisted the second glass.

The next afternoon I went to Turtle Bay with my overnight bag, parked it downstairs in case the plan backfired, and went to the living room where I found Kate examining the script of *Love Affair*. "I have no idea what this scene is supposed to be about," she kept saying. "Let's ask him when he gets here," I said, "and see if it can be rewritten."

Beatty was all charm at dinner, attentive to his hostess and even a little nervous. He spoke of the house he had found for her in California—not far from the studio and even closer to his house, at the top of Benedict Canyon. The Warners' private jet, he said, would be available at noon to fly us to Burbank. Norah was in a swivet, barely able to keep her eyes off him as she ran trays up and down the stairs. I asked if there was still time to tinker with the script; and the producer and cowriter assured Kate that she would not have to film a word of it until she was satisfied. Hepburn came around. She said she would fly to California and appear in the picture. A little after eight, she was ready to retire and asked where I'd be spending the night. I said that Warren had a suite at the Carlyle for me but that I would prefer to stay on the fourth floor. "Good idea," she said. "Save the forty-five bucks!"

"Forty-five bucks?" I laughed. Realizing she was way off, Kate tried again. "Sixty-five?"

Kate said her "good nights" and went upstairs, followed by Norah, who had already packed most of Hepburn's clothes for the journey.

I went downstairs to get my bag and to show Warren out. He felt good about the way the evening went. "But listen," I said. "It's not over. She's going to wake up tomorrow and refuse to go." I suggested he put Erik Hanson on alert, and I told Warren to be ready to return to the house himself at nine for the final round of persuasion. Winter weather had arrived in New York, and Norah beamed at the thought of three weeks in Los Angeles—with Warren Beatty no less.

The next morning I went downstairs at seven-thirty to get my breakfast tray, which I brought up to Kate's room. She was propped up in bed, pouring another cup of coffee and poring over the script. "It's really terrible," she said. "I read it and read it, and it makes absolutely no sense. Here," she said, throwing her copy across the bed, "you play it." I acted out the scene, which included some drivel likening the promiscuous Beatty character to a duck. Kate rolled her eyes. "It'll be fine once you get out there," I said reassuringly.

"Out where?" she asked blankly.

"L.A."

"L.A.? I'm not going to L.A." I said I was under the impression she was, that she had told Warren Beatty that she was, and the Warners' jet was scheduled to take off at noon. "Well," she insisted, "I will not be on it."

The next few hours were bedlam. I called Warren a little after nine, and when the operator patched me through to his room, it sounded as though I had awakened him. I said he had better come over right away, that Hepburn was back at square one. He said he would be there in an hour. I suggested he get Erik Hanson over to the house as well. Norah efficiently finished Hepburn's packing and put the house in order. I continued to tell Kate that she should make the trip and that she could "get sick" and return home if she wanted, but that it might just be some fun.

She would not budge, clearly waiting to be wooed one more time by Beatty. He arrived a little after ten, and restated how important it was to him and the movie that she appear. But it really wasn't until Erik Hanson, the financial adviser, arrived that she was moved into action. In a sharp tone, he argued that there was no good reason for her to stay home, that she had nothing to do there but sit around and look at the same four walls. Here was an opportunity, he said, for her to travel in great comfort and work under ideal circumstances. A little before noon, Norah, Warren, Kate, and I were packed in a limousine on our way to the airport—in dead silence.

Kate looked miserable, sad and tired, like some exotic animal that had been bagged. "Now Warren," I asked, for Hepburn to hear, "if, at any time, Kate wants to come home, she can come home, right?" Right, he said; he'd arrange for the jet to take her back. "And there's still plenty of time to work on the script, right?" Right. "And there's plenty of time to get the costumes fitted, right?" Right.

The stewardess greeted us as we entered the Warners' jet; and as soon as we had settled into the comfortable seats, we took off. A buffet of salads and meats was set up; and it was one of the few times I saw Kate eat food that hadn't been prepared in her own house. After lunch, she looked exhausted and said she wanted to lie down. Norah covered her with a blanket on a daybed in the front of the cabin, and she fell asleep. During the flight I spoke to Beatty about the script. He asked a few questions about Hepburn's career, which made me think he might be rewriting some of her dialogue. He brought up Elia Kazan's name, not realizing that Kate had worked with him. Kazan had, of course, unleashed Beatty onto the public in *Splendor in the Grass,* a galvanic film debut. "Kate was in his other 'grass' movie," I said, *The Sea of Grass.* After a two-hour nap, Hepburn awoke—her face looking somewhat the worse for having slept on it, irritating some of its small lesions. A look of shock came over Beatty.

He spent the balance of the flight making conversation with Hepburn, trying to get her to warm up to him. As I sank into a nap myself, I heard only his icebreaker: "I was just thinking," he said, "you and I both did Elia Kazan's 'grass' movies."

Later in the flight, while I was sitting with them, he brought up the name of Shirley MacLaine. "Bad girl," Kate said, presumably remembering something she had heard, because I didn't think they had ever met. Warren dropped the subject. A few minutes later, when he changed seats, I told Kate that MacLaine was Beatty's sister. "Oh dear," she said, then laughed for the first time that day.

Upon our arrival we were ferried off in limousines—our luggage in a separate car—to a secluded, spacious house at the top of Benedict Canyon. It seemed to meet all of Hepburn's criteria. It sat behind a gate and had a beautiful tree in the courtyard; the rooms were large and bright, with comfortable furniture in neutral colors; the large master bedroom was within shouting distance of what would be Norah's bedroom, and it opened onto a large patio with a pool; the living room had a big fireplace. Norah was giddy, having left slushy New York behind her; and when Warren told her a team of assistants stood at the ready to run any errands, I could practically see her praying for the filming to go over schedule. After walking through the house, Kate said, "It's awful. Let's go home."

Promptly insisting he would find her another house, Beatty asked what the problems were. The chair in the living room was in the wrong place for her to enjoy the fire, and the house looked too boring and bare. I suggested that Beatty leave her alone for a few hours, to allow her to make it her own. When he returned, I was just moving a potted tree from another room onto a low ledge by the fireplace, and Kate had showered and changed into a crisp white outfit and was holding a Scotch, sitting in a comfortable chair that had been moved to face the hearth.

The three of us ate a small dinner, after which I said I had to go home. Hepburn had assumed I was staying at the house, but I explained that I lived only ten minutes away myself, that Norah was on the premises, and that I would be back the next morning for breakfast, as though we were in New York together. I asked if the assistant on duty could drop me off at my house, but Beatty volunteered to drive me. We were hardly out the driveway, when he said, "My God, her face looks like a fruitcake. Is it always that bad? What is it, skin cancer?" I said the blotches were probably the result of many years of outdoor sports. "And what is that grease she puts on her face?" I said that it was some formula she had been using for years, really little more than petroleum jelly with lanolin. "My God," he said, "that can't be good for her."

As soon as we hit Mulholland Drive, he reached for the car phone and called a doctor, who immediately got on the line and to whom he described her condition. They began to discuss long-term treatment for Hepburn's condition and short-term remedies in the week they had before shooting. When he had finished his call, he told me that he had an active interest in medicine, that he tried to keep up-to-date on all the latest cures and treatments and which doctors and hospitals were best in their fields. "Are you a hypochondriac as well?" I asked. He laughed and said, "A little."

I asked Beatty what the schedule would be like for Hepburn during this week before shooting, as the most important thing for the moment was to keep her occupied. "Her life may have slowed down in New York," I explained, "but she has a routine there, and all her time is accounted for. So I think you should make sure there's some activity for her every day." I explained that until she was before the cameras, I could be there to have breakfast with her every morning and dinner at night, but that he would have to see that her days were filled. He said there would be no problem—what with showing her the set, costume fittings, and the like.

He dropped me off at my house, and I said I would be at the Hepburn Command Center at eight the next morning. As I got out of the car, Warren leaned to the right and yelled through the passenger window, "I don't know how to thank you."

"Look," I said, "I'm doing this mostly for Kate. But think of something."

With that, he turned off his motor, got out of the car, and rushed over to give me a bearhug. Then, without a word, he drove down the hill toward home.

I spent a few hours every morning that week at Hepburn's house. Trying to duplicate our regimen, I sat in her bedroom while she finished breakfast and we discussed the newspapers. She seemed tired and disoriented and unsteady on her feet. Thinking part of the problem was that she wasn't getting any exercise, I took a long swim every day; and a few times I was able to induce her into the pool as well. Although Beatty did come up with an activity each day, that still left the bulk of the time unfilled, with nothing for Hepburn to do but sit around and moan. She suffered from spells of vertigo.

Even so, late mornings she wanted to go out on drives. I thought they would exacerbate her dizziness, but she said inactivity was worse. The first day she wanted to look at some of the houses in which she had lived. I drove her to the cottage she shared with Tracy on the Cukor estate, which had recently been bought and remodeled into a charmless house. It bore so little resemblance to what it had been, Kate had no idea where we were until she looked at the street sign. "Do you know who lives there?" she asked. No, I told her; but I was sure they would be thrilled to let her look around if she wanted. "Let's," she said. As I got out of the car, I saw her staring sadly at the place. As I opened her door to help her out, she said, "Let's not."

We drove up Doheny Drive a few blocks, to my house—three storeys perched on stilts, modern, and with a big view of the city from the mid-Wilshire area to the ocean. It was a beautiful clear day. She got as far as the entrance on the top floor, marveled at the vista, and said, "Where's the fireplace?" When I told her I had none, her interest in the place waned. I started to lead her down the stairs to show her the rest of the house, especially my office. Not two steps down, she changed her mind. "I'd rather not know," she said, beginning a familiar refrain.

"Know what?" I asked.

"That you live somewhere," she said in a slightly wistful tone.

She wanted to leave the house right away and carry on our tour of the canyons. Hepburn remembered every turn up every small street, stopping at one address or another, seldom getting more than a glimpse of a driveway. Later in the ride, she asked out of the blue, "How can you live in a house without a fireplace?"

That night Annette Bening accompanied Warren to Hepburn's house, and the four of us had dinner. The meals Norah prepared were the same she served in New York. Annette was charming and courtly with Hepburn. When she and Warren left, Kate asked, "Who's the girl?" That, I explained, was her costar in the movie— a very good actress and Warren Beatty's wife. "His wife!" she said. "He has a wife?" Yes, I explained; after years of his being Hollywood's most eligible bachelor, with countless celebrated romances, he married her. "Poor girl," said Kate. I asked why she said that, that I thought they both seemed in love. "Hmmm," observed Kate. Then, without missing a beat, she added, "With the same man."

The second day our driving tour took us to the top of Tower Road. She wanted to see the wonderful house in which she had lived in the thirties, one later owned by Jules Stein, the founder of MCA, the entertainment empire. She asked who the current owner was, and I said, Rupert Murdoch. "Hmmmm," she nodded knowingly, "this is a place for somebody who feels that he owns the world." Big gates with the letter "M"—reminding me of the gates outside Xanadu in *Citizen Kane*—barred entry onto the property; but Kate asked me to try to get us in. I buzzed a half-dozen times from the gate, but there was no response. "This is New Year's Eve," I said. "Everybody's probably away." That was good, she said, instructing me to drive around to the back of the property. There was a chain-link gate ajar, through which we were both able to squeeze, thus setting foot on the grounds. After a few steps, however, we were met by a more formidable fence.

"We need some of those big wire-cutters," she said. I apologized for not traveling with metal shears. "What about a bat, or something," she said, suggesting that we could probably pry the locked gate open. After I struck out again, she scrounged around for a big stick. Not until we had rattled the chain-link fence for several minutes did she abort our mission. We tried the front gate one more time, then retreated down the hill.

Before going out to a New Year's Eve party that night, I returned to Kate's house to have dinner with her and the Beattys—at five-thirty. In honor of the occasion, Kate had me open a bottle of champagne. We all hoisted our glasses to good things in 1994, all except Annette . . . who at the last minute picked up her glass and, as though talking to herself, quietly said, "Well, the doctor said a small glass of wine would be all right." It would not make the columns for a few months, but I drove off that night thinking the Beattys were expecting a second child.

That weekend, just before she was to begin shooting, Kate talked of going home. She said she was tired of Los Angeles; and the deal was that she could return whenever she wanted. Over breakfast the conversation veered to where it had been weeks ago, to the script. We read her scene aloud, and she kept saying, "It just doesn't make any sense." I asked her what was unclear and suggested she improvise some dialogue of her own. She asked me to do the same. "Why don't you tell him," she said, referring to Beatty, "that you and I discussed the script, and you've come up with a few suggestions that you thought would help the film." I said that as the star, producer, and cowriter, he might not take kindly to "my" suggestions, but that I would speak to him.

After I had typed up the fresh pages, Beatty asked me to come to the house to discuss them. He said he liked them, then insisted on discussing even the most innocuous lines, word by word. I suddenly realized why so many years elapsed between each of his pictures. Then he asked what the possibilities were of her saying a line in his version of the script, "Fuck a duck."

I asked him what the point was, as the line was neither necessary nor funny and was, frankly, a little tasteless. "But would she ever say it?" he asked. I said the sheer shock value of the line would probably hold some appeal for Hepburn. In *Coco*, I told him, her character had come down a staircase after a fiasco of a fashion show and said, "Shit!" I also said that, while that had been some twenty years earlier, she had disappointed a lot of fans. "But do you think she'd say it?" Warren repeated, clearly intent on working the line into the script. I said she probably would, but why upset some of the people who would be coming to the movie to see her?

"Nobody's coming to this movie to see her," Beatty said.

"I'm sorry?" I said, having obviously misheard him.

"I said nobody's coming to this movie to see Hepburn."

I stared at him, waiting for him to crack a smile but quickly realized he was dead serious. I replayed the past few months in my mind, wondering what the exigency of getting Katharine Hepburn into this movie had been about if it wasn't somehow to raise interest in the film. Suddenly I understood that this entire casting expedition had been little more than an exercise in vanity. "Well," I said, "when the movie comes out in video and the distributor wants a third name on the box and the video stores shelve a copy in the 'Katharine Hepburn' section, some of her fans might be disappointed to hear her say that line."

"But," Warren asked, ending the discussion, "you think she'd say, 'Fuck a duck?'"

Yes, Warren. Only one or two bits out of the pages I had brought over made their way onto the screen. And I did leave him with one further suggestion, which had to do with the moment when Warren and Annette's characters say goodbye to his aunt for the last time. "Kate's got a very theatrical wave," I said. "Look at the end of *Summertime*." I suggested that this could be a touching moment for Hepburn's fans—"I mean, not that anybody's going to see this movie because of her."

Beatty proceeded to tell me that he didn't understand why Hepburn didn't seem to be enjoying herself in Los Angeles, regarding the trip as more of an "opportunity." He said that the weather was certainly better than New York's, the movie provided her with something to do, and "she'll be working with the greatest living director in the world." While a successful television director named Glenn Gordon Caron was nominally the man calling the shots on this picture, I knew that Beatty himself intended to direct the Hepburn scenes. And so, once again, I looked for even a suggestion of irony. "I'm sorry?" I said.

When I saw once again that this was no laughing matter, I said, "Well, it's true, Cukor and Huston and Ford are all dead," naming just a few of the giants with whom she had worked. "But what about Billy Wilder and Kurosawa and David Lean?"

"I mean guys who are still working," Beatty contended.

"How about Stanley Kubrick?"

"Yeah," he conceded, "but he hasn't made a picture in years." I refrained from even introducing such names as Martin Scorsese, Francis Ford Coppola, Steven Spielberg, Mike Nichols . . .

Beatty and I saw each other again on Sunday night, for dinner at Hepburn's. Kate's mood seemed lighter than it had all week. She had been applying a salve one of Beatty's doctors had prescribed, and her skin had noticeably improved. Everybody was aglow with anticipation. As Warren and I left her, she called out to me, "I hope he's paying you a lot of money." Warren only laughed . . . all the way out the door.

On Monday shooting began. I had never seen Hepburn work on a set, and so I instinctively kept my distance during the days. To help her maintain her rhythm, I joined her almost every night for dinner, at which time I would find her in a robe with her hair in a towel. A few old friends occasionally appeared as well. Warren dropped by every night, and used me to compliment her indirectly, telling me in her presence how great her performance was. I had to leave at the end of the week for a writers' conference, and two nights before my departure, Kate asked if I might visit her on the set. I said I would try. Warren seemed eager for me to drop by as well—to show, I felt, how regally she was being treated.

I drove to Warner Brothers the next day at noon, arriving between camera setups. Kate was in her large soundstage dressing room, where her hair and makeup teams were tending to her. She looked great—more alert and alive than she had in months. Norah was on hand, assistants catered to the star's every whim, and the crew was hurrying to set their lights and camera, so that Miss Hepburn would not be kept waiting. But that's not what excited her so. It was the work. "As you can see," she said, swiveling in her makeup chair to face me, "they're treating me all right. So you don't have to stay." An assistant director came in to announce that they were ready to film again, and Kate said by way of dismissing me, "We've got to play now."

I saw Beatty and told him that I was leaving, that I felt my presence while she was working would make her uncomfortable. He suggested that I stand on the other side of the black curtain behind the set, where one could watch the proceedings on a television monitor. There I stood in the wings, alongside a slightly forlorn, sweet-faced, heavyset man who was also watching the screen intently, as Warren directed Hepburn in the scene. She did several takes, working off cue cards at first, then improvising a little on her own. By the third or fourth take, she seemed to be playing to the crew, and obviously winning their approval, as she brought more to the scene than was actually there.

She had a way of reading the most banal lines as though they were fraught with some meaning—sometimes by pausing a little here, speeding up a little there; and the moments full of import, she simply tossed off. She provided a slightly different reading on each take, but she always made a point of understating, avoiding the obvious. When the scene was finished, the man by my side introduced himself and thanked me for my part in getting Hepburn to Los Angeles. Then I realized I was talking to the director, who, evidently, was not allowed on the set during Hepburn's scenes.

As I was leaving the soundstage, a posse of executives entered, wanting to get their first glimpses of Katharine Hepburn. From the sidelines, I watched Beatty escort them over and saw how she utterly charmed them—shaking each hand, laughing at their comments, thanking them for all their accommodations. She even posed for a team photograph, flinching only once, when one of the young executives put his arm around her.

That night over dinner, Warren carried on about how she had snowed "the suits." Hepburn explained that that had been part of her job since David Selznick had brought her to Hollywood sixty years ago. When Warren raved about her ability to improvise in the scene they had done later that afternoon, I reminded him that much of the final sequence of *Woman of the Year*, in which Tess Harding is alone in the kitchen trying to make breakfast with some culinary props, had been improvised as well. As he left that night, Warren kissed Kate on the cheek, looked deep into her eyes, and said, "If I had only met you thirty years ago."

After he left, Kate said to me, "Was that supposed to be a compliment?"

By the time I returned from my trip, Hepburn had finished her work on *Love Affair*. Beatty and company had treated her magnificently, and she was obviously pleased to have completed the job. She returned home as soon as possible, which was fortunate . . . because less than forty-eight hours later, the Northridge earthquake seriously rocked the house in which Hepburn had been staying, sending lamps and vases to the floor. The Beattys' house atop the city, where I had first dined with them five months earlier, was destroyed.

The following September, Dominick Dunne wrote a profile of Warren Beatty for *Vanity Fair*, which detailed how Beatty had seduced Hepburn into appearing in his film. What struck me most in the article was a line toward the end of the piece, when Beatty was reflecting on stars and personalities and the subject turned to Howard Hughes. "What you must always remember about Howard," Beatty said, "is that he was deaf."

The following month I was invited to a screening of *Love Affair*, at which Beatty and I never quite found each other. The movie played even cornier than I had expected, and for me its only moments of relief came when Hepburn appeared on the screen. (Her participation in the film was billed as a "Special Appearance by.") While her dialogue still didn't add up to much—and she did, somewhat haltingly, utter the pointless "Fuck a duck" line—she looked good and made a strong impression, especially at the moment when she waves goodbye. I found it most touching, because again, instead of the obvious, waving big, she sat alone and simply looked down at her aging hands.

On my birthday that December, I received a dozen enormous crimson roses from "Warren and Annette." Four years later, he showed up at a publication party for *Lindbergh,* which my brother

Jeff threw. Except for the occasional chance encounter with Warren Beatty in the years between and since, I have never again seen or heard from "the movie star."

Katharine Hepburn's phone still rang, and scripts continued to appear at her door. A producer I had never met called me one afternoon to ask if I might use my influence in getting her to consider playing the role of Aunt March in a remake of *Little Women*—a film that would feature Winona Ryder in Hepburn's former role of Jo. I said it seemed dubious because I thought she had no intention of becoming a character actress—even as she approached ninety. ("Please tell them," Kate said, "I would never even think of competing with Edna May Oliver"—who had played Aunt March in 1932.) Instead, Hepburn trekked to Canada to star in one or two more forgettable television movies, her powers of concentration diminishing as the tremors in her head and hands increased. She continued to talk of future projects, decrying the quality of what was being written for older actors.

With each of my visits east, there came a moment of shock upon seeing her. Norah would usually try to prepare me for the changes I would find upon climbing the stairs to the living room. But Kate's hair, still pulled back and piled high, looked whiter and wispier, her eyes grayer, and her body heavier, the result of her inability to exercise. Conversation became more difficult, what with her having less to report and her increasing difficulty remembering things. She seemed to be working hard to maintain her carriage, thrusting her jaw forward. "So noble," I could hear Irene Selznick saying in her succinct way, "—heartbreaking." Whenever I stood next to Kate, I was taken aback, seeing that she was several inches shorter than when I had met her. Her energy waned; she suffered from dizziness; she often seemed depressed.

The next year I found her in the Manhattan Eye, Ear and Throat Hospital, checked in under Phyllis Wilbourn's name. Norah had suggested to me that nobody really knew what the problem was, but that she was receiving a few visitors. Upon entering the large room, I heard a doctor addressing her in a peculiarly hostile tone, while a grim nurse looked on. "Nobody's allowed in here," the doctor said as I entered. "He is," Kate corrected, as I went over to the chair in which she was sitting, wearing her familiar pajamas and ratty red robe. "He's my friend."

"What's going on?" I asked, hoping to clear some of the obviously unpleasant air.

"They say I'm a drunk," Kate whimpered, a tone I had never heard her emit.

"Now, nobody said that," the doctor quickly asserted.

"Yes, you did," Kate said. "You called me an alcoholic and said that I can't drink again." With that, she turned to me, her eyes watering. "You've known me a long time, Scott Berg," she said. "Do you think I'm a drunk?" I said she was not a drunk, and I asked the doctor and nurse if they might leave us alone for a moment. Then I went over to give Kate a hug, and she put her arm around my waist, pressed her head into my stomach, and cried. "I don't know why I'm here," she said.

She wasn't disoriented. In fact, she seemed sounder of mind than she had been in my last few visits. It was more that she didn't know what was wrong with her, and nobody else seemed to know either. She just felt bad. I knew she was on a number of prescription drugs, and I couldn't help thinking they were all somehow interacting, contributing to her general funk. "Look, Kate," I said, "there's no doubt in my mind—you don't have a drinking problem . . . but as long as you're taking all these pills, it seems to me you've got to stop drinking any alcohol. I mean, that's what killed your friend Judy Garland . . . and Marilyn. That's just common sense." And common sense was still enough to trump any argument with Hepburn.

She was soon home, with some changes in her various drugs; and Kate entered that phase in old age of "good days and bad days." Sometimes, good hours and bad hours. More often than not, Norah answered the telephone, usually in a state of agitation over some minor emergency with Miss Hepburn.

While never far from Kate's thoughts, Phyllis Wilbourn gradually withdrew from the scene, as she required increasing amounts of bedrest and care from her team of attendants. During a visit to Fenwick in early 1995, I saw her sitting in a chair, staring out at the Sound, crying. I walked over to comfort her and asked what was wrong. "I'm just very worried," she said. "Nothing will ever be the same."

"Why do you say that?" I asked. "What are you worried about?"

"The abdication," she said. "That changes everything. And he was our most handsome king."

"Look on the bright side," I said consolingly. "He evidently wasn't very happy; and now he gets to spend the rest of his life with the woman he loves." That cheered Phyllis up a little. As I held her hand, I added, "I'm sure he and Mrs. Simpson will have a long, happy life together."

"Do you really think so?" Phyllis asked.

"I know so," I said with enough authority to put her worries to rest.

Another weekend, I flew to Connecticut to attend the wedding of Dick Hepburn's son Mundy (an artist who worked with glass) and Joan Levy (an artist who worked on canvas). The bride was dressed as a Druid princess, and Kate was in relatively fine form. She was a little unsure on her feet but, with the support of a cane, completely ambulatory. She looked tired but was attentive, as she selected a comfortable chair from which to watch the ceremony. At one point, she noticed a man across the room snapping photographs of her and asked me to stand directly in front of her, with my back to the camera, so that I would obstruct his view. Driving back to Fenwick, I asked what had been the purpose of the bride's costume. "To prove she's insane enough to marry into this family," she replied.

In April 1995 Joan Levy called to tell me that Phyllis had died in New York City. I called Kate not only to offer my condolences but to find out how she was taking the loss. "What did she die of?" I asked.

"What's the difference?" Kate said. "She stopped breathing, and she's dead. And that's that."

Kate maintained her brave front until May eleventh. On what would have been Phyllis's ninety-second birthday, a few Hepburns and some intimate friends celebrated her long life of loving companionship by burying her ashes in a cemetery at West Hartford, alongside other Hepburns. During the brief ceremony at the grave— as rain came down—Kate suddenly dropped to her knees and sobbed. I never heard her raise Phyllis's name again.

In late winter of 1996, Hepburn was taken to Lenox Hill Hospital with pneumonia. Reports on the radio and television were fatalistic. My phone calls to the house and to her brother Dr. Bob were more encouraging. Within a few days, in fact, Kate had asked for an ambulance to take her from the hospital to Fenwick, where oxygen tanks, a hospital bed, and round-the-clock nurses were waiting. Meantime, *The National Enquirer* splattered a ghoulish picture of her across its cover, quoting her as saying, "Don't be sad—I'm going to join Spencer. . . ."

Hepburn pulled through, as she would after a few other small bouts that year. But each attack compromised her vitality; and each siege brought out an army of tabloid reporters, who camped at the end of the Hepburn driveway—on "deathwatch." The crafty ones got hold of the telephone number inside the house and tried to wrest any information from whomever answered the phone.

My visits became increasingly quiet, as Kate's ability to converse continued to diminish. She seemed to understand what was being said, but she seemed to lack the strength to respond. Direct questions seldom elicited more than a few words, which sometimes seemed to be in response to something that had been asked earlier . . . or unasked at all. Unless there was a third person present, these encounters became difficult, for they basically demanded that the guest engage in a monologue. During one of my trips that year, I found Tony Harvey. We sat on either side of Kate all afternoon and chatted, which she followed as though observing a tennis match. After a while, however, Tony and I noticed that her attention had shifted to a box of Edelweiss chocolate I had brought from California. One by one, she took every piece of chocolate out of the box, and then, one by one, put every piece back. Tony and I kept talking, though he raised an eyebrow and looked heavenward.

In 1997, Joan Levy called me in Los Angeles to say that Kate had suddenly taken a turn for the worse and that she was sinking fast. Again I called Kate's brother Bob, who said that this, in fact, looked like the end and that there seemed little for anybody to do. Kate had become very weak, wasn't eating, and her "systems were shutting down." I said I could catch a plane out later that day to come say goodbye, but Bob advised against it. "At this point, I'm not sure you'll make it in time," he said. "And even if you do, I'm not sure what you'll find."

I found Kate the next morning, in her bedroom—sitting in a chair, in a fresh pair of pajamas, a shawl around her shoulders— looking old but fine. "Do you know who I am?" I asked, as I entered the room, sunshine pouring through every window. "No," she said, the light in her eyes. As I stepped out of the shadow of the entry and closer to where she sat, she looked up and into my face, and a big tear rolled down her left cheek. One of the nurses leaned toward me and whispered, "When she heard you were coming today, she asked me to put some lipstick on her."

"What's all this business about you dying?" I asked.

"I'm not," she said, in what was clearly an effort. Then she looked a little ashamed that she was evidently incapacitated, a state belied by the animation in her eyes.

I spent the day in Fenwick, mostly in the company of the household staff, the nurses, and, later, Cynthia McFadden, who had been visiting regularly. After our morning meeting, Kate napped. Like the doctors, everyone was puzzled by Hepburn's condition—what ailed her and how she kept springing back. They worried because she had not eaten much in days.

When she awoke, Cynthia and the others, knowing that I had to return to Los Angeles, suggested that I go upstairs and spend some time alone with her. The general consensus in the house was that she had pulled through this bout, but the end was surely close. Again, I found her sitting upright in her chair, with a tray of untouched food.

I sat by her side and asked if she wanted to eat. Like a child, she turned her head away and said nothing. I told her that I was so happy to see her but that I hated to find her this way. She sat stock-still and seemed to look through me. Winding into what I thought might very well be my last goodbye, I told her how much her friendship had meant to me over the years but how I hoped it would continue. She still looked away, now into the blazing fire. "Look, Kate," I said leaning in very close to her and talking in a low voice, "you and I have talked about death a lot . . . and I know you've always been interested in the Hemlock Society and all those books on how to kill yourself. And maybe that's where you are now. And if there's anything I can do to help you . . . well, actually, if you're ready to go now, the best thing you can do is just keep up what you're doing. Don't eat. Starve yourself. Just don't eat."

Suddenly her head snapped in my direction, and her eyes burned into mine. With her right hand she grabbed mine and put it on her left forearm. "I'm not weak," she said, shaking her flexed arm for me to feel. It was unbelievably firm. "I'm not dying," she said. "I'm strong."

"Well," I said, "you really do feel strong. But you don't seem to be able to pick up a fork. And people are worried that you're not eating, even when they try to feed you. And you can't stay strong unless you eat. And I'm saying if you're not eating because you're ready to go, well then, don't eat—"

Without having to search for words, she continued to look me in the eyes . . . and then, without making any other move, she simply opened her mouth. For the next few minutes, I fed her soup, macaroni and cheese, and coffee ice cream, which had melted, until she emptied the plate and two bowls. As she ate, I talked about how she had to start building herself up. I discussed yoga with her, and told her how Alice Roosevelt Longworth practiced postures and stood on her head into her nineties. "Can't," she said. I explained that anybody could, that there was always a movement of some part of the body, to say nothing of the breathing, that one could practice. I demonstrated a few basic exercises.

By the time she had finished eating, I realized I had to leave, in order to catch my plane home. I hugged her goodbye, and she held her cheek pressed against mine, then looked into my eyes until hers began to tear again. I said I would try to get back soon, but it might not be for a few months. As I started for the door, she spoke the longest sentence I had heard from her that day. "Are you still loved?" she asked.

I assured her that I was, that my longtime relationship had never been more fulfilling. "Good," she said, then added, "I've been loved too." I knew she was speaking of Spencer Tracy, but I couldn't resist adding, "By more people than you know."

Downstairs, everyone was anxious to know how I had found her. "She's not going anywhere," I said. "We're all going to die. I mean, none of us knows how long we're going to stick around. But I know this, she's not going anywhere, at least for a while."

"What did she say?" Cynthia asked. Realizing the conversation might have been personal, she stopped herself from pressing and said it was all right if I didn't want to share what had gone on. I reported the headlines, that she had eaten her entire lunch . . . and that until then, I had thought she wanted to die. But now, I reiterated, "She's not going anywhere."

During the next year, I completed, published, and promoted my biography of Lindbergh—a book that I probably wouldn't have been able to write had Kate not written to Anne Morrow Lindbergh on my behalf a decade earlier. My visits to Fenwick dwindled in number, but we communicated through family members and staff. The reports were always gloomier than what I would find in reality. Her mind wandered; but it seemed to me that she was just going on short voyages in her memory, maybe her imagination. More unusual, I thought, was what happened to her face.

Now each time I saw her, I thought of a short story by F. Scott Fitzgerald, "The Curious Case of Benjamin Button," in which a man was born old and progressively youthened, until he died an infant. As Hepburn's immobility increased, her physiognomy uncreased. Treatments for her skin left her visage taut and pink; her eyes seemed bigger and more expressive, lighting up at small things—positively childlike. She smiled a lot.

In the middle of May 1999—just days after her ninety-second birthday—I found myself in New York with a few free hours in which to drive to Fenwick for lunch. Kate's courtly friend David Eichler— himself in his late eighties, and looking a good decade younger—was up from Philadelphia; and Kate's sister Peg happened to visit that day as well, having driven down from Canton Center with a young Irishwoman, who brought a guitar. After a lunch of hot dogs with honey mustard and the standard macaroni and cheese, the girl pulled her chair right up to Kate's and began to play and sing. Kate gazed into her eyes through the entire song, as if in a daze. As soon as the tune was finished, her eyes widened, and she said, "Great. Another." The young woman obliged. After another encore, she and Peg left, while David and I commented to Kate on the beauty of the girl's voice. She seemed not to know what we were talking about; and David said to me sotto voce, "Her short-term memory's completely gone."

He left us alone for a while, during which time I carried on what passed in those days for conversation, a gentle soliloquy, which could occasionally draw a few syllables or sounds of response. When I at last announced that I had to leave, she said, "Is that wise?" I said I wasn't sure about that. And so she asked, "Is that necessary?" I said it was.

On my way out, I decided to drop in on Dick Hepburn, whose own declining health had kept him bedridden—sometimes asleep, I was told, as much as twenty-three hours a day. His nurse at the other end of the house told me that I was in luck, that he had just awakened.

I rapped on his door and found him in red pajamas, sitting upright on the side of his bed, motionless and staring into space. I entered, making polite conversation . . . until he said, "Present yourself." I assumed that meant that I should stand before him. As I did, he held out his hand and said, "It is a pleasure to see you, Mr. Berg. Thank you for calling on me." Then he lay down . . . and before I had left the room, he was sound asleep, snoring.

Ten days later I was able to steal away to Fenwick for another afternoon, where I had the pleasure again of seeing Peg, who had traveled this week with her granddaughter Fiona—a poetic soul who had been diagnosed with cystic fibrosis for more than a decade and had already outlived all medical expectations by years. She was there—carrying a portable oxygen tank—with her husband and beautiful child and talking hopefully of getting a lung transplant. Peg's great friend Don Smith, a music teacher and choirmaster, was visiting as well, as was Dr. Bob Hepburn. Over hot dogs and macaroni, the conversation was largely about the recent shooting at Columbine High School in Littleton, Colorado. Peg had plenty to say about guns (too many unenforced laws against) and child-rearing (not enough parents taking responsibility for). Somehow, this swirl of subjects triggered a nostalgic twist in the conversation, a rarity in any Hepburn house.

While Kate's mind seemed to wander, Bob and Peg told stories of their parents and their childhoods. Then Peg spoke of giving the government a sample of her blood, because the remains of some soldiers had recently been found in Southeast Asia, possibly including those of her son Tom, who had been missing in action for almost three decades. Finally the conversation turned to the other Tom—Peg, Bob, and Kate's oldest brother. For several minutes they mused in the most matter-of-fact tones about the circumstances of his death in the twenties. I looked over at Kate, who had turned away from us and stared instead toward the fire, her face wet with tears. I grabbed a tissue and blotted her eyes.

After the other guests left, I sat alone with Kate for a few minutes and commented on the stories that had surfaced that afternoon—the sickness, the shooting, the deaths. I wasn't expecting her to respond; I was just filling the silence. Then she spoke. "Life," she said quietly and with some difficulty, as though it were hard to unclench her teeth, ". . . not easy." One of Kate's caretakers entered the room and announced that it was time for some exercise. "We go out to play, don't we?" she said. Kate smiled broadly and said, "We do."

Kate had said to me literally dozens of times over the years that she didn't fear death—"the big sleep," she called it. It was dying she was afraid of. As I looked at her that day, I realized she no longer had anything to fear. She had survived the great race without much suffering; she had come through relatively unscathed. Of course, her life, like everybody else's, had had its share of disappointments and even tragedies. But she had approached the finish line free of most of the indignities of old age. Her days were blurring from one to another, but into her tenth decade, she was well-cared-for and comfortable—with few pains and with every need met. Loving people surrounded her.

After more than ninety years of challenges—personal, professional, emotional, and physical—Kate was surrendering, and seemed happy doing so. "Life's tough for everybody," I heard her say more than once, "and that's why most people become its victims." She lived most of her life as a contestant in that great struggle, always pushing herself hard, riding the wave and sometimes swimming ahead of it. "The natural law is to settle," she once said. "I broke that law."

Because Hepburn lived so long, for so many years ahead of her time, most of her fans forgot or failed to realize that she broke other "laws" in her lifetime as well. The biggest was that she refused to live as a "woman" in what was very much a man's world. She conducted her acting career as any freelance actor might, seldom seeking the protection of a studio or manager or agent. She conducted her personal relationships with that same independent spirit. Her initial response to any interdiction was always, "Says who? Just watch." In so doing, she became a hero, someone men and women of all ages had to admire.

At the end of the *Esquire* interview I had conducted when we had first met in 1983, I asked Hepburn why she thought she had endured professionally, indeed flourished, for so long while all those around her lasted only a few years or decades at best. It was one of the few questions that ever made her pause before answering. After a few seconds, she said, "Horsepower."

When I showed her my finished, and ultimately unpublished, piece, with her interview bracketed by my commentary, I provided my own answer to the question, with which she took issue. I wrote that "Katharine Hepburn inspires because she speaks directly to the heart in a most intelligent manner. The reason for her staying power is that for the last half century, she—above all—has provided a treasury of images which represent timeless human values: courage, independence, truth, idealism, and love. She is romance."

"Christ," Kate argued. "I'm not romance. That's Marilyn."

"No," I said, "Monroe is sex and an object of lust . . . and a victim. You told me that the times you met her, she always reminded you of a 'lonely leaf blowing in the wind.'"

"Garbo, then," she counteroffered.

"No," I said, "I think she's mystery . . . and also a victim."

"Well, then, I don't understand what you mean."

"Eva Lovelace, Jo March, Terry Randall with their artistic yearnings," I said; "Alice Adams with her social aspirations; Linda Seton, Tracy Lord, Tess Harding, Pat Pemberton, Bunny Watson getting whacked over the head by love; Rosie Sayer, Jane Hudson, Lizzie Curry, all desperate for love; Mary Tyrone, Christina Drayton, Ethel Thayer, even Eleanor of Aquitaine, all remembering the early glory of their love—don't you see, they're all dreamers, believers, adventurers, women of spirit who remain true to themselves but manage to change and grow and give to another person. That's what I mean by romance."

"Okay," she said. "I won't argue with you."

"Well, that's a first."

"You always have to have the last word, don't you?"

"Yep."

When I first met Kate, she often kidded that she would not live long enough to see the year 2000. "Don't be ridiculous," I'd say to her. "Lillian Gish is in her nineties, and you're tougher than she is."

"Oh, no," she said. "Nobody's tougher than Lillian. She did all those stunts in the Griffith pictures—facing storms and running across the ice floes. She was there at the beginning. She blazed the trail. She was the tough one." Miss Gish died in 1993 at the age of ninety-nine . . . and Katharine Hepburn lived to see what the world celebrated as the new millennium.

January 1, 2000, turned out to be just another day of another year for her. When she and I had talked about that future date, I'm sure she had never foreseen her life reduced to such inactivity. At first, it pained me to witness her body breaking down; but then I began to find joy in her longevity. I found solace just in seeing her living on with grace and dignity, delighting in even the smallest quotidian offerings of life—the sun rising over the lighthouse at Fenwick, a good meal, a warm fire, family and friends, a sound sleep under a lot of covers with a cool breeze and the sound of the waves blowing in—listening to the Song of Life.

XI

Queen Anne's Lace

That first time I rang the doorbell at 244 East Forty-ninth Street and walked up the stairs for the second time—after I had been sent to the bathroom—I faced not only Katharine Hepburn but also several arrangements of flowers. They were all huge arrays of king-sized blossoms—anthuriums, birds-of-paradise, African daisies, star lilies, gladioli, and agapanthus—large enough for a hotel lobby; there were two cachepots, each containing a monstrous red amaryllis. "A big room like this wants big flowers," she said during the course of our conversation. "They're really the only ones I care for."

When I returned to Turtle Bay after my first visit to Fenwick, whole new shipments of flowers were arriving from friends and fans, and Kate fussed only over the arrangements of small blooms—precise arrangements of baby iris, sweet william, African violets, purple dendrobium, and Madagascar jasmine, known as wax flowers. "I really don't care for those big arrangements," she declaimed. "The smaller flowers are so much more beautiful."

One week she was passionate about white roses; the next week she couldn't stand them. "I really think the rose is the most over-rated flower in the world," she argued with complete sincerity one afternoon. "That seems a bit harsh, Kate," I said. "I'm sure they're doing the best they can."

Only one flower was above reproach, never debated nor denigrated: Queen Anne's lace—*Daucus carota*—known in North America as the wild carrot and in Britain as cow parsley. "A popular name," *The*

Oxford English Dictionary says, "for various umbelliferous plants bearing clusters of small white flowers." From afar, what distinguishes Queen Anne's lace is the large, flat white flower, sometimes the size of a butter plate, which is actually a cluster of smaller flowers formed by small stalks growing out of the central stem. A field of them does, indeed, look as though somebody has strewn a delicately woven mantilla across the ground.

"Have you ever looked at Queen Anne's lace," Kate asked me during our first walk around Fenwick, "I mean really looked at it, up close, and studied it?"

I had not. Upon our uprooting a bunch of them, however, she provided me with an inspirational lesson. "Aren't they just thrilling?" Kate effused, pushing all the blossoms together so that they formed one large, flat-topped flower. "They're beautiful," I concurred.

"But that's not the best part," Kate said. "Turn one of them over."

I did, and I saw a genuine marvel of nature, the underside of Queen Anne's lace, an extraordinarily intricate network of tiny stalks—"pedicels," they're called, Kate told me—interwoven into a mesh that was at once strong and complex but also delicate and simple, perfectly symmetrical. This cross-hatching design of countless small spokes created a magnificent whole much greater than all its parts. "Now how can anybody look at that," Kate asked, grabbing the flower from me and gently brushing her fingers across the fragile infrastructure, each tiny but tough filament connected to a smaller one, "—and not believe in God?"

I looked at Kate with some astonishment, only to realize—as I would repeatedly over the years—that Kate was being absolutely literal. "I mean," she expounded, "how can anybody look at this and not believe there is some higher power, some divine force at work in the universe greater than Man, some god that created it, that created all this, that created us?"

319

As we toured Fenwick that day, and a few times after that over the next two decades, I was able to lead Kate to the subject of religion. In truth, it was not one with which she was especially comfortable. She was always more at home with the physical than the metaphysical, with the earthly rather than the cosmic. "I believe," she told me—though she was always vague about what, exactly, she believed in. "I would have to say that I don't believe Man is the Supreme Being," she said; but she seldom revealed herself to be more spiritual than that.

"What about Jesus Christ?" I asked. "Do you believe he was the son of God?"

"I believe he lived," she said without hesitation. "And I believe he was an exemplary human being who walked the earth . . . and if more people practiced what he preached, this world would be a better place. And I'd say a lot of people have done terrible things in his name. But was he the son of God? Well, I don't think I could honestly say. . . ."

"And Heaven and Hell?" I asked.

"I don't really believe in Heaven and Hell," she said, "—but in the here and now, and that we are meant to live in such a way that we can hope there is always something better than what we currently have. I believe how I act today will affect the way I am tomorrow."

"And one day I'll die," she said, "and that doesn't frighten me. I think it will be fine, perfectly fine . . . because I'll just be taking a long, wonderful nap. But until I do . . . I intend to tire myself out."

"A long, wonderful nap?" I queried. "Does that mean you think you'll then wake up . . . and come back to life? Do you believe in reincarnation?"

She laughed, responding only with a look that suggested I had gone berserk.

Kate was never one to speak in abstractions. For all her wisdom, she was seldom one to philosophize. But in my last long conversation with her, the evening of her nephew Mundy's marriage—when we were alone and she seemed strangely pensive—I could not resist asking, "So what do you think it's all about? Life, I mean. What's the purpose? What are we doing here?"

I would have felt embarrassed asking such trite questions had Kate not spared me by answering without hesitation. "To work hard," she said, "and to love someone." Then she paused.

But that was not all. "And to have some fun," she added. "And if you're lucky, you keep your health . . . and somebody loves you back."

She was proud of her answer. And as I just stared at this woman in front of me, then in her late eighties, her head shaking terribly that night, and her moist eyes looking right into mine, she said, "Now, don't tell me you're going to argue with that, Scott Berg! Just once, for God's sake, you might think I'm right about something . . . and you won't insist on having the last word!"

I got up from my chair, walked over to the couch, kissed her on the forehead, and threw another log on the fire along with a piece of driftwood, which crackled and sparked into a small pyrotechnic display of reds and yellows and blues. I returned to my chair, and then we both just sat there in complete silence until the fire burned out.

Dick Hepburn died in October 2000. Kathy Houghton informed me of a small memorial service that was to be held in the little church at Fenwick. I wanted to attend—to salute Dick and to check on Kate. A few weeks later, I found her looking none the worse for his death, but she barely spoke. During that afternoon's ceremony, she remained in the reclining chair recently installed in the living room, with Peg at her side.

After a series of warm eulogies in the very plain, unheated chapel, most of the several dozen congregants walked back to the Hepburn house, where food had been set out. Kate was still sitting quietly with Peg, whom I relieved for the next hour, serving as an usher to the steady procession of people who came in, one or two at a time, to pay their respects. When we were alone, Kate asked why all those people were there; and I said because Dick had died. With unexpected vehemence, she said, "You have misinformation." I marveled at her powers of denial.

And, in that moment, I realized that until then most of us around Kate had been exercising those same powers in relating to her. Norah stifled her tears as she admitted that Miss Hepburn had failed to recognize her on this particular visit. I counted the months, no years, since I had had an actual conversation with Kate, a genuine volley of more than two sentences; and I had blithely accepted the fact that her daily physical activity had declined to little more than moving from her bedroom to the stair lift to the living-room recliner and back. Peg told me that in my absence that afternoon, she had asked Kate how I had met her in the first place. "At a dance," she had replied, "in Philadelphia." Peg and I laughed, wondering what decade she was imagining. Sadly, the fireplaces at Fenwick had sat cold for years, ever since oxygen tanks had been parked at Kate's side.

I made efforts (not always successful) to see Kate whenever I traveled east, and my visits invariably followed a medical scare or rumor of her demise. She watched some of the television coverage of September 11, 2001, and seemed to understand the violent attack on Manhattan that day. "But we're not in New York," she comfortably observed.

Over the next twenty months, I saw her condition remain stable, relatively still and stressless. But when I called on her ninety-sixth birthday, she could not speak into the phone; and those around her all asked in somewhat ominous tones when I was visiting next.

I arrived in Fenwick eighteen days later, on May 30, 2003, and Kate's appearance alarmed me. Her eyes widened as I entered the living room and sat beside her; but they appeared sunken, their bright light extinguished. She managed a weak smile of recognition, but she looked weary and miserable. A tube carrying oxygen was fixed to her nostrils. A dramatic weight loss suggested that she had not been eating.

Hong, who had been filling Norah's shoes in Connecticut for years, and Norah herself, who was spending as much time in Fenwick as possible, said that in the past few weeks Miss Hepburn had ingested little more than liquefied yogurt and nutritional drinks. Every now and then, she showed interest in a small piece of toast with jam, which she would hold up to her mouth for two minutes at a time—sometimes putting it down, sometimes swallowing it whole. I kept thinking of my conversation with her a few years prior, about her own ability to hasten her departure from life by not eating, and wondered if she had taken to questioning every mouthful. Or had eating simply become a burden, maybe even painful? When I asked about her new diet, Hong and Norah hastily urged me to talk to the circumspect Erik Hanson.

I called him from the kitchen and learned the recently diagnosed truth, that a very aggressive tumor—large and hard—had been discovered in Kate's neck. Various medical options had been considered; and, after factoring in her age and diminished quality of life, it was decided to let nature take its course. When I pressed Erik for further details from the doctors, he simply said, "Any time. Maybe tomorrow . . . but, with Kate, who knows? But we're not talking years." Nurses were administering over-the-counter drugs to quell any pain.

In saying goodbye to Kate that afternoon, I held her hand for several minutes as I told her, hardly for the first time, how much she meant to me. And I whispered into her ear that it was all right for her to "let go" whenever she wanted, that if she were tired, she could simply go to sleep—during the day, when there was always a friend or family member by the side of her chair, or at night, when a nurse kept bedside vigil. I didn't fool myself, thinking my words would make much difference; they were just my way of saying that she would not be alone, and that everyone around her felt she had long since displayed more than a lifetime of strength and courage.

Within two weeks, getting beyond the chair in her bedroom became too much of a challenge; and Kate's intake of liquids decreased. I monitored her condition daily by telephone. On the afternoon of Sunday, June 29, 2003, Cynthia McFadden thoughtfully placed the call I had been anxiously awaiting. After showing us for almost a century how to live, Katharine Hepburn showed us, at last, how to die.

I think about Kate often, as I will for the rest of my life. Lately, I'll admit, I've been having a little fun steering myself time and again into the same daydream, one of my own deliberate invention: It's a balmy night in June, and I'm in a white dinner jacket at the Merion Cricket Club in Haverford, Pennsylvania, just outside Philadelphia, for the first promenade of the summer. A lively band breaks into a bouncy new Cole Porter tune. Suddenly, a striking young woman appears—fresh from Bryn Mawr—with big, luminous eyes and high cheekbones. A gentle breeze blows through her auburn hair. We notice each other; and, with her long legs, she is striding right toward me . . .

PN 2287 .H45 B47 2004
Berg, A. Scott
Kate remembered